Descriptosaurus

Now in a fully updated third edition, *Descriptosaurus* is the first book for creative writing that is a thematic expansion of a dictionary and a thesaurus; it provides children with a comprehensive resource with which to expand their descriptive vocabulary, experiment with language and sentence structure and build up narratives based around settings, characters and creatures.

Descriptosaurus positions the word, zooms in on it to examine the meaning, expands it into phrases, and then provides alternatives in words, phrases and sentences. The model was created and refined over a number of years as a result of feedback from children inside and outside the classroom as to the resources they required to inspire and assist them with their writing. For reluctant writers or those faced with blank page syndrome, it provides essential starting points to encourage putting pen to paper, not only inspiring children, but also building their confidence, encouraging them to use, apply and create using the correct grammatical structures, and adding colour to their writing through evaluation and experimentation.

New features for this updated third edition include:

- ★ Sample poems
- ★ Word banks and model sentences to provide a step-by-step process for development of vocabulary and understanding of phrase, clause and sentence structure
- ★ Contextualised grammar and punctuation instruction and guidance
- ★ Units of work where the models can be incorporated in a creative focus
- ★ A companion website containing all the features of the book, games, planning sheets and vocabulary builders.

This is an ideal resource to dramatically improve children's creative writing for all KS2 primary and KS3 secondary English teachers, literacy coordinators and parents. It would also make an excellent classroom book for PGCE students, particularly Primary PGCE with English specialism.

Alison Wilcox has extensive teaching experience in schools in England and Scotland. Colleagues describe her methods as 'innovative and inspirational to even the most reluctant of writers'.

Descriptosaurus

Supporting Creative Writing for Ages 8–14

Third Edition

Alison Wilcox

Routledge
Taylor & Francis Group
LONDON AND NEW YORK

Third edition published 2018
by Routledge
2 Park Square, Milton Park, Abingdon, Oxon OX14 4RN

and by Routledge
711 Third Avenue, New York, NY 10017

Routledge is an imprint of the Taylor & Francis Group, an informa business

Second edition published 2013 by Routledge
First edition published 2009 by Routledge

British Library Cataloguing in Publication Data
A catalogue record for this book is available from the British Library

Library of Congress Cataloging in Publication Data
Names: Wilcox, Alison, author.
Title: Descriptosaurus : supporting creative writing for ages 8–14 / Alison Wilcox.
Description: Third edition. | Milton Park, Abingdon, Oxon : Routledge, [2017]
Identifiers: LCCN 2017016949 | ISBN 9781138093027 (hardback) |
ISBN 9781315107110 (ebook)
Subjects: LCSH: English language—Synonyms and antonyms—Dictionaries. |
Creative writing (Elementary education)
Classification: LCC PE1591 .W487 2017 | DDC 372.62/3—dc23
LC record available at https://lccn.loc.gov/2017016949

ISBN: 978-1-138-09302-7 (hbk)
ISBN: 978-1-315-10711-0 (ebk)

Typeset in Myriad Pro
by Apex CoVantage, LLC

Visit the companion website: www.routledge.com/cw/wilcox

MIX
Paper from responsible sources
FSC www.fsc.org FSC® C013056

Printed and bound in Great Britain by
TJ International Ltd, Padstow, Cornwall

To my mum and dad – two of the strongest and most loyal people I have ever known. Thanks for everything.

Contents

Contents

Acknowledgements

My name might be on the front cover, but to complete this book took the help and support of a great many people. Thanks to Andrew, Robert and Kitty for their patience and understanding; to my wonderful parents, Ann and John, for their unwavering belief; my sister, Trish, for her support and all the laughs along the way; and to my friend, Gail, who always seems to know when I need a 'shoulder.'

Bruce Roberts at Routledge has been the mastermind behind the *Descriptosaurus* series and, as always, I owe him an immense gratitude for his wise words, guidance and support. Thanks to Lucy Stewart of Routledge for all her support, input and hard work.

My thanks also to Jenni Mayo and Oakworth Primary School and all its inspirational, dedicated teachers and staff who were willing to let me into their classrooms to experiment with the new system – in particular, Ben Fawcett and Claire Wimbles. To be able to try something new requires the support, humour and patience of a teaching assistant who has the ability and willingness to try something different and the flexibility to make changes when required. Thanks Brenda, I loved working with you.

Finally, I would like to thank Scarlett and her mum, Jo. I really enjoyed the opportunity of working with you both.

Preface

ORIGINAL AIM

My aim has always been to provide resources that facilitate the teaching of creative writing in such a way as to enthuse and engage the children, to relieve the pressure on teachers, who spend many hours of their 'spare time' creating their own differentiated resources, as well as ideas and guidance for parents, and a structure to enable pupils to work independently.

When I first decided to write *Descriptosaurus* it was because my experience of teaching creative writing to children had revealed that many had great imaginations and lots of ideas but lacked the descriptive vocabulary to communicate these effectively.

The original focus of *Descriptosaurus* was to provide children with a comprehensive resource to help them to expand their descriptive vocabulary and to demonstrate how words, phrases and clauses could be incorporated in a variety of sentence structures.

DESCRIPTOSAURUS: GENRE SERIES

In the *Descriptosaurus* genre series – *Action & Adventure*, *Ghost Stories*, *Myths & Legends*, and *Fantasy* – I set out with a new system I called S/C-I-R (Setting/Character, Interaction, Reaction) to tackle the issues I had encountered with disjointed pieces of description: action scenes that were merely a list of actions with no description of setting, other characters or emotions; excellent descriptions of setting, but the character(s) did not move through (interact with) the setting.

This was also an attempt to provide a contextualised alternative to the prescriptive, repetitive focus on textbook grammar in response to the introduction of the SPAG tests, which shifted the focus to knowledge of the language and the labelling of its component parts rather than its application. By taking a number of sentences or phrases for setting, interaction and reaction, combining them into a descriptive paragraph of a scene, and then experimenting with different ways of combining the sentences, openers and length, children learn about grammar but also, more importantly, its purpose and impact on flow, sense and expression.

WHY WRITE A THIRD EDITION OF *DESCRIPTOSAURUS*?

Learning grammar as knowledge in preparation for specific assessments may result in decent scores, but it does not necessarily follow that this knowledge will be demonstrated in pupils' everyday or creative writing. The process that is used to succeed in the tests is temporary and shallow, with little guarantee that pupils progress to understand, evaluate, apply and create.

As with all assessments, the challenge we face is to balance the need to prepare for the SPAG tests with teaching those skills as part of completing and improving a creative writing task so that children know that the ultimate aim is to be able to use the skills and knowledge in a real context.

I found the artificial sentences in grammar books that were concocted to illustrate a target sentence structure rarely captured the attention or imagination of the children, but using the same target structure in contextualised sentences that related to the creative text being composed and discussing their impact had a very positive effect on engagement and enthusiasm.

I therefore felt it was necessary to develop the *Descriptosaurus* model further, to not only incorporate models for the coordination and subordination requirements of the National Curriculum, but also provide models that teach children how to embed description and imagery in their writing by using a variety of phrases and structures. These models can then be used to accumulate grammatical knowledge and, at the same time, discuss the grammatical skills involved in changing the structure of a sentence and its impact. In the words of Ted Hughes: 'the example goes like magic through all their writing . . . if you do it regularly. This is the only successful method I found of teaching grammar . . .'.

The ability to link ideas within sentences by combining and sequencing clauses enables pupils to structure and connect ideas. However, partly as a result of the identification and labelling required by the SPAG tests, this emphasis on cohesion results in paragraphs of sentences that are formulaic, having been cultivated to follow the same basic patterns. Little time and consideration is available for studying and practising how to manipulate and elaborate sentences to create more precise, varied and effective writing.

Teaching children how to manipulate sentence structure produces powerful, precise and able writers. The more they practise, using modelled sentence types, the more fluid their writing will become. They need to be introduced to new vocabulary and literary techniques and given the chance to:

- Use them repeatedly in context to understand how to use them appropriately.
- Experiment with different sentence structures and length to evaluate the effect on the quality of their writing, not merely complete an exercise in a textbook where they have to choose the appropriate conjunction to make a compound sentence.

NEW FEATURES

POETRY

Poetry is an effective way of demonstrating the use of the vocabulary and phrases from *Descriptosaurus* to model the various target sentence structures. This enables pupils to approach the task in small, manageable steps, and to focus on:

- word choice
- the target phrase or clause
- the sentence structure.

Poetry is also an excellent form to focus on impact rather than merely cohesion.

The new edition includes a number of poems that I have developed as a starting point, but the process can be used with any poetic structure being studied.

SENTENCE MODELS: DFI

Once the poem is complete, the next stage is to provide a *model of the target sentence structure* and give children time to experiment with inserting combinations of the vocabulary they have chosen.

These poems and sentence models can, therefore, be used not only to practise the target structure but also to manipulate and elaborate it, and to consider the impact on meaning and effect. While imitating sentence patterns children also become aware of punctuation.

Part 5 includes modelled sentence structures. These have been split into three sections: Detail, Flow, Impact (DFI). Where appropriate, I have assigned beginner, intermediate and advanced labels to the models rather than year group, as a pupil who has not mastered compound sentences will find it difficult to access a model on how to use subordination. Likewise, a child who has absorbed advanced sentence structures from their independent reading should have the opportunity to experiment with that structure, but with the support of a modelled sentence that demonstrates the correct structure and punctuation.

The website also includes display cards for each of the sentences to facilitate demonstration and discussion. In addition, each sentence has been split into individual word flash cards for sentence construction and manipulation.

ACTION FRAMES

For many years, I have been frustrated that a final piece of creative writing never seems to match up to the fantastic, imaginative ideas for a story that pupils are able to articulate during the initial brainstorming session. I have tried many different methods of planning to try to remedy this situation, and whilst I found that there was more evidence of these ideas being included in the story, the problem of maintaining the threads of the story, the creativity and descriptive language remained.

A method that proved to be very successful was to take sections of the story and write action frames. This can be done for the pupils' own writing or from a class text. Breaking the frame down into a series of movements and reactions enables pupils to describe the scene more effectively and in detail, but also to apply the skills they have previously learned in respect of grammar. In addition, this exercise also facilitates the inclusion of discussion and drama. An example is included using a wolf chase, which can be combined with the resources for 'Little Red Riding Hood'. To demonstrate how part of a class text can be taken as a writing stimulus, a scene from *The Silver Sword* by Ian Serrailler is included on the website.

DESCRIPTIVE PARAGRAPHS: S/C-I-R

Applying and combining the sentences for flow and impact are also essential skills. To enable pupils to practise this skill, this edition has included a number of S/C-I-R passages for discussion, which have also been broken down into individual sentences for combining into a passage. The passages have been designed to provide opportunities for cross-curricular writing.

The current obsession with fronted adverbials is having a negative impact on the quality of creative writing in schools. These S/C-I-R sentences expose pupils to various sentence structures, lengths and openers; enable them to discuss how to develop the sentences into a descriptive passage using various techniques that have been studied as part of the grammar curriculum; experiment with the techniques, and discuss the results in terms of flow and impact. These exercises embed the grammar being studied and enable pupils to master the concepts in context.

CONCLUSION

It is important that we do not lose sight of the fact that children need to be able to *use* grammar as a tool to help them *improve their writing*. By actively noting new vocabulary and phrases gleaned from their independent and class reading, writing down key sentence patterns, highlighting punctuation, and storing them in a writing journal, children will eventually have all the tools they need when they find their own voice.

By including these sentence models, as well as providing children with ideas and descriptive vocabulary, I hope to fully engage them with the tasks rather than merely the mechanics of the language; to tap into their imaginations; add colour to their writing by evaluating and experimenting with vocabulary and figurative language, and then frame it by examining the elements of grammar and punctuation. Studying and creating a text should be an holistic experience rather than a functional, formulaic, technique-gathering exercise.

Introduction

WHAT IS A DESCRIPTOSAURUS?

Descriptosaurus is a new and innovative model of creative writing that is a thematic expansion of a dictionary and a thesaurus.

To be creative when writing, it is first necessary to have the requisite knowledge and skills: the vocabulary to describe and the structure to organise ideas.

Descriptosaurus provides children with a comprehensive resource to help them expand their descriptive vocabulary, experiment with language and sentence structure and build up narratives based around the following areas:

★ Settings – landscapes, settlements and atmosphere
★ Characters – appearance, emotions and personality
★ Creatures – appearance, abilities and habitats.

A dictionary teaches children the meaning of words and a thesaurus expands their vocabulary. *Descriptosaurus* teaches them how to describe a setting using their senses; how to describe a character using expressions, voice and movement, to add detail, depth and colour to their writing.

It positions the words – whether for appearance, expression, landscape, smell or sound – classifies them as nouns, adjectives and verbs, zooms in to examine their meaning and then expands them into phrases and sentences. It shows how they can be used and provides alternative sentence structures.

The model was created – and continues to evolve, with additional components and models being added to each new edition – as a result of feedback from children about the resources they require to inspire and assist them with their writing. For reluctant writers or those faced with the 'blank page syndrome,' *Descriptosaurus* provides invaluable starting points to encourage putting pen to paper.

Alison Wilcox has extensive teaching experience in schools in England and Scotland. Colleagues describe her methods as 'innovative and inspirational to even the most reluctant of writers.' She is also the author of the *Descriptosaurus* genre series, which includes *Action & Adventure, Ghost Stories, Myths & Legends* and *Fantasy*. In addition to writing, Alison continues to work for periods as a full-time teacher, and has collaborated with the National Literacy Trust on two very successful creative writing competitions.

WHY IS DESCRIPTIVE WRITING IMPORTANT?

The importance of children being able to express their ideas using good descriptive language is widely accepted, not just for creative writing, but also for non-fiction.

Developing descriptive language to communicate effectively is an essential tool across the curriculum. History is concerned not merely with dates and facts, but with describing and interpreting past events. In Geography, children need to be able to describe the world around them. In Science, they need to observe carefully and then be capable of describing what is happening in an experiment. In all areas of the curriculum, children need the vocabulary to enable them to describe and interpret.

To be able to describe effectively, we first need to be taught how to look and listen. We need to learn the vocabulary to use in order to express our ideas. As well as encouraging children to use interesting language, *Descriptosaurus* aims to improve children's observation skills in both their own environment and their reading.

We describe sights and events differently because we see and interpret things differently. To any situation or piece of writing we bring our own personality, experience and imagination. As educators, both parents and teachers, we need to open children's eyes to the world around them, stimulate their imaginations and sow the seeds of effects that can be achieved in their writing. With the vocabulary, knowledge and understanding of how to use language to achieve depth and colour in their writing, children will grow in confidence and motivation to experiment, find their 'voice' and develop their own style of writing.

WHO SHOULD USE *DESCRIPTOSAURUS?*

Although the age range for *Descriptosaurus* is 8–14, it is beneficial for older children, or even adults, who need assistance with vocabulary or who who suffer from 'blank page syndrome'.

WHERE CAN *DESCRIPTOSAURUS* BE USED?

Descriptosaurus is a resource that can be used at home or school by pupils, parents and teachers.

Although consideration has been given to specific curricula, *Descriptosaurus* is a general tool applicable to any creative writing syllabus in any territory where there is a desire to improve descriptive writing.

WHY IS *DESCRIPTOSAURUS* A USEFUL TOOL FOR PARENTS?

We all agree that there is no substitute for reading to improve children's writing. However, we live in a world dominated by the moving image, be it television, mobile phones or games consoles. As a teacher, I have encountered the problems reluctant readers face when challenged to write creatively. As a parent, I have encountered the problems of developing a 'reading habit' at home alongside an obsession to use their fingers to operate a keyboard or console rather than turn a page.

How then can we develop children's writing when there is a reluctance to read or engage with a text? The answer is to feed the children's imaginations with pictures, sounds and games, and use *Descriptosaurus* to describe what they see, hear, smell, touch.

One of the main rationales for developing the *Descriptosaurus* model into a book was in response to comments from other parents regarding the advantages enjoyed by my own children having an English teacher as a parent. Parents and teachers have never been under as much pressure as they are today, with the demands of SATS and 11 plus exams to improve writing levels. Parents felt relatively confident about helping their children with grammar, maths and science because these had rules, a method and a right or wrong answer. They found creative writing to be very different. Many of these parents felt that their own descriptive vocabulary was inadequate and thus struggled to assist their children with writing tasks.

Not only have I witnessed a marked improvement in the descriptive writing of the children using a *Descriptosaurus,* I have also noted an increase in confidence in their parents.

IDEAS FOR PARENTS

PLANNING

When children bring home any piece of writing, the most important assistance a parent can provide is getting them to plan it carefully.

Get the children to mind map words and phrases to answer the questions:

- ★ *Who* (appearance, personality, and emotions – expressions, voice, body language)
- ★ *Where* (senses – sights, sounds, smell, touch)
- ★ *When* (atmosphere – time of year or day, weather).

Planning sheets, which structure this process, can be downloaded from the companion website at www.routlege.com/cw/wilcox.

Frames for action, and character and setting descriptions, including modelled writing – can be found on the companion website. These frames break the text into bite-size tables, which make it easier to focus on the quality of the writing.

'How to use this book' is also a useful guide.

FILMS

This is an opportunity to use the moving image to improve creative writing.

Watch a film together and examine how:

- ★ atmosphere and suspense are achieved using
  - ☆ weather
  - ☆ light/dark
  - ☆ sound
- ★ the body language and tone of a character is used to express their emotions.

MAKING THE MOST OF JOURNEYS OR FAMILY LEISURE TIME

When embarking on a journey, use the following as boredom busters.

- ★ Audio books are a great way of passing the time and develop descriptive vocabulary and discussion.
- ★ Use a sentence from the Prompt Cards section for a game of 'What happened next?' or 'Where is it?' Each player can take it in turns to contribute an idea to each of the

questions. The benefit of sharing ideas, imaginations and discussion should not be underestimated. Children can also be encouraged to create their own Prompt Cards and questions.

★ The alternative version of 'I Spy' on the companion website is a great, fun way of improving children's vocabulary.
★ Playing 'I Can' helps improve children's understanding of how using senses in their descriptive writing can dramatically improve the quality of their work.
★ The 'Character Profile' cards can be used to create interesting and even bizarre characters.
★ When stuck in a traffic jam, an amusing game to pass the time is to make up character profiles for the occupants of neighbouring vehicles. Where are they going? What are they going to do? What is their job? What sort of house do they live in? What is interesting about them? Are they famous, a secret agent, etc.? How are they feeling? This is a good way of getting children to notice body language. For example, are they drumming their fingers on the steering wheel?

PHOTO ALBUMS, SCRAPBOOKS

Collect photos, postcards, leaflets, travel brochures, pictures from newspapers and magazines.

Make an album of old photos. Instead of listing where the photo was taken, who is in the picture – describe the scene. There may be an opportunity here to practise using dialogue by imagining what the people in the photos are thinking or what they are saying to each other.

Use cuttings and leaflets to produce a scrap album. Collect a list of words and phrases to describe the settings and characters.

The companion website includes a number of additional elements, ideas, frameworks and models to assist with the description of setting and character:

★ *Tour Guide* demonstrates how to develop a description of a setting.
★ *Missing Person* demonstrates how to develop a description of a character.

See also *Guess the Portrait* in the 'Games' section of the companion website.

CHARACTER CHARADES AND 'DON'T MOVE'

These can be played at home and are great fun.

SENTENCE STRUCTURES

Many parents receive feedback that to improve their writing their children need to use *conjunctions*. For many, this has proved a minefield. Model sentences have been included for each element, and the companion website includes the sentences on individual display cards and on flash cards, where each sentence has been broken down into individual words.

IDEAS FOR TEACHERS

PLANNING

When planning a piece of creative writing, use planning sheets, mind maps, etc. to collate words and phrases to answer the questions:

★ Who (appearance, personality, and emotions – expressions, voice, body language)
★ Where (senses – sights, sounds, smell, touch)
★ When (atmosphere – time of year or day, weather).

For more ideas go to the following sections on the companion website:

★ Writing tips to build atmosphere, tension and suspense
★ Hooks to build interest and tension
★ Mountain Pyramids
★ Little Red Riding Hood
★ Scene Setters
★ The Wolf
★ Creature description using the opening of *The Iron Man*
★ Emotion Riddle
★ Missing Person
★ Tour Guide
★ S/C-I-R
★ Planning sheets
★ Action frames, description frames for setting and character (*these include a model, outline and blank forms*).

TRADITIONAL STORIES, MYTHS OR LEGENDS

Take a traditional tale, such as 'Red Riding Hood', in which the structure is already in place, and get the children to fill in the descriptive detail.

Detailed lessons plans are included in 'Lessons plans for descriptive writing' on the companion website.

Part 5 of the book has been based on a wolf chase to demonstrate how a basic story can be innovated.

Myths and legends can be used in much the same way. For example, the journey through the tunnel to meet the Minotaur.

Resources for developing a creature description are included in the companion website. They include a poem, plan, vocabulary bank, and a model of how to incorporate the description in the structure of an existing text. The Coming of the Rhinogasaurus uses the opening from Ted Hughes' *The Iron Man*.

'I SPY'

The alternative version of 'I Spy' on the companion website is a great, fun way of improving children's vocabulary.

'I CAN'

Playing 'I Can' helps improve children's understanding of how using senses in their descriptive writing can dramatically improve the quality of their work.

WHAT HAPPENED NEXT?

Use a sentence from the Prompt Cards section for a game of 'What happened next?' or 'Where is it?' Children can also be encouraged to create their own Prompt Cards and questions.

Prompt Cards are designed to stimulate and aid creative writing, and encourage the inclusion of a range of senses in description. The questions scaffold the structure and description. The benefit of the Prompt Cards is that they can be used as a quick-fire verbal planning burst or for modelling, but also as a piece of descriptive writing, a poem or to scaffold a story.

They are designed to stimulate children's imagination by getting them to consider a number of different settings and atmosphere – use their senses to build a detailed picture of the setting and create different scenarios and characters that could apply to the sentence prompt. If the children need help with ideas or vocabulary, they can use the main *Descriptosaurus* text to assist them.

The same technique can be used with the sentences in *Hooks* (companion website).

CHARACTER DETECTIVES

Pick a sentence from the Character Profile Cards.
Centre it in a mind map and develop a profile.
See also *Missing Person*.

WHERE AND WHEN PAIRS GAME

Give the children a number of Setting and Atmosphere Cards. Challenge them to arrange them in pairs by matching a setting card with an atmosphere.

STORY SEQUENCING

The Prompt Cards can be combined with the Character Profile Cards and used in a warm-up activity. Divide the class into groups and give each group a number of cards.

Set the children the challenge of organising the cards into a story, using the connectives to link the descriptions.

SENTENCE STRUCTURE

The cards can also be used for an activity for examining sentence structure and also punctuation. For example:

- ★ Varying the length of the sentences to build tension
- ★ Changing the sentences so that the children make a series of simple, compound or complex sentences
- ★ Changing the order of the sentences.

CHARACTER CHARADES AND 'DON'T MOVE!'

We continually reinforce to children the need to 'show not tell' when developing their characters. These are two easy and fun games that can be used to get the children to really think about character traits and use speech, tone of voice, expressions and movement to describe their characters, but also to devise situations where the character's reaction and their interaction with other characters clearly demonstrates the character's personality. There are six levels and the characters and vocabulary get progressively harder. The children may need to look up some of the words in a dictionary to find the meaning and an easier synonym. The games, therefore, also work as vocabulary builders.

LOCATION POSTERS

These can be completed in groups for different settings and displayed as prompts. For example, forests, mountains, beaches, islands, water (sea, river, waterfalls), cities, towns, villages.

- ★ A–Z lists for nouns, adjectives and verbs. The work on 'I Can' can be recorded and used to produce these posters.
- ★ Senses mind map (sight, sounds, smells, touch). The work on the Prompt Cards can be used as planning sheets for this activity.

WANTED POSTERS

Use the Character Profile Cards to produce:

- ★ A Missing Person poster for a missing hero/heroine. A Missing Person report form, together with a description frame model, outline and blank form (see companion website), provides a framework, outline and model.
- ★ A Wanted poster for a dangerous criminal.

Challenge the children to describe the personality, abilities and exploits of the characters to explain why they need to be found.

Extension: The characters are in disguise. The children now need to think of distinguishing features, voice, movements and gestures in their description.

GUESS THE PICTURE/PORTRAIT

Collect a selection of pictures (could be taken from studies in history, space or geography).

- ★ Give each pair or group a selection of three/four numbered pictures.
- ★ Pairs/groups label the pictures with important details that will help identify them.
- ★ Using their notes, describe the picture to the rest of the class, who have to guess which of the numbered pictures is being described.

Extension: Each group adds extra detail to develop a class description of the picture.

Portraits: It is also a useful exercise to develop skills in describing characters. www.npg.org.uk is an excellent source.

ADVERT FOR A HERO/HEROINE

The task for the hero/heroine can be linked to a historical topic. For example, join an expedition to search for an Egyptian tomb. It can also be linked to a study of legends, where the children can first analyse the personality, abilities of the hero/heroine in the legend and use this information to develop their advert.

Challenge the children to describe the task and the characteristics required to secure the job. They should also include a description of the setting and the perils likely to be encountered.

Extension: Write a Curriculum Vitae and an accompanying letter asking to be considered for the expedition, task or job.

TRAVEL BROCHURES, ADVERTISING PAMPHLETS

Collect photos, postcards, leaflets, cuttings from newspapers, magazines, brochures and store in a Setting/Character file.

Make a travel brochure/advertising pamphlet for:

- ★ an adventure holiday
- ★ a relaxing beach holiday
- ★ a ghost-hunting expedition.

POETRY

The grammar elements of the literacy curriculum have been incorporated into a variety of poetic forms. Using these is an effective way to demonstrate the use of vocabulary and phrases from *Descriptosaurus* to model the various target sentence structures. It also enables pupils to approach the task in small, manageable steps, by focusing on:

- ★ word choice
- ★ the target phrase or clause
- ★ the sentence structure.

DETAIL, FLOW AND IMPACT (DFI)

Models for each target sentence structure, themed for a forest setting.

SETTING/CHARACTER, INTERACTION AND REACTION (S/C-I-R)

Use the S/C-I-R passages to discuss detail, flow and impact and the techniques used. Combine the individual sentences into a descriptive paragraph of an action scene, and then experiment with different ways of combining the sentences, openers and length.

The exercise can be extended to changing tenses, including adverbs, etc.

How to use this book

A. WORDS

List nouns, adjectives and verbs that will give you ideas and vocabulary to describe your setting and characters.

Example: A forest where the character is in danger.

If you think of **thick, dark, trapped**, your description could be:

He was trapped in the thick, dark forest.

Does this sentence paint a vivid picture for the reader? No. How can it be improved?

★ Imagine you are looking at your setting through a camera. Zoom in and describe to the reader what you can see.

★ Use the words in the book to search for vocabulary to paint a more detailed picture.

WORDS	
Nouns	Forest, jungle, woodland, trees, treetops, trunks, branches, roots, logs
	Sky, ceiling, canopy, umbrella, blanket
	Floor, carpet, paths, tunnels
	Leaves, buds, berries, blossoms, flowers, petals, stems, vines, creepers, ivy, brambles, thorns, twigs
	Bluebells, snowdrops, daffodils, poppies, gorse, heather, hawthorn, rhododendrons
	Sun, wind, dew, icicles, mist, fog, shadows
Adjectives	Tall, huge, vast, towering
	Beautiful, majestic, stunning, spectacular, magnificent
	Brown, yellow, green, emerald, pink, red, scarlet, crimson, fiery, orange, bronze, purple, blue, white, silver
	Bright, vivid
	Dark, black, gloomy, shadowy, misty, eerie, ghostly
	Thick, dense, spidery, impenetrable
	Rough, sharp, thorny, spiky, barbed, gnarled, twisted, bent
	Dead, rotting, decaying
Verbs	Stood, rose, spread, stretched, arched
	Knotted, tangled, twisted, choked, strangled
	Blocked, trapped, grasped, scratched
	Burst, erupted, crept, wriggled, writhed
	Hung, swayed, tossed, danced, hopped, floated, fluttered
	Lit, painted, covered, cloaked, shrouded

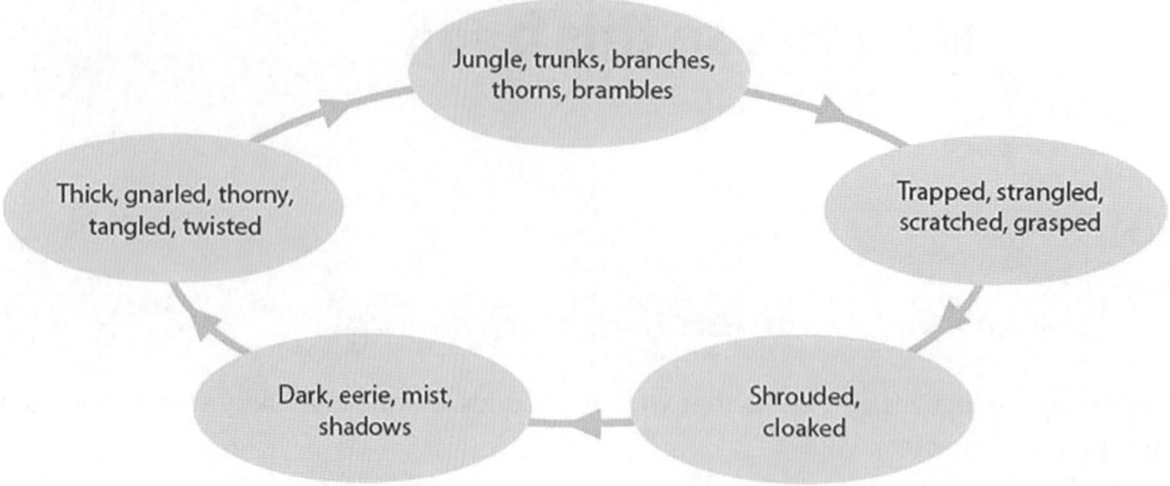

B. PHRASES

- **Nouns and adjectives:** ideas on how to combine nouns and adjectives.
- **Verbs:** ideas on how to use verbs.

PHRASES – NOUNS AND ADJECTIVES

- Magnificent forest of tall trees
- Like a crowd of vivid green umbrellas
- Huge canopy of treetops like a green blanket
- Emerald green leaves
- Fiery scarlet autumn leaves
- Vivid green stems
- Beautiful, green cloaks
- Like fluttering, emerald ribbons
- Brightly coloured creepers like party streamers
- Blazing carpet of bluebells
- Clumps of snowdrops
- Clusters of purple blossoms
- Red and orange berries
- Spikes of quivering, yellow petals
- Bright red rhododendron flowers
- Like a carpet of jewels – rubies, sapphires and opals
- Glistening icicles
- Dew-soaked grass like a field of liquid diamonds
- Thick jungle of dense forest
- Dark, tangled maze of tunnels and secret paths
- Spidery knot of trees and bushes
- Thick, gnarled trunks
- Huge, thick limbs
- Bleached skeletons of dead trees
- Roots like enormous, wooden tentacles
- Like ghostly, stooped figures
- Like feathery shadows
- Sharply pointed tips like fingernails
- Carpet of decay
- Rotting leaves and dead branches
- Writhing carpet of buzzing, crawling insects
- Blanket of fog
- Eerie, greenish gloom

PHRASES – VERBS

- Spread out above him
- Stretched as far as the eye could see
- Framed the deep blue sky
- Impossible to find a way through
- Couldn't tell one part of the forest from the rest
- Formed dark tunnels
- Created secret paths
- Hid many secrets
- Swayed to the rhythm of the wind
- Danced on gusts of frosty air
- Tossed their branches
- Flung their leaves up to the sky
- Arched in the wind
- Trailed their leaves on the ground
- Hung like swaying feathers
- Waved like hundreds of tiny hands
- Floated to the ground
- Creepers hung between the branches
- Alive with splashes of red and orange berries
- Covered in butterflies
- Stretched like a carpet of jewels
- Lay like a carpet of confetti
- Cloaked with purple heather
- Dotted with red poppies
- Sun danced on the leaves
- Bathed in light
- Dripped stalactites of colour
- Shone with patches of misty light
- Painted the ground with flickering shadows
- Branches spread and twisted together like a prehistoric beast
- Ivy choked the twisted tree
- Thorns knotted amongst the trees and bushes
- Twisted and grated against each other like rusty hinges
- Blocked the path
- Strangled the paths
- Littered the ground
- Burst from the ground
- Wriggled across the forest floor
- Shrouded in mist
- Cloaked in a blanket of darkness
- Tore at their arms and legs
- Grasped at her ankles like bony fingers
- Pressed in on him on all sides
- Trapped her in its thorny grasp

Use these ideas to think of other ways of using the words, perhaps in your own similes and metaphors.

Example: Brambles were thorny spiders' webs

Tore at her ankles like barbed spikes on a trap.

Jungle, trunks, branches, thorns, brambles, thick, tangled	**Dark, eerie, mist, shadows, shrouded, cloaked, covered**	**Trapped, strangled, grasped**
Thick jungle of dense forest	Cloaked in mist	Strangled the paths
Thick, gnarled trunks	Like ghostly, stooped figures	Impossible to find a way through
Huge, thick limbs		Trapped in their thorny grasp
Spidery knot of trees and bushes		Pressed in on her from all sides
Spread and twisted like some prehistoric beast		Tore at her arms and legs
		Grasped at her ankles like bony fingers

C. SENTENCES

These model how:

★ to combine the phrases in sentences;
★ to vary the type and length of sentences to make your writing more interesting.

There are three main types of sentence, which, when used together, produce different effects and make your writing more interesting.

★ **Simple sentence:** has one **clause**. (A clause has a **subject** and a *verb*.)

Example: The **forest** was *cloaked* in mist.

They are useful because they can create suspense, mystery and excitement.

★ **Compound sentence:** two or more simple sentences joined by a ***conjunction*** (***and, or, but, so, for, yet***), or separated by a comma, semi-colon (;) or colon (:).

Too many simple sentences can make your writing sound very jerky and boring to read.

Example: The forest was a dark, tangled maze. It was impossible to find a way through. The dead branches rose up out of the mist. They grasped her ankles like bony fingers.

It is important to join sentences together to add variety and make your writing flow.

If we join some of these simple sentences together, the writing will flow more easily.

The forest was a dark, tangled maze and it was impossible to find a way through. The dead branches rose up out of the mist, grasping at her ankles like bony fingers.

★ **Complex sentence:** has a main clause and one or more subordinate clauses (information added to the main clause, but does not make sense on its own).

☆ Example: Subordinate clause is at the beginning of the sentence.

Rising out of the mist, the branches grasped at her ankles like bony fingers.

These are important because they can create variety and different effects and can be used to add detail or description.

☆ Example: Subordinate clause is in the middle of the sentence.

The branches, ***which rose out of the mist***, grasped at her ankles like bony fingers.

CAUTION

Do not just copy a sentence from the book, as it may not fit into the rhythm of your writing or produce the intended effect.

SENTENCES

The majestic trees stood tall and proud.

The trees were joined together like a crowd of vivid green umbrellas.

The magnificent trees flung their branches up to the sun to frame the deep blue sky.

A white blanket of snowdrops danced on gusts of frosty air.

They were welcomed by wave after wave of the gently nodding heads of daffodils.

The ground was painted with red poppies and yellow gorse.

The hedge was alive with splashes of red and orange berries.

Hanging from every branch were icicles that glistened like liquid diamonds.

The branches swayed to the rhythm of the wind and their leaves fluttered like graceful butterflies.

The petals had been shaken off the bush and lay like a carpet of pink confetti on the floor.

As they entered the wood, they were greeted by the bowed heads of a blazing carpet of bluebells.

It was impossible to move quickly through the spidery tangle of trees and bushes.

The brambles and thorns tore at their arms and legs.

The forest floor was a writhing carpet of buzzing, crawling insects.

An eerie, greenish gloom filled the clearing.

Patches of misty light shone through the gaps in the trees.

The leaves glowed in the early morning light like hundreds of tiny hands.

The bonfire blazed in the background. A thousand flickering shadows painted the ground.

Rotting leaves hid the roots that wriggled across the ground.

The forest was a dark, tangled maze and it was impossible to find a way through.

The branches of the thick, tangled trees had spread and twisted to form dark, overhead tunnels and created secret paths.

The ceiling of thick branches shut out the sky and covered the path in darkness.

The dead branches rose up and grasped at her ankles like bony fingers.

The branches twisted and grated against each other like rusty hinges.

Like some prehistoric beast, the huge, twisted limbs of the tree guarded the entrance.

Pressing in on her from all sides, it seemed that the forest was trying to trap her in its thorny grasp.

As it drifted through the forest, the fog made eerie shapes and shadows.

Cloaked in mist, the trees looked like ghostly, stooped figures.

RESULT

'She was trapped in a thick, dark forest' could now become:

> The forest was cloaked in mist. She was trapped. She was surrounded by a thick jungle of tangled trees, gnarled branches and thorns. They had spread and twisted together. It was impossible to find a way through. She tried to pass. The thorns grasped at her ankles. They tore at her arms and legs.

or

> The forest was cloaked in mist and she was trapped and surrounded by a thick jungle of tangled trees, gnarled branches and thorns, which had spread and twisted together, so it was impossible to find a way through and, as she tried to pass, the thorns grasped at her ankles and tore at her arms and legs.

or

> Cloaked in mist, the trees were like ghostly, prehistoric creatures. It was impossible to find a way through. She was trapped in a thick jungle of tangled trees, gnarled branches and thorns that had spread and twisted together. Grasping at her as she tried to pass, they tore at her arms and legs, clutching her in their thorny grasp.

Which one is easiest to read and paints the best picture?

TIPS

The key to good writing is careful planning. When thinking about who, when and where, using *Descriptosaurus* will give you ideas and vocabulary to:

★ use your senses to paint a vivid picture of your setting – sights, sounds, smells and touch
★ describe a character using appearance, voice, movement and emotions.

Part 1
Settings

Landscapes

1

Forests and woods

WORDS

Nouns	Forest, jungle, woodland, trees, treetops, trunks, branches, roots, logs
	Sky, ceiling, canopy, umbrella, blanket
	Floor, carpet, paths, tunnels
	Leaves, buds, berries, blossoms, flowers, petals, stems, vines, creepers, ivy, brambles, thorns, twigs
	Bluebells, snowdrops, daffodils, poppies, gorse, heather, hawthorn, rhododendrons
	Sun, wind, dew, icicles, mist, fog, shadows
Adjectives	Tall, huge, vast, towering
	Beautiful, majestic, stunning, spectacular, magnificent
	Brown, yellow, green, emerald, pink, red, scarlet, crimson, fiery, orange, bronze, purple, blue, white, silver
	Bright, vivid
	Dark, black, gloomy, shadowy, misty, eerie, ghostly
	Thick, dense, spidery, impenetrable
	Rough, sharp, thorny, spiky, barbed, gnarled, twisted, bent
	Dead, rotting, decaying
Verbs	Stood, rose, spread, stretched, arched
	Knotted, tangled, twisted, choked, strangled
	Blocked, trapped, grasped, scratched
	Burst, erupted, crept, wriggled, writhed
	Hung, swayed, tossed, danced, hopped, floated, fluttered
	Lit, painted, covered, cloaked, shrouded

1 *Landscapes: forests and woods*

PHRASES – NOUNS AND ADJECTIVES

- Magnificent forest of tall trees
- Like a crowd of vivid green umbrellas
- Huge canopy of treetops like a green blanket
- Emerald green leaves
- Fiery scarlet autumn leaves
- Vivid green stems
- Beautiful, green cloaks
- Like fluttering, emerald ribbons
- Brightly coloured creepers like party streamers
- Blazing carpet of bluebells
- Clumps of snowdrops
- Clusters of purple blossoms
- Red and orange berries
- Spikes of quivering, yellow petals
- Bright red rhododendron flowers
- Like a carpet of jewels – rubies, sapphires and opals
- Glistening icicles
- Dew-soaked grass like a field of liquid diamonds
- Thick jungle of dense forest
- Dark, tangled maze of tunnels and secret paths
- Spidery knot of trees and bushes
- Thick, gnarled trunks
- Huge, thick limbs
- Bleached skeletons of dead trees
- Roots like enormous, wooden tentacles
- Like ghostly, stooped figures
- Like feathery shadows
- Sharply pointed tips like fingernails
- Carpet of decay
- Rotting leaves and dead branches
- Writhing carpet of buzzing, crawling insects
- Blanket of fog
- Eerie, greenish gloom

PHRASES – VERBS

- Spread out above him
- Stretched as far as the eye could see
- Framed the deep blue sky

- Impossible to find a way through
- Couldn't tell one part of the forest from the rest
- Formed dark tunnels
- Created secret paths
- Hid many secrets
- Swayed to the rhythm of the wind
- Danced on gusts of frosty air
- Tossed their branches
- Flung their leaves up to the sky
- Arched in the wind
- Trailed their leaves on the ground
- Hung like swaying feathers
- Waved like hundreds of tiny hands
- Floated to the ground
- Creepers hung between the branches
- Alive with splashes of red and orange berries
- Covered in butterflies
- Stretched like a carpet of jewels
- Lay like a carpet of confetti
- Cloaked with purple heather
- Dotted with red poppies
- Sun danced on the leaves
- Bathed in light
- Dripped stalactites of colour
- Shone with patches of misty light
- Painted the ground with flickering shadows
- Branches spread and twisted together like a prehistoric beast
- Ivy choked the twisted tree
- Thorns knotted amongst the trees and bushes
- Twisted and grated against each other like rusty hinges
- Blocked the path
- Strangled the paths
- Littered the ground
- Burst from the ground
- Wriggled across the forest floor
- Shrouded in mist
- Cloaked in a blanket of darkness
- Tore at their arms and legs
- Grasped at her ankles like bony fingers
- Pressed in on him on all sides
- Trapped her in its thorny grasp

1 *Landscapes: forests and woods*

SENTENCES

The majestic trees stood tall and proud.

The trees were joined together like a crowd of vivid green umbrellas.

The magnificent trees flung their branches up to the sun to frame the deep blue sky.

A white blanket of snowdrops danced on gusts of frosty air.

They were welcomed by wave after wave of the gently nodding heads of daffodils.

The ground was painted with red poppies and yellow gorse.

The hedge was alive with splashes of red and orange berries.

Hanging from every branch were icicles that glistened like liquid diamonds.

The branches swayed to the rhythm of the wind and their leaves fluttered like graceful butterflies.

The petals had been shaken off the bush and lay like a carpet of pink confetti on the floor.

As they entered the wood, they were greeted by the bowed heads of a blazing carpet of bluebells.

It was impossible to move quickly through the spidery tangle of trees and bushes.

The brambles and thorns tore at their arms and legs.

The forest floor was a writhing carpet of buzzing, crawling insects.

An eerie, greenish gloom filled the clearing.

Patches of misty light shone through the gaps in the trees.

The leaves glowed in the early morning light like hundreds of tiny hands.

The bonfire blazed in the background. A thousand flickering shadows painted the ground.

Rotting leaves hid the roots that wriggled across the ground.

The forest was a dark, tangled maze and it was impossible to find a way through.

The branches of the thick, tangled trees had spread and twisted to form dark, overhead tunnels and created secret paths.

The ceiling of thick branches shut out the sky and covered the path in darkness.

The dead branches rose up and grasped at her ankles like bony fingers.

The branches twisted and grated against each other like rusty hinges.

Like some prehistoric beast, the huge, twisted limbs of the tree guarded the entrance.

Pressing in on her from all sides, it seemed that the forest was trying to trap her in its thorny grasp.

As it drifted through the forest, the fog made eerie shapes and shadows.

Cloaked in mist, the trees looked like ghostly, stooped figures.

2

Mountains

WORDS

Nouns	Top, peak, summit
	Slope, climb, drop, ascent, descent
	Rock-face, rocks, slabs, boulders, pillars, arches, ridges, humps
	Snow, ice, clouds, mist, fog, blanket, cloak, veil
	Streams, waterfalls, valleys, meadows
Adjectives	Tall, high, huge, soaring, enormous, massive, gigantic, towering
	Amazing, majestic, magical, spectacular, breathtaking, enchanting, magnificent, picturesque, snow-capped
	Sharp, pointed, rough, stony, rocky, uneven, rugged, jagged, savage, shark-finned
	Steep, vertical, sheer
	Dangerous, deadly, harsh, hostile, imposing, lethal, perilous, threatening, ominous, menacing, treacherous
	Black, dark, gloomy, inky, creepy, ghostly, shadowy, eerie, haunting
	Slippery, polished, shimmering, glinting
Verbs	Rose, fell, soared, towered, framed, surrounded
	Burst, thundered, erupted, pierced, slashed, gashed
	Carved, worn, sculpted, split, torn, ripped, cracked, shattered
	Sparkled, shimmered
	Covered, hidden, wrapped, enveloped, swathed, shrouded
	Climbed, crawled, crept, edged, slid, scrambled, slithered

PHRASES – NOUNS AND ADJECTIVES

- Majestic mountains
- Huge, snow-capped mountains

2 *Landscapes: mountains*

- Magical world of shimmering snow
- Spectacular views
- Paths of shimmering pillars and arches
- Cascading waterfalls
- Lush, green meadows
- Green valleys
- Streams like silver ribbons
- Wooden chalets
- Picturesque mountain village
- Black, deadly mountains
- Huge, hostile mountains
- Towering peaks
- Savage summits
- Bleak, perilous peaks
- Shark-finned ridges
- Snow-capped summit
- Like gigantic spearheads
- Like the humps of a gigantic dinosaur
- Like menacing, black daggers
- Enormous peaks like arrowheads
- Hunched shoulders of the craggy mountain
- Black boulders of jagged rock
- Haunting maze of glinting ice and rock
- Inky black maze of steep, rugged paths
- Shattered, jagged boulders and unstable rock-falls
- Steep, rocky slopes
- Sheer drop
- Veil of mist
- Ghostly blanket of dark clouds

PHRASES – VERBS

- Rose to meet the sky
- Surrounded by breathtaking summits
- Soared above her
- Towered above the village
- Framed by the mountain's majestic peaks
- Had a spectacular view
- Split, cracked and carved by the magic of nature
- Thundered towards the sky
- Pierced the sky
- Slashed the land
- Loomed ahead
- Burst out of the forest

- Rose like a black beacon
- Erupted in sharp points
- Huddled tightly together
- Crowded in on them
- Crushed them in its stony mouth
- Walls glistened with damp
- Polished into dangerous, slippery slopes
- Shattered by nature into jagged blades
- Blocked the path
- Shrouded in mist
- Enveloped in thick storm clouds
- Hostile peaks jumped out of the mist
- Gloomy, brooding summit lay in wait
- Wound his way over
- Edged their way to the top
- Scrambled up the sheer, rugged slopes
- Slithered down the bare slopes
- Tore their hands and knees on the jagged rocks

SENTENCES

Towering, snow-capped mountains rose to meet the sky.

He was surrounded by the soaring summits of the majestic mountains.

A magical world of shimmering snow towered above the wooden chalets of the mountain village.

From high up on the summit of the mountain, they had a spectacular view of green meadows and streams like silver ribbons.

Split, cracked and carved by the magic of nature, the rocks had created a path of shimmering pillars and arches.

The huge, hostile mountain pierced the sky.

Mountains, like gigantic spearheads, towered above her.

The top of the mountain was covered by a ghostly blanket of dark clouds.

The steep slopes rose towards the shark-finned ridges of the huge mountain.

The snow-capped summit of the mountain soared above her and to reach it she knew she would have to climb the sheer, deadly slopes.

Enormous boulders of jagged rock blocked the path and he had to wind his way over and through the inky black maze.

Like huge black daggers, the savage summits burst out of the trees.

The mountains loomed ahead like a giant black shadow, their peaks like huge, pointed black teeth waiting to crush him in their stony mouth.

The steep path glistened with damp – polished by nature into dangerous, slippery slopes.

He was faced by a haunting maze of ice and rock, glimmering white, stark and hostile.

3

Caves

WORDS

Nouns	Mouth, opening, entrance
	Hill, rock, path, tunnels, maze, labyrinth, gallery
	Ceiling, roof, walls, floor
	Crystals, diamonds, icicles, stalactites, stalagmites
Adjectives	Giant, enormous, amazing, spectacular, magnificent
	White, shimmering, glittering
	Dark, black, gloomy, shadowy, ghostly, eerie
	Slippery, damp
Verbs	Bent, wound, twisted, turned, coiled
	Hung, rose, covered
	Glistened, shimmered, polished

PHRASES – NOUNS AND ADJECTIVES

- ★ Entrance to an enormous cave
- ★ Huge, shimmering stalactites
- ★ Stalagmites like giant spikes
- ★ Glittering gallery of white crystals
- ★ Entrance to the cave was like a ghostly, black hole
- ★ Like a silent, screaming mouth
- ★ Inky black maze of dangerous, slippery paths
- ★ Low, dark tunnels

PHRASES – VERBS

- Wound underground
- Tunnels twisted and turned
- Hung from the roof
- Floor covered in stalagmites
- Crystal spikes rose from the gloom
- Hidden behind thick, tangled vines
- Glistened with damp
- Polished into dangerous, slippery paths
- Lit only by the narrow beam of light from the torch

SENTENCES

The tunnel suddenly opened out into a glittering gallery of white crystals.

Hidden behind thick, tangled vines was the mouth of a low cave.

The cave was a winding, underground maze of low, dark tunnels.

Stalagmites, like giant crystal spikes, covered the floor and rose out of the gloom.

Hanging from the roof, like enormous diamonds, were huge, shimmering stalactites.

The cave was a black hole – a silent, screaming mouth in the face of the rocky hill.

Lit only by the narrow beam of light from the torch, the cave was a ghostly, black hole.

Where water had leaked in from the rocks, the walls and floor glistened with damp.

4

Beaches, islands, volcanoes and deserts

SECTION 1 – BEACHES

WORDS

Nouns	Shore, cove, bay, dunes Sand, shingle, pebbles, rocks
Adjectives	Small, large, long, narrow, thin, strip, wide, arc Golden, white, sandy, powdery, pebbly, rocky
Verbs	Stretched, surrounded Lined, framed, sheltered Sloped, descended Shimmered

PHRASES – NOUNS AND ADJECTIVES

- ★ Long, narrow beach
- ★ Small, sheltered cove
- ★ Pebbly bay
- ★ Sugar white, sandy beaches
- ★ White pebble beaches
- ★ Long arc of powdery, white sand
- ★ Huge, sandy dunes
- ★ Lush, green forest
- ★ Large umbrella palm trees
- ★ Vivid blue sea
- ★ Sheer cliffs
- ★ Emerald jewel of coral reefs and diamond dust beaches

PHRASES – VERBS

- Stretched for miles
- Backed by huge, sandy dunes
- Surrounded by a lush, green forest
- Shaded by palm trees
- Sloped gently down to the sea
- Reached by scrambling down a steep, winding path
- Shimmered in the heat

SENTENCES

The beach was long and narrow and sloped gently down to the sea.

He was surrounded by sugar white beaches and a vivid blue sea that stretched for miles.

The emerald jewel of coral reefs and diamond dust beaches was enclosed by a lush green forest.

The beach was a long arc of golden sand, sheltered by dunes and large umbrella palm trees.

The small, sheltered cove was reached by scrambling down a steep, winding path.

SECTION 2 – ISLANDS

WORDS

Nouns	Sea, lagoon, reef, bays, coral, fish Rocks, cliffs, caves Heather, palm trees Bones, skeletons, relics
Adjectives	Small, large, long, thin, narrow, wide, flat, rocky Shallow, deep Tropical, rainbow, multi-coloured, blue, turquoise Wild, overgrown, rocky, black, barren, volcanic, eerie, moon-like, lifeless, sinister, ancient
Verbs	Surrounded, circled Shadowed, guarded

PHRASES – NOUNS AND ADJECTIVES

- Tropical island
- Rocky island slopes
- Pure, white beaches
- Purple heather
- Beautiful coral reef

- Brilliant turquoise lagoons
- Tropical, rainbow-coloured fish
- Wild and overgrown
- Eerie, lifeless island
- Barren and rocky
- Pillars of rock at the entrance to the bay
- Jigsaw of human and animal skeletons
- Relics of an ancient world
- Sinister view of volcanic peaks and a moon-like landscape

PHRASES – VERBS

- Ablaze with purple heather
- Palm trees swayed in the breeze
- Circled by a shallow, blue lagoon
- Teeming with multi-coloured corals and tropical fish
- Guarded by steep, rocky cliffs
- Littered with bones
- Haunted by bats
- Echo of pain and death lingered

SENTENCES

It was an eerie, lifeless island guarded by steep, rocky cliffs.

The rocky island slopes were ablaze with purple heather.

They had arrived in a paradise of tropical islands, with swaying palm trees, pure white beaches and brilliant turquoise lagoons.

The island was circled by a shallow lagoon on a beautiful reef teeming with multi-coloured corals and tropical fish.

The island was a time capsule. Wherever they went they found relics of an ancient world.

Littered with bones, the shore was a jigsaw of human and animal skeletons.

SECTION 3 – VOLCANOES

WORDS

Nouns	Cone, crater, fountain, cauldron
	Clouds, steam, bubbles, fumes, fire, smoke, ash, rocks, lava, mud
Adjectives	Smoky, black, choking, red, white-hot
	Spitting, hissing, belching, smouldering
	Menacing, throbbing, awesome, deafening
Verbs	Shook, trembled, bubbled, exploded, erupted, crashed, rained
	Hissed, roared, boomed

PHRASES – NOUNS AND ADJECTIVES

- White-hot steam
- Choking fumes
- Fountain of fire like a throbbing wound
- Smoky black haze
- Towering, black clouds of ash and smoke
- Smouldering ash and rocks
- Cauldron of spitting bubbles, hissing steam and belching fumes

PHRASES – VERBS

- Rose up in a cone
- Crater loomed ominously over the town
- Ground trembled and shook
- Rained from the sky
- Flooded the sky
- Followed by a deafening boom

SENTENCES

The air was thick with choking fumes.

The earth trembled and shook and sent everything crashing to the ground.

It was hard to breathe and hard to see in the smoky, black haze.

Huge black clouds blocked out the sun, and darkness fell.

Torrents of sizzling, smouldering ash and rocks rained from the sky.

As the volcano erupted, there was a deafening boom and the ground trembled and shook.

A fountain of fire, like a throbbing wound, flooded the sky.

Looming ominously over the village, the crater and its plume of vapour was a silent, menacing reminder of its awesome power.

SECTION 4 – DESERTS

WORDS

Nouns	Sand, dunes, horizon Heat, furnace, wind, storm
Adjectives	Rocky, flat, thorny, bare, stark, barren Burning, shimmering, savage, merciless, endless
Verbs	Burnt, baked, shimmered Blew, flung, whipped

4 *Landscapes: beaches, islands, volcanoes and deserts*

PHRASES – NOUNS AND ADJECTIVES

- ★ Land of burning sands
- ★ Sea of sand
- ★ Desert was a furnace
- ★ Stark and barren
- ★ Rocky and spiked with thorny bushes
- ★ Endless, flat horizon
- ★ Burning, merciless desert of glare and death

PHRASES – VERBS

- ★ Stretched as far as the eye could see
- ★ Shimmered in the heat
- ★ Baked by day and chilled by night
- ★ Wind flung the sand into their throats and eyes
- ★ Whipped up mile-high walls of sand
- ★ Endless, flat horizon was suddenly broken by . . .

SENTENCES

The desert was a furnace. It was a land of burning sands.

Huge sand dunes had been blown away by the sand storm and dumped elsewhere.

The endless, flat horizon was suddenly broken by a group of tall rock pillars like giant mushrooms.

The desert spread out before him – a sea of sand, shimmering with heat.

It was a burning, merciless desert of glare and death.

5

Ground and paths

SECTION 1 – GROUND

WORDS

Nouns	Ground, earth, grass, leaves, twigs, moss, lichen, frost, ice, snow Dust, cracks Mud, bog, marsh, swamp
Adjectives	Cold, white, crisp, sparkling, shining Hard, frozen, solid Green, lush Dry, red, brown, dusty, baked, arid, scorched, parched, barren Wet, muddy, swampy, boggy, waterlogged, slippery, squelchy, slimy, gooey
Verbs	Sparkled, glittered, glinted, gleamed Burned, roasted, withered Split, cracked, crunched, groaned Trapped, held, swallowed Fell, slipped, scrambled, clawed, struggled, sunk

PHRASES – NOUNS AND ADJECTIVES

- ★ Fairytale world
- ★ Crisp carpet of snow
- ★ Glittering ice
- ★ Glinting, white frost
- ★ Hard with black frost
- ★ Autumn's crisp leaves
- ★ Lush, green grass

- Dry, red ground
- Enormous cracks in the scorched earth
- Baked ground was as dry as cork underfoot
- Withered, dead leaves and dry twigs
- Like muddy soup
- Squelching, slimy mud
- Slippery moss and lichen
- Wet, slippery leaves
- Gooey slime

PHRASES – VERBS

- Sunk into the lush, green grass
- Cloaked in snow
- Crunched beneath her feet
- Sparkled with frost
- Nothing grew on the baked earth
- Roasted by the sun
- Wind blew a cloud of dust along the road
- Feet crunched on the withered, dead leaves
- Fell back in a mud-slide
- Swallowed her feet
- Held her in its squelching, slimy grasp
- Struggled to gain a foothold
- Slipped and clawed her way through the gooey slime
- Ice groaned and cracked
- Split like a lightning bolt
- Seeped through his boots

SENTENCES

The snow made a crisp carpet beneath their feet.

They had entered a fairytale world, where the ground and hills were cloaked in snow.

Above her, clouds like fluffy cotton balls drifted across the sky and below, autumn's crisp leaves crunched under her feet.

The land was barren. Nothing grew on the dry, red ground.

The months without rain had caused enormous cracks to appear in the scorched earth.

The ground was as dry as cork underfoot and her feet crunched on the withered, dead leaves and fallen twigs.

She slipped and clawed her way through the gooey slime.

The ground was like muddy soup and swallowed her feet in its squelching, slimy grasp.

She scrambled up the vertical bank, which was slimy with damp leaves and mud.

The ground was covered in frost and glinted dangerously.

The earth was hard with black frost that seeped through his sodden boots and spread ice into every limb.

Below his feet, the glittering ice cracked and groaned, until finally it split like a lightning bolt.

SECTION 2 – PATHS

WORDS

Nouns	Track, trail, path, footpath
Adjectives	Wooded, grassy, ancient, forgotten Narrow, wide, steep, winding Rough, rutted, pot-holed, bone-shaking, dusty, muddy, slimy
Verbs	Ran, led, followed, headed, veered Wound, twisted, turned, coiled Climbed, dipped, dropped, plummeted

PHRASES – NOUNS AND ADJECTIVES

- Wooded path
- Ancient mule track
- Narrow, winding coastal path
- Dirt track
- Steep, winding mountain trail
- Forgotten path
- Rough, pot-holed cattle trail
- Bone-shaking trail
- Rough path through heather and gorse

PHRASES – VERBS

- Dipped and climbed across the hills
- Coiled round the mountain
- Climbed steeply up the side of the mountain
- Disappeared into the menacing peaks
- Plummeted into the woods
- Ran parallel to the shore
- Followed the twists and turns of the river
- Led down to the stream
- Led them through the forest
- Veered to the left
- Ran between a tunnel of high bushes
- Hidden in the brambles

5 *Landscapes: ground and paths*

- Strangled by thorns and creepers
- Holes like craters gouged in the surface

SENTENCES

A grassy path headed down to the left.

The dusty, rugged path wound steeply up the side of the mountain.

The narrow path followed the river and wound through the wood.

The ancient mule track twisted and turned and snaked its way steeply to the top.

The rough track dipped and climbed across the hills through the heather and gorse.

The path suddenly veered to the left and they had a fleeting view of the vivid, blue sea stretching as far as the eye could see.

They followed a rough track between the fields of golden corn, until they came to a stile.

Beyond the gate, a flight of narrow, rough steps led down to a stream.

He searched for a way forward and finally came across what seemed to be a forgotten path, hidden by thorns and creepers and leading deep into the forest.

The bone-shaking trail was covered in holes like craters, which were filled with mud and water.

They followed the narrow, winding coastal path until they came to a wooden fence. Suddenly, the land fell away in a steep slope and then plunged into the sea.

6

Streams, rivers, lakes and waterfalls

WORDS

Nouns	Forest, mountainside, hills, slopes, banks
	Cliffs, rocks, pebbles
	Depths, current, rapids, waterfall, fountain
	Spray, mist, foam
	Plants, weeds, rubbish, fumes, chemicals
	Sunlight, moonlight, starlight
Adjectives	Deep, shallow, long, narrow, wide, broad
	Clear, silver, crystal, pearly, white, glassy, blue
	Silky, sparkling, glinting, glistening, glittering, gleaming, flickering
	Calm, peaceful, tranquil, soothing
	Dark, grey, brown, gloomy, inky, greasy, oily, murky
	Swollen, stormy, bulging, restless, boiling, foaming, churning, frothing, swirling
	Wild, raging, deadly, savage, thunderous, pounding, ominous, threatening, menacing
Verbs	Wound, flowed, twisted, turned, weaved, snaked
	Glided, spilled, meandered, ambled, tumbled, toppled, splashed
	Fell, dropped, danced, hopped
	Whispered, murmured, burbled, rippled, bubbled, trickled, gurgled
	Blocked, choked, trapped, polluted
	Rushed, sped, swept, gushed, burst, flooded, pounded, blasted, crashed, hurtled, plunged, cascaded, rampaged
	Roared, thundered

6 *Landscapes: streams, rivers, lakes and waterfalls*

PHRASES – NOUNS AND ADJECTIVES

- Long and narrow
- Deep, wide lake
- As clear and smooth as glass
- Calm and crystal clear
- Peaceful blue waters
- Like a long, snaking ribbon
- Like lines of sparkling silver
- Huge curtain of shimmering silver
- Glimmering like a lazy, grey snake
- Pearly white in the shadow of the moon
- Like thousands of tiny diamonds on the water
- Silky, watery stairs
- Curtain of sparkling, dancing water
- Misty spray
- Leaping foam
- Soft bubbling of a stream
- Trickle of running water
- Ripple of a stream tumbling down the hill
- Music of invisible fountains
- Dark, oily river
- Gloomy and murky
- Grey, restless water
- Bulging blister of churning, grey water
- Brown, frothing and polluted
- Eerie, green, underwater forest
- Wild current
- Torrents of water
- Huge clouds of wild, flying spray
- White, swirling foam
- Raging, foaming falls
- Pounding roar
- Deadly sound of roaring rapids

PHRASES – VERBS

- Wound down the mountainside
- Danced down the slopes
- Flowed down the hill as dozens of little waterfalls
- Rushed down the mountain like watery stairs
- Twisted and turned through the forest
- Meandered through the village

- Toppled over moss-covered rocks
- Gurgled over the pebbles
- Burbled as it hopped and danced down the rocks
- Whispered as it fell
- Glistened with a million diamonds of light
- Shimmered in the flickering starlight
- Sparkled in the midday sun
- Choked with weeds
- Polluted by rubbish and chemicals
- Dived into an eerie, green world
- Strangled by a spidery web of weeds
- Impossible to see anything in the murky depths
- Swollen and flooding its banks
- Churning, grey water
- Rushed savagely
- Plunged and cascaded down the mountain
- Cascaded over the top of the falls
- Rampaged down the rocks
- Battled against the boulders that barred its way
- Hurtled into the misty void below
- Blasted into a white, swirling foam
- Sent huge clouds of spray hundreds of feet into the air
- Roared as it hurtled over the edge
- Blanketed everything with its pounding roar
- Thundered endlessly over the lip of the rock
- Ate mile upon mile of ground
- Destroyed everything in its path

SENTENCES

The lake was a huge curtain of shimmering silver.

The cold, clear water of the stream wound down the mountainside.

He could hear the soft bubbling of a stream in the distance.

The water in the lake was calm and crystal clear and sparkled with a million diamonds of light in the midday sun.

Shimmering in the flickering starlight, the river was a long, snaking, silver ribbon.

The mountain streams made winding lines of sparkling silver as they danced down the slopes.

There was a trickle of running water as the river flowed down the hill as dozens of little waterfalls.

From every hill came the gurgling of water – the music of invisible fountains as the river tumbled down the slopes.

The waterfall was a silky, watery stairs that whispered as it fell.

6 *Landscapes: streams, rivers, lakes and waterfalls*

He was surrounded by a curtain of dancing water, which sent a spray like thousands of tiny diamonds dropping from the sky.

Clear and as smooth as glass, the stream twisted and turned through the forest.

The river was swollen and flooding its banks.

The grey, churning water of the lake blended with the stormy sky.

From below came the deadly sound of roaring rapids.

The lake was long and narrow and wound between the towering, ghostly mountains.

The river was brown and frothing, polluted by rubbish and chemicals.

It was impossible to see anything in the murky depths of the oily river.

The wild current swept past and flung the water into the air as it tumbled over the edge.

A torrent of water thundered endlessly over the lip of the rock and filled the river with its hammering roar.

The water was turned into wild, flying foam as it rampaged down the rocks.

Roaring fiercely, the river hurtled over the edge into the swirling mist below.

She had dived into an eerie world: an underwater forest of murky, green water, strangled by a spidery web of weeds.

Torrents of water plunged over the top of the cliffs into the once calm waterhole, turning into a raging, foaming falls and sending huge clouds of spray hundreds of feet into the air.

7

Sea and waves

WORDS

Nouns	Ocean, sea, surface, depths, coast Island, shore, bay, cove, harbour, beach, sand, rocks, rock-pool, pebbles, seaweed Waves, breakers, rollers, swell, crests, surf, foam, spray, mist Sunlight, breeze, wind
Adjectives	Blue, turquoise, green, emerald, white, silver, clear, crystal, vivid Calm, smooth Shimmering, sparkling, glittering Grey, black, dark, inky, murky Cold, icy, chilly, stormy, restless, churning, foaming, boiling Huge, vast, enormous, giant, massive Brutal, fierce, merciless Roaring, deafening, thunderous
Verbs	Rippled, creased, wrinkled Rolled, trickled, flicked, lapped, curled, coiled, crept, slid, danced Slapped, sucked, swished, sloshed, splashed Foamed, boiled, swirled, churned, heaved Tugged, sucked, dragged, trapped Grew, rose, curled, arched, bent, tumbled, tossed, lurched Marched, raced, galloped, soared, surged Struck, tossed, beat, battered, pounded, hammered, crashed, smashed, pummelled Groaned, rumbled, growled, roared, boomed, thundered

7 *Landscapes: sea and waves*

PHRASES – NOUNS AND ADJECTIVES

- Turquoise ocean
- Emerald surface
- Vivid blue water
- Shimmering blue waves
- Crystal clear water
- Like a rare jewel
- As smooth as silk
- Circles of soft, white foam
- Picture postcard of paradise
- Slap and suck of water on sand
- Like the swish of a curtain
- Splash and slosh of the waves
- Dark, cold water
- Grey, churning surface of the waves
- Black world of the deep, restless ocean
- Massive waves
- Booming breakers
- Enormous, curling rollers
- Crest was a huge arch
- Like galloping foam horses
- Massive crest of churning foam
- Icy mist
- Boiling, hissing foam
- Foaming, yellow sand
- Swirling, white spray
- Spray like a bleeding mist in the setting sun
- Watery grave
- Warning groan and rumble of the huge waves

PHRASES – VERBS

- Caught sight of the sea far below
- Sparkled like a rare jewel
- Silver streaks of light danced across the water
- Blazed with all the colours of the rainbow
- Rippled softly in the breeze
- Wrinkled the surface of the water
- Rolled onto the beach
- Slid onto the sand
- Coiled around the rocks
- Flicked lazily at the rocks

- Rippled onto the sand
- Lapped against the side of the boat
- Crept into the rock pools
- Trapped by the black world of the vast ocean
- Tugged at him and sucked him into its swirling surface
- Dragged into its inky depths
- Soared high in the air
- Bent first one way and then the other
- Curved towards the beach
- Rose in a huge arch above the boat
- Roared as they raced to the beach
- Crashed against each other
- Marched towards the island
- Surged into the harbour
- Flung the boats from side to side
- Wrenched the boats from their anchors
- Threatened to bury it in a watery grave
- Pounded the shore mercilessly
- Crashed against the rocks
- Pummelled and tossed by the brutal power of the waves
- Churned the beach into foaming, yellow sand
- Deafening roar as the wave thundered into sight
- Boom of the waves echoed through the air

SENTENCES

The sea around the island was a shimmering blue.

The water in the bay was a vivid, pure green.

She looked down through the crystal clear water to the powdery, white sands below.

The emerald surface of the sea glittered with a million diamonds of sunlight.

The waves slid, like the swish of a curtain, onto the powdery white sand.

The waves curled and lapped against the side of the boat.

The blue sea sparkled like a rare jewel and rippled softly in the breeze.

The crystal waves creased the surface of the sea and rolled gently into the cove.

Lapping gently onto the shore, the waves sent circles of water dancing around the rocks.

Crystal clear and as smooth as silk, the turquoise ocean was a picture postcard of paradise.

It was quiet except for the soothing, rhythmic splash and slosh of the waves creeping into the rock pools.

He caught sight of the dark, cold water of the sea far below.

She was surrounded by a black blanket of swirling sea and stormy sky.

The booming breakers battered the shore.

7 *Landscapes: sea and waves*

Ahead and below them it was dark. They were trapped by the black world of the deep, restless sea.

The sea was dark, heaving and choked with seaweed.

The tumbling breakers crashed onto the rocks and left an icy mist as they were dragged back to sea.

A mass of churning foam rose in an arch high above the boat and threatened to bury it in a watery grave.

The hissing foam pounded the rocks and covered them in an icy mist.

As it thundered into sight, the roar of the wave was deafening.

The waves roared in from the sea, surged into the harbour, flung the boats from side to side and wrenched them from their anchors.

He was caught in the heaving, murky water, which tugged at him, sucked him into its swirling surface and dragged him into its inky depths.

The waves rose higher and higher; thundered nearer and nearer; broke into a roar of boiling foam and raced to the shore like galloping foam horses.

The spray from the waves looked like a bleeding mist in the red light of the setting sun – their thunderous roar like a wounded animal.

Like two giants locked in combat, the waves crashed against each other, soaring high in the air, bending first one way and then the other.

Settlements

8

Cities, towns and villages

WORDS

Nouns	Cafes, restaurants, shops, malls, stalls, markets, art galleries, museums, skyscrapers, offices, hotels, factories, houses, flats
	Streets, alleys, lanes, arcades, squares, centre, parks, village green
	Graffiti, rubbish, smoke, fumes, soot, smog, damp, mould, grime, waste, chemicals, pollution
Adjectives	Small, little, big, large, huge
	Busy, lively, bright, colourful, exciting, vibrant, electric, dynamic, cosmopolitan
	Quiet, sleepy, quaint, leafy, picturesque
	Crowded, cramped, empty, deserted
	Old, ancient, new, modern, Victorian, Georgian
	Dark, black, grey, ugly, dirty, stinking, polluted
	Run-down, crumbling, rotting, decaying, ruined, haunted
Verbs	Lived, built, constructed
	Spread, sprawled, huddled, nestled, hidden, shadowed, overlooked
	Buzzed, bustled
	Covered, painted, sprayed, blackened

PHRASES – NOUNS AND ADJECTIVES

- Busy, colourful city
- Bustling market town
- Quaint fishing village
- Sleepy little village
- Small, quaint town on the coast
- Old market town

8 Settlements: cities, towns and villages

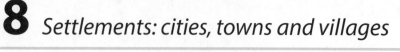

- Sprawling concrete jungle
- Ruined ghost village
- Stinking, polluted place
- Run-down part of the city
- Cobbled squares and arcades
- Wide, tree-lined streets
- Leafy lanes
- Warren of narrow, twisting alleys
- Labyrinth of secret, underground tunnels and cellars
- Scores of shops, art galleries and museums
- Shopping malls
- Pavement cafes
- Market stalls
- Georgian buildings
- Victorian cottages
- Modern skyscrapers
- Big, ugly factories
- Towering chimneys
- Blocks of flats
- Red-brick houses
- White houses with brightly coloured doors and shutters
- Houses with thatched roofs
- Vibrant, cosmopolitan atmosphere
- An exciting mix of smells and sounds from around the world
- Haven from the noise and pollution of the city
- Houses built from cardboard
- Empty shells
- Pile of stones and shattered walls
- Boarded-up windows
- Empty, gaping window frames
- Crawling damp and mould
- Black veil of smoke
- Soot and smog
- Rotting rubbish and broken glass
- Plastic bags, crisp packets and empty drink bottles

PHRASES – VERBS

- Lived in a run-down part of the town
- Spread out before him like a concrete jungle
- Surrounded by gentle hills and leafy lanes
- Huddled around the village green
- Overlooked the sea
- Nestled at the foot of the mountain
- Seemed an unlikely place for . . .

- Bustling with tourists
- Buzzing with pavement cafes and street musicians
- Alive with smells from the food stalls
- Sprayed with graffiti
- Wood covered the windows
- Lined with rotting rubbish
- Grime and pollution clung to the houses
- Blackened by soot and smog
- Smoke spewed from the factories
- Waste pumped and dumped into the river

SENTENCES

It was a quaint town, with narrow, cobbled streets.

The picturesque market town was surrounded by gentle hills and leafy lanes.

The sea-side town was a small, enchanting haven from the polluted city.

Ahead of him on the rocky coast was a quaint fishing village.

The ancient town was a warren of tunnels and narrow, twisting alleys, and a maze of buildings.

It was a colourful, cosmopolitan city. The street markets filled the air with an exciting mix of smells and sounds from around the world.

The wide, tree-lined streets were bright and cheerful, lined with pavement cafes and alive with the sounds of street musicians.

The city was bustling with tourists, eager to explore the scores of shops, art galleries and museums.

Nestling around the village green, the sleepy village seemed an unlikely place for an adventure.

The village was no more than a pile of stones and shattered walls.

She lived in a run-down part of the city. Wood, not glass, filled the windows. Graffiti covered the walls. Rotting rubbish and broken glass lined the streets.

Plastic bags and crisp packets flapped like streamers from the trees. Empty drink bottles rattled in the gutter.

They could see the city spread out before them, with its black veil of smoke and towering chimneys.

Most of the houses had been built from cardboard, or anything that could be rescued to provide shelter.

The houses were crowded together and blackened by soot and smog.

It was a ghost town of deserted houses crawling with mould and damp – empty shells with gaping windows like haunted eyes.

Years of grime and pollution clung to the houses, spewed from the big, ugly factories that shadowed the streets.

A warren of secret, underground tunnels and cellars was used to move around the city and to hide from invaders in times of danger.

9

Roads

WORDS

Nouns	Motorway, highway, route, road, street, lane, alley, passageway
	Maze, warren, labyrinth
	Cars, traffic, fumes, pollution, dust, pot-holes
Adjectives	City, town, country, coastal, mountain, desert
	Wide, narrow, flat, steep, straight, winding, twisting
	Quiet, busy, noisy
	Dirty, pot-holed, bone-shaking
	Dangerous, perilous
Verbs	Drove, followed
	Circled, wound, bent, twisted, turned, curved, coiled, meandered
	Clogged, jammed

PHRASES – NOUNS AND ADJECTIVES

- Winding mountain roads
- Quiet country lanes
- Narrow, dusty roads
- Wide, straight motorways
- Roads like strings of spaghetti
- Warren of narrow, twisting alleys
- Arrow-straight desert road
- Pot-holed road
- Series of perilous curves like a coiled spring
- Patchworks of lush, green fields
- Golden fields of corn

- Streams of noisy traffic
- Cars and fumes
- Clouds of dust

PHRASES – VERBS

- Drove from village to village
- Route took him through . . .
- Along winding, country roads
- Followed the coast for miles
- Circled the city centre
- Through narrow village streets
- Twisted and turned
- Crabbed along the mountain
- Started downwards in a steep descent
- Jammed with traffic
- Carried streams of noisy traffic
- Belched out fumes
- Jostled their way forward
- Shuddered along the road
- Struck huge pot-holes
- Clouds of dust sprayed the windscreen

SENTENCES

She drove from village to village along the winding country roads.

His route took him through quiet country lanes and patchworks of lush green fields.

The narrow, winding road followed the coast for miles, past sandy bays and a shimmering turquoise sea.

The arrow-straight desert road shimmered in the intense heat.

It was a huge, dirty city clogged with fumes and traffic.

The city centre was circled by wide motorways carrying streams of traffic belching out fumes, but never moving very fast.

Like strings of spaghetti, roads circled and split the town.

The road started downwards in a steep descent and crabbed along the mountain in a series of perilous curves, twisting and turning like a coiled spring.

The car shuddered along the bone-shaking trail. Clouds of dust sprayed the windscreen and the car leaped into the air as the front tyres struck the pot-holes.

10

Gardens

WORDS

Nouns	Wall, fence, railings, hedge, bush, trees
	Gate, arches, pillars, lanterns, statues
	Brick, gravel, stones, grass
	Woodland, wilderness
	Lawn, flowers, plants, shrubs, blossoms
	Oak tree, rose bushes, apple tree, maple tree, willow tree, palm tree, lilac, clematis, honeysuckle, jasmine, lavender, rhododendrons, bedding plants
	Patio, deck, tree house, pond, fountain, flower pots, hanging baskets, window boxes
	Barbed wire, steel spikes, rubbish, junk, weeds, brambles, thorns, ivy, creepers, moss, lichen, slime
Adjectives	Long, wide, thin, narrow, straight, winding, sweeping
	Green, bronze, orange, pink, scarlet, red, white, purple, blue, rainbow-coloured
	Bright, beautiful, vivid, vibrant, tropical, stunning, spectacular, magnificent
	Neat, manicured
	Brown, yellow, dying, wilting, shrivelled
	Dark, gloomy, sinister, ghostly, eerie, mysterious
	Wild, overgrown, long, high, knee-high, tangled, spidery
	Prickly, thorny, needle-sharp, razor-sharp
Verbs	Grew, hung, spread, covered, brimmed
	Lined, flanked, arranged, surrounded
	Hid, shielded, guarded, shadowed, loomed
	Crept, overflowed, choked, tangled, strangled
	Spilled, spewed, flapped

PHRASES – NOUNS AND ADJECTIVES

- Long, sweeping drive
- High stone walls
- Twisted metal railings
- Metal fence three metres high
- Heavy gates studded with iron bolts
- High, wooden, electric gates
- Huge stone pillars
- Arched gateway
- Carpet of lush, green grass
- Magnificent oak trees
- Beautiful wilderness of huge trees and wild flowers
- Pots brimming with brightly coloured flowers
- Baskets of flowers like balls of blazing colour
- Magnificent pond
- Rainbow-coloured tropical fish
- Wild and overgrown
- Sinister hedge of prickly, tangled branches
- Wild, tangled and mysterious
- Long, knee-high grass
- Brown grass and wilting flowers
- Needle-sharp steel spikes
- Razor-sharp barbed wire
- Full of junk and rubbish bags
- Plastic bags instead of blossoms
- Battered, rusty, old furniture

PHRASES – VERBS

- Set in acres of woodland
- Shielded by high, red-brick walls
- Surrounded by twisted metal railings
- Impossible to see behind the high, wooden gates
- Wall topped with . . .
- . . . guarded the gate
- . . . loomed the ghostly shadow of the house
- Shielded the house from the road
- Swept up to an enormous manor house
- Ran through the middle of lush, neat lawns
- Oak trees lined the drive
- Lined with rose bushes
- Guarded by enormous stone lions
- Flooded by the light of huge, bronze lanterns

- Stood either side of the front door
- Hung from the walls
- Brimmed with brightly coloured flowers
- Arranged in symmetrical rows and colours around the lawn
- Spread its enormous limbs over the centre of the garden
- Covered in pink clematis flowers
- Glowed yellow and bronze
- Steeped in shadow
- Strangled the path
- Crept and wriggled over the drive
- Dripped with slime
- Choked with weeds and ivy
- Wilted in the sticky heat
- Spilled their contents over the path
- Flapped on the bushes

SENTENCES

The long gravel drive ran through the middle of lush, neat lawns.

The manor house was surrounded by high, red-brick walls.

The gates to the long, sweeping drive were flanked with statues of enormous stone lions.

The wooden gate was hidden by a huge maple tree.

The arched gateway dripped with slime.

It was impossible to see what lay behind the high gates.

The gate was set in the wall and cunningly hidden in the shadows.

Weeds and ivy had eaten their way into the cracks of the wall and spread their tentacles into every crevice.

Bushes crept and wriggled over the drive, which was now just a thin strip steeped in shadow.

The warehouse was surrounded by a tall fence, at least three metres high, topped with steel spikes and razor wire.

The drive was paved, but grass grew in every crevice and moss clung to the surface like mould on bread.

They looked through the twisted railings and in front of them in the gloom were dark, crumbling stones, thorny bushes and knee-high grass. Beyond loomed the ghostly shadow of the house.

The back of the house was a huge carpet of lush, green grass.

Grassy slopes rolled down from the house to a beautiful wilderness of huge trees and wild flowers.

Huge terracotta pots, brimming with brightly coloured flowers, sat either side of the front door.

Brightly coloured plants were arranged in symmetrical rows and colours, and bordered the edge of the lawn.

Honeysuckle clung to the majestic oak tree, which spread its enormous limbs over the centre of the garden.

The front garden was wild and overgrown.

Plastic bags instead of blossoms flapped on the bushes.

It was a spidery tangle of trees, bushes, weeds and long, knee-high grass.

The grass was withered and brown, and the flowers wilting, starved of water and choked with weeds.

The garden was full of junk: battered, old furniture, rusty metal frames and rubbish bags ripped and spewing their contents on the ground.

11

Buildings

WORDS

Nouns

House, manor, farmhouse, cottage, bungalow, villa, flat

Height, floors, storeys

Stone, brick, timber, wood, tiles, slate, thatch, metal, glass

Walls, roof, chimney, gutter, windows, shutters, balcony, porch, door, bay window

Window-boxes, hanging baskets, flowers, herbs, roses, jasmine, honeysuckle

Adjectives

Old, ancient, new, modern, Georgian, Victorian

Detached, semi-detached, terraced

Tall, high, low, long, small, big, large, huge

Wooden, stone, red-brick, whitewashed, white, cream, grey, black, peach, pastel-coloured, brightly coloured

Warm, cosy, charming, inviting, welcoming, peaceful, impressive, luxurious

Empty, bare, deserted, lifeless, haunted, strange, sinister

Dirty, dusty, dark, gloomy, neglected

Wild, overgrown, derelict, ramshackle, rickety, boarded up

Verbs

Lived, rented, inhabited, lodged, resided

Located, situated

Made, built, constructed

Painted, decorated

Leaked, crumbled, clogged, smashed, shattered

PHRASES – NOUNS AND ADJECTIVES

- ★ Farmhouse was over four hundred years old
- ★ Street of terraced Victorian houses
- ★ Modern semi-detached house
- ★ Old detached cottage
- ★ Modern block of flats
- ★ Huge, luxurious mansion
- ★ Red-brick manor house
- ★ Georgian town house
- ★ Tall, imposing house
- ★ Ten-storey tower block
- ★ Single-storey villa
- ★ Wooden hunting lodge
- ★ Derelict factory
- ★ White, stone bungalow with a green tiled roof
- ★ Whitewashed farmhouse
- ★ Black and white front
- ★ Peach fronted
- ★ Tall, arched windows
- ★ Bay window at the side of the front door
- ★ Row of floor-to-ceiling windows
- ★ Beautifully carved white shutters
- ★ Arched, wooden porch
- ★ Window-boxes and hanging baskets
- ★ Charming, inviting home
- ★ Cosy cottage
- ★ Rickety old cottage
- ★ Huge, dirty, ramshackle place
- ★ Derelict building
- ★ Deathly, haunted place
- ★ Wild and overgrown
- ★ Pile of stones and shattered walls
- ★ Crumbling chimneys and hanging gutters
- ★ Peeling paint
- ★ Rotting sills
- ★ Broken windows
- ★ Empty, gaping window frames
- ★ Only ragged traces of glass in the windows

PHRASES – VERBS

- ★ Situated at the end of a narrow dirt track
- ★ Built in a peaceful haven

- Set in ten acres
- Surrounded by strange, sinister countryside
- Set right in the heart of the forest
- Located in the centre of the town
- On the outskirts of the city
- Circled the gated park
- Lived in a street of . . .
- Lived in a cosy cottage
- Made out of great, stone slabs
- Built of brick
- Made entirely of wood
- Arched with roses
- Framed with elegant shutters
- Flanked by a sweetly scented herb garden
- Smothered in honeysuckle and jasmine
- Filled with brightly coloured flowers
- Stood empty and lifeless
- Clogged with rotting leaves
- Jutted out of rotting sills
- Roof leaked like a colander
- As if gnawed by hundreds of starving rats

SENTENCES

The wooden hunting lodge was set right in the heart of the forest.

She lived in an old, terraced cottage at the end of a narrow dirt track.

The farmhouse was over four hundred years old. It was made out of great stone slabs and had a red tiled roof.

She lived in a street of terraced Victorian houses, each with a bay window at the side of the front door.

The red-brick manor house was set in ten acres of woodland. It was a tall, imposing house and its numerous towers made it look like a fortress.

The hotel was a modern glass and metal building, ten storeys high.

The modern, semi-detached house was in a quiet cul-de-sac and shielded from the road by a line of pine trees.

They had rented an impressive single-storey villa. Its front was painted peach and the windows were framed by carved white shutters.

It was a charming, inviting home with an arched wooden porch covered in honeysuckle and flanked by a sweetly scented herb garden.

The house was falling down. It was a pile of stones, shattered walls and empty, gaping window frames.

The place felt evil. It was the type of place that made people quicken their step as they passed.

Ivy clasped the walls of the house and curled through the roof.

It was a rickety old cottage with dark green moss spreading across the walls like mould on bread.

The house was nearly derelict. Its stonework was decayed and crumbling, its windows boarded up, paint peeling and sills rotting.

It was a huge, dirty, ramshackle place, with broken windows and a roof that leaked like a colander.

Only ragged traces of glass remained in the windows – sharp spears jutting out of rotting sills.

The derelict building stood lifeless. Its crumbling chimneys and hanging gutters were clogged with rotting leaves and the walls were pitted, as if they had been gnawed by hundreds of starving rats.

12

Doors, halls, corridors and stairs

SECTION 1 – DOORS

WORDS

Nouns	Yard, courtyard, gate, door, knocker, handle Bolts, nails, symbols
Adjectives	Wooden, oak, glass, stained-glass, metal, iron, steel, brass, ancient Front, back, side Low, high, heavy, light
Verbs	Led, faced, opened, blocked Studded, carved

PHRASES – NOUNS AND ADJECTIVES

- Heavy oak door
- Low, ancient-looking door
- Metal gate
- Steel-shuttered door
- Door with stained-glass panels
- Carved with ancient symbols
- Studded with black nails
- Large brass handle
- Knocker in the shape of . . .

PHRASES – VERBS

- Blocked by a metal gate
- Towered above them
- Rattled in the wind

- ★ Led to a door with stained-glass panels
- ★ Led from the yard into the main part of the house
- ★ Faced by a low door
- ★ Set deep in the wall
- ★ Opened out onto a large hall

SENTENCES

The entrance was blocked by a metal gate carved with ancient symbols.

The heavy, metal door opened out onto a vast, wood-panelled hall.

The front step was set deep in the wall and led to a door with stained-glass panels.

A steel-shuttered door towered above them and rattled in the wind.

They went through a heavy, oak door, which led from the courtyard into the main part of the house.

Where the path ended, they were faced by a low, ancient-looking door studded with sharp, black nails.

SECTION 2 – HALLS, CORRIDORS, STAIRS

WORDS

Nouns	Entrance, hall, hallway, corridor, steps, stairs, staircase
Adjectives	Narrow, wide, long, vast, spiral Dark, dimly lit, gloomy, eerie, draughty, echoing White, cream, red, wooden, stone, marble Polished, luxurious
Verbs	Entered, led, opened Twisted, turned, spiralled Echoed, creaked, rattled

PHRASES – NOUNS AND ADJECTIVES

- ★ Dark flight of narrow stairs
- ★ Stone steps
- ★ Wide staircase
- ★ Spiral stairs
- ★ Creaking stairs
- ★ Narrow hallway
- ★ Vast, echoing entrance hall
- ★ Long, dimly lit corridor
- ★ Draughty corridor
- ★ Polished white marble floor
- ★ Luxurious red carpet

12 *Settlements: doors, halls, corridors and stairs*

PHRASES – VERBS

- ★ Entered a narrow hallway
- ★ Ahead was a flight of stairs
- ★ Led up to the first floor
- ★ Climbed the stone steps
- ★ Entered a vast entrance hall
- ★ Opened onto a long corridor
- ★ Swept dramatically down to the entrance hall
- ★ Twisted and turned sharply
- ★ Spiralled to the rooms upstairs
- ★ Changed direction at every corner
- ★ Steeped in a thick, eerie darkness
- ★ Wind tore through the draughty corridor

SENTENCES

The door opened onto a long, dimly lit corridor.

The wooden stairs spiralled their way to the rooms upstairs.

The glass doors opened out onto a lobby of polished white marble.

Her feet sunk into the luxurious red carpet.

The wide staircase swept dramatically down to the entrance hall.

They went up the stone steps into the vast, echoing entrance hall.

She was faced with a long corridor steeped in a thick, eerie darkness.

He had entered a narrow hallway and ahead of him was a flight of stairs leading up to the first floor.

A bitter wind tore through the draughty corridors and rattled the windows.

The staircase was dark and gloomy and every step she took was followed by a creaking echo.

The spiral stairs twisted and turned sharply, changing direction at every corner.

13

Rooms

WORDS

Nouns

Kitchen, lounge, sitting room, dining room, family room, study

Ceilings, beams, walls, floor, floorboards, windows

Curtains, wallpaper, carpet, tiles, furniture, tables, chairs, sofa, shelves, fireplace

Haven, retreat

Shadows, cobwebs, dust, dirt, grime, mould, slime, bats, rats, spiders, mice

Sunlight, streetlamps, roof lights, condensation

Adjectives

Large, enormous, small, tiny, square, rectangular

Warm, homely, snug, relaxing, welcoming, peaceful, bright, light, gleaming

Cold, stuffy, dusty, bare, dirty, damp, old, battered

Dark, gloomy, dim, lifeless, strange, eerie, sinister, squalid

Verbs

Furnished

Painted, decorated, scrubbed, polished

Torn, peeled, hung, dripped, covered, encrusted

Lit, shone, smeared, fogged, flickered

PHRASES – NOUNS AND ADJECTIVES

- ★ Large, rectangular kitchen
- ★ Small, square lounge
- ★ Large, modern kitchen of glass and metal
- ★ Wooden beams and a stone floor
- ★ Roaring fire
- ★ Colourful rugs

- Large floor cushions
- Enormous, carved coffee table
- Gleaming, scrubbed and polished wood
- Warm, welcoming room
- Heart of the house
- Welcoming retreat
- Relaxing haven
- Light and homely
- Bright and airy
- Sinister, evil place
- Dusty and bare
- Place of shadows and whispers
- Dark and lifeless
- Lights shimmered with cobwebs
- Cloud of dust hung over everything
- Dark, green moss
- Old, battered furniture
- Wallpaper was torn and peeling
- Dirty, threadbare carpet
- Dimly lit room
- Buzzing strip light
- Ground thick with rats
- Carpet of writhing hair
- Bodies of dead flies

PHRASES – VERBS

- Furnished with a huge oak table and sideboard
- Painted cream
- Tastefully decorated
- Bathed in sunlight
- Crackling fire sealed the room against the rain outside
- Covered in cobwebs
- Encrusted with grime
- Smeared with dirt
- Covered with a layer of crawling damp and mould
- Curtains closed, dirty dishes piled high in the sink
- Spilled out of the bin
- Crumpled and scattered everywhere
- Trampled into the floor
- Lights flickered
- Fogged with condensation
- Gloomy light filtered through
- Bathed in a strange, orange light from the streetlamps

- Only sign of life was . . .
- Bats haunted the ruins
- Eyes watched and ears listened in the shadows

SENTENCES

The room was light and homely.

The large, rectangular kitchen had wooden beams and a stone floor.

It was a small, cosy lounge with a low, sloping ceiling.

The study had a wooden floor and was painted cream.

The high-ceilinged dining room was furnished with a huge oak table and sideboard.

The room was a relaxing haven, furnished with comfy, deep leather couches and large floor cushions.

A fire crackled in the open fireplace, making the living room a snug retreat from the grey, hissing veil of rain outside.

The kitchen was a warm, welcoming room of gleaming, scrubbed and polished wood.

The furniture was old and battered and the carpet dirty and torn.

The light flickered as if the bulbs were coming to the end of their days.

The old house was dark and forbidding. The only sign of life was a torn curtain hanging across one of the upstairs windows.

The ground was so thick with rats that it seemed to be covered in a carpet of writhing hair.

A buzzing strip light hung from the ceiling. Its casing was peppered with the bodies of dead flies.

The big house was dusty and bare. All the stairs and corners were secretive places, covered in cobwebs. A place of shadows and whispers.

It may have once been a pleasant, comfortable room, but damp, dirt, disuse, mice and spiders had made it their home.

The windows were dirty and smeared with a layer of crawling damp and mould, and only a gloomy light could filter into the room.

There was a wild, overgrown feel to the place, which made it easy to imagine the spirits of the dead haunting it. He imagined eyes watching him, ears listening.

It appeared that no-one had lived in the house for some time. The wallpaper was torn and peeling, the carpet threadbare, the lights shimmering with cobwebs, and a cloud of dust hung over everything.

The place was in chaos – curtains closed; dirty dishes piled high in the sink; rubbish spilling out of the bin; books, papers and clothes scattered and crumpled.

Atmosphere

14

Time of day

SECTION 1 – DAWN

WORDS

Nouns	Sky, horizon, sun, moon, rays, beams, darkness Grass, trees, branches, bushes, hedges, leaves, water Mist, dew, clouds, frost Birds, song, chorus, alarm call, echo
Adjectives	Pink, yellow, orange, red, gold, bright First, eastern Black, dim, inky, grey, silver, colourless, ghostly, eerie
Verbs	Dawned, burst, exploded, blazed Warmed, bathed, shimmered, glittered Welcomed, rustled, echoed Rose, crept, clung, spread, covered, shrouded

PHRASES – NOUNS AND ADJECTIVES

- ★ Dawn's first rays of sunlight
- ★ Rim of pale pink on the eastern horizon
- ★ Glorious explosion of pink and yellow
- ★ Pink clouds like candy floss
- ★ Millions of sparkles like diamonds
- ★ Dew-soaked leaves
- ★ Gleaming frost
- ★ Crystal patterns on the icy windows
- ★ Echo of the dawn chorus
- ★ Dim, grey hour

- Dying moonlight and rising mist
- Ghostly, silver light
- Bushes were still inky black
- Rising sun like the mouth of an enormous, blazing tunnel
- Clinging dew like a shimmering spider's web

PHRASES – VERBS

- Dawned fine and bright
- Sky changed to orange and then to red
- Exploded in a blaze of pink and gold
- Forest bathed in dawn's first rays
- Sun burst onto the water
- Light stroked the hedges
- Glittered on the leaves
- Warmed the air
- Birds rustled in the treetops
- Nature came to welcome the new day
- Time of day when nothing moves
- Things crept out of the darkness
- Washed with a ghostly, silver light
- Horizon was aflame with the rising sun
- Clinging dew bent the blades of grass

SENTENCES

A rim of pale pink had formed on the eastern horizon.

The first rays of morning sunlight were an alarm call for the forest.

The sky changed to orange and then red, and the sun rose in a glorious explosion of pink and gold.

The morning light stroked the hedges and glittered on the dew-soaked leaves.

Crystal patterns frosted the early morning windows and glittered like starlight on the roofs.

As the sun rose, millions of sparkles like diamonds burst out onto the water, making it dance and shimmer.

Birds moved in the treetops, branches swayed and leaves rustled as nature greeted the sun and the new day.

As the first calls of the dawn chorus echoed across the land, the eerie, damp gloom of the night was replaced by the soft light of dawn.

The next morning dawned misty and damp.

The dawn streets were washed in a ghostly, silver light.

The clinging dew bent the shivering blades of grass.

The dew spread from blade to blade, clinging to the grass and hedges like a shimmering spider's web.

It was that dim, grey hour when things were just creeping out of darkness, the bushes still inky black, and the sky colourless and cheerless.

Just visible on the eastern horizon, the rising sun was like the mouth of an enormous blazing tunnel.

SECTION 2 – DAY

WORDS

Nouns
Sun, sunlight, haze, rainbow
Clouds, rain, gale, thunder, squall

Adjectives
White, blue, amber, brilliant, wispy, fluffy
Grey, silver, black, gloomy, grim, dim, crimson
Thick, dense, heavy, swollen, stormy, ominous, malicious, menacing

Verbs
Drifted, travelled, glided
Rushed, scudded
Lit, blazed, tinted, dotted
Covered, blanketed, drowned

PHRASES – NOUNS AND ADJECTIVES

- Clear, blue sky
- Shimmering blue sky
- Cloudless sky
- Wispy white clouds
- Clouds like fluffy cotton balls
- Glorious rainbow
- Golden haze
- Grey thunder clouds
- Dense, black rain clouds
- Swollen and an ominous black
- Clouds like a torn veil
- Great crumpled mountains of cloud
- Dark and threatening a gale
- Screaming frenzy of rain and thunder
- Angry crimson lines like wounds in the sky
- Sun was a dim, pale eye, behind a socket of grey haze

PHRASES – VERBS

- Grey of dawn replaced by a clear, blue sky
- Clouds drifted slowly across the sky
- Sun blazed beneath the clouds in a golden haze

- Lit by a glorious rainbow
- Clouds scudded over the mountains
- Distant squall blanketed the sun
- Moon swung between light and an eerie gloom
- Clouds rushed at him like the crest of a killer wave

SENTENCES

Wispy white clouds dotted the vivid blue sky.

Clouds, like fluffy cotton balls, drifted slowly across the sky.

Beams of light tinted the clouds with blazing colours of red and amber.

The rain had passed and the grey sky was lit by a glorious rainbow.

Great, icy grey mountains of cloud glided like mist over the ground.

The sky was as grey as a thunder cloud and grim with the menace of rain.

The moon swung between light and an eerie gloom, as the dense, black rain clouds drifted across the sky.

The clouds had swollen and grown an ominous black, rushing at him like the crest of a killer wave, threatening to drown him in their stormy embrace.

SECTION 3 – NIGHT

WORDS

Nouns	Sky, moon, twilight, stars, clouds
	Curtain, blanket, shadows, beams, torch, candle
	Buildings, hedges, trees, branches
	Creatures, predators, bats
Adjectives	Black, velvet, dark, inky, grey, dull, gloomy, moonlit
	Ghostly, eerie, silent, nocturnal
	Red, fiery, dangerous, menacing, malicious
	Amber, golden, bright, sparkling, blazing
	Warm, humid, balmy, chilly
Verbs	Lit, bathed, washed, drenched, painted
	Glowed, sparkled, shimmered, flickered
	Faded, sunk, fell, cascaded, disappeared
	Watched, waited, hid, lurked, huddled, glided, quivered, flitted

PHRASES – NOUNS AND ADJECTIVES

- Last rays of the sun
- Hazy, golden mist

- Soft, fading light
- Black, velvet sky
- Blazing stars like heavenly fires
- Warm breeze
- Night air like a warm blanket
- Warm and humid
- Gloomy, ghostly grey
- Eerie, silver light of the full moon
- Dark and eerily silent
- Darkness on either side of the torch was like a wall
- Chilly, black wave of darkness
- Leafy shadows
- Branches like thrusting limbs
- Tree trunks like prison bars
- Invisible predator
- Secretive, nocturnal creatures

PHRASES – VERBS

- Dusk was falling
- Splashed with a gentle light
- Painted the hills
- Sparkled like a diamond necklace
- Glittered in the sky
- Lit up the sky
- Darkness fell like a curtain
- Stretched around and above him
- Steeped in darkness
- Like a blanket putting out a candle
- Inky fingers of darkness clung to his ankles
- Moon was drowned in heavy clouds
- Cast leafy shadows on the ground
- Bathed the land in a ghostly reflection of daylight
- Only a fleeting glimpse of the full moon to guide them
- Hid what might lay behind the trees, watching and waiting
- Full of dangerous, flitting shadows
- Branches whispered in the silence
- Bats flitted in the moonlight
- Shimmered in the distance like ghostly eyes
- Air quivered with anticipation
- Brought the fear of the invisible predator
- Imagined all sorts of terrors lurking in the misty night

14 *Atmosphere: time of day*

SENTENCES

The moon washed the land in a gentle light.

The last rays of the sun painted the hills with a hazy, golden mist.

The stars glittered like a diamond necklace in the black, velvet sky.

The night was pierced in thousands of places with sparkling, rainbow-coloured light.

The day had been hot and the night sky lay like a warm blanket over the land.

There was no moon, but the sky was lit up by the blazing stars cascading out of the night sky.

Although the sun had gone and dusk was falling, there was still some heat left from the day and the forest glowed with a gentle warmth.

The moon was drowned in heavy clouds.

The ground was full of dangerous, flitting shadows.

The trunks of the trees were framed against the moon like the bars of a prison.

The approach of dusk brought the secretive, nocturnal creatures gliding into the night.

The sun fell like a sinking stone and a black cloak was drawn across the sky.

The moon glowed behind the clouds and bathed the land in a ghostly reflection of daylight.

There was a small circle of light from the torch, but either side was like a wall of darkness.

The shadows of the trees seemed to lean towards each other, whispering in the silence.

The trees stood silent and dark, hiding what might lay behind, watching and waiting.

They only had a fleeting glimpse of the moon to guide them as it scudded across the horizon, appearing briefly from behind the dark clouds.

The air seemed to be quivering with anticipation as a curtain of darkness was drawn across the sky, bringing with it the fear of an invisible predator.

The beam from the light cast a thin strip of flickering light in front of him, whilst behind the inky fingers of darkness clung to his heels.

15

Seasons

SECTION 1 – SPRING

WORDS

Nouns	Sleep, slumber, growth Sun, river, pond, hills Fields, hedges, trees, branches, leaves, bracken, ferns, buds, shrubs, shoots, stems, flowers, blossoms Tulips, crocuses, daffodils, bluebells, poppies, snowdrops Blackbirds, magpies, thrushes, sparrows, wrens Lambs, calves, foals, ducklings, goslings, cygnets, squirrels, spawn, tadpoles, frogs
Adjectives	New, fresh, crisp Green, emerald, red, crimson, scarlet, ruby, yellow, orange, amber, blue, turquoise Bright, colourful, vivid, vibrant, sparkling, dazzling Young, gangly, unsteady, quivering
Verbs	Woke, roused, stretched, unfurled Pushed, burst, sprouted, erupted, bloomed, blossomed Painted, decorated, heaped, sprinkled, shimmered Shouted, sang, smiled, waved, danced, fluttered Rushed, darted, scuttled, scampered, lurched, waddled

PHRASES – NOUNS AND ADJECTIVES

- ★ Starkness of winter
- ★ Spring was in the air
- ★ One of those spring days when . . .

- Fresh morning sun
- Emerald shoots
- Clumps of snowdrops
- Blazing carpet of bluebells
- Flowers were like piles of jewels
- Fresh, green finery of spring
- Quivering colour of spring
- Vivid, sparkling treasures of spring
- Vibrant sights and sounds of spring
- Symphony of songbirds
- Gangly foals
- Clusters of spawn

PHRASES – VERBS

- Winter had relaxed its grip
- Woken from their wintry slumber
- Waking world of new growth and colour
- Searched for light
- Pushed towards the sun
- Erupted with emerald shoots
- Unfurled and stretched
- Burst with blossoms
- Shouted and sang
- Danced in the light breeze
- Nature had painted the hills
- Decorated winter's bare branches
- Alive with quivering colour
- Heaped like piles of jewels
- Sprinkled tiny diamonds on the rivers
- Stretched as far as the eye could see
- Rushed to their nest
- Scampered up the trees
- Foamed in the pond
- Lurched unsteadily on their new legs

SENTENCES

She was enveloped by the vivid, sparkling treasures of spring.

Bracken and ferns unfurled and stretched. Creepers crawled out of hiding in search of the sun.

The scent of the bluebells was flung like wafts of perfume into the air.

The forest floor was a carpet of bluebells dancing in the breeze.

They were welcomed by wave after wave of the gently nodding heads of daffodils.

Winter had relaxed its grip and the world was waking to new growth, colour and sound.

The colours of spring shouted and sang – rubies and emeralds, sapphires and opals.

The ground was erupting with emerald shoots, woken from their wintry slumber.

Crocuses smiled their greeting and tulips waved as they pushed their way towards the sun.

It was as if, overnight, nature had painted the hills in reds, yellows and greens and sprinkled tiny diamonds on the rivers to shimmer and dance in the fresh morning sun.

Squirrels scampered up the trees to the melody of the songbirds marking their territory.

Magpies rushed to hide their stolen treasure in the fresh, green cloak covering winter's bare branches.

The fields were full of lambs, calves and foals lurching unsteadily on their new legs.

Hidden in the branches, the open, anxious beaks of the baby sparrows pushed their way out of the nest.

SECTION 2 – SUMMER

WORDS

Nouns	Sun, air, warmth, heat, rays, beams, breeze
	Sky, earth, land, ground, hills, fields, forest, trees, rivers, streams
	Grass, flowers, stems, blossoms, corn, poppies, gorse, heather, honeysuckle
	Butterflies, bees, crickets, birdsong, echo, symphony
	Glare, furnace, temperature, atmosphere
Adjectives	Warm, balmy, hot
	Fresh, clean, sweet
	Clear, blue, hazy, golden
	Yellow, purple, red, pink, copper, green
	Vivid, dazzling, brilliant, shimmering
	Dry, burning, baking, fierce, stifling, searing
	Wet, steamy, humid, still, motionless, merciless, oppressive, intolerable
	Dizzy, thirsty
Verbs	Burst, blazed, poured, flooded, cloaked, drenched
	Painted, gleamed, glittered, shimmered
	Hung, fluttered
	Burned, blasted, crashed, soared, pounded
	Clung, drifted, coiled
	Parched, blistered, soaked, sapped, wilted

15 *Atmosphere: seasons*

PHRASES – NOUNS AND ADJECTIVES

- ★ Cloudless sky
- ★ Shimmering, dazzling blue
- ★ Sun's glittering rays
- ★ Midday sun
- ★ Hazy, golden mist
- ★ Brilliant light
- ★ Air was fresh and sweet
- ★ Gentle breeze
- ★ Air thick with the scent of honeysuckle
- ★ Smell of freshly mown grass
- ★ Aroma of barbecued food
- ★ Symphony of joyous birdsong
- ★ Echo of clicking crickets
- ★ Lazy humming of bees
- ★ Red blossoms
- ★ Spikes of yellow and white flowers
- ★ Vivid green stems
- ★ Pink and white of blossoming trees
- ★ Purple heather
- ★ Golden corn, red poppies and yellow gorse
- ★ Dazzling glare
- ★ Burning beams of light
- ★ Baking hot
- ★ Hot and steamy
- ★ Stifling, dry heat
- ★ Sun's merciless heat like an invisible hammer

PHRASES – VERBS

- ★ Blazed from a clear, blue sky
- ★ Poured in through the windows
- ★ Bathed the room in a brilliant light
- ★ Flooded warmth into the land
- ★ Painted the hills with a hazy, golden mist
- ★ Glittered on the water
- ★ Shimmered over the fields in a haze
- ★ Trees fluttered in the warm breeze
- ★ Tickled his face like a feather
- ★ Splashed with red poppies and yellow gorse
- ★ Alive with splashes of red and bright orange berries
- ★ Cloaked with purple heather
- ★ Covered in butterflies

- Hung in masses from vivid green stems
- Crashed down fiercely
- Burned like a furnace
- Soaked into the land
- Earth itself seemed to burn
- Temperature soared
- Everything in its path cowered
- Drifted through the air in a misty haze
- Beat down on them
- Heat coiled itself round him
- Settled on his sweating body
- Pounded at his senses
- Blinded by the sunlight
- Blistered their lips and skin
- Mouth was parched and skin dry
- Sapped their energy
- Cowered under the hammer blow of the sun's glare
- Every bit of moisture had been stolen by the sun

SENTENCES

The sky was a shimmering, dazzling blue.

Red blossoms hung in masses from vivid green stems.

The golden corn was splashed with red poppies and yellow gorse.

The hedge was alive with splashes of red and bright orange berries and the hills cloaked with purple heather.

The sun poured in through the windows and bathed the room in a brilliant light.

The sun blazed from a cloudless sky and millions of sparkles, like diamonds, glittered on the water.

The sun's rays drenched the forest and painted the hills with a hazy, golden mist.

The gentle breeze tickled his face like a feather and brought with it the smell of freshly mown grass.

The air around him was filled with the scent of honeysuckle and the symphony of joyous birdsong.

Among the clicking of crickets and the lazy humming of bees, the aroma of barbecued food lingered in the air.

It was stifling hot and the air was still.

The hot, wet air was like an invisible hammer pounding at his senses.

The sun's rays crashed down fiercely on his eyes and blinded him with its dazzling glare.

The humid air coiled itself around him and settled on his sweating body.

The searing sun blinded them and blistered their lips and skin.

The sun beat down on her, stealing the moisture from her mouth and sapping her strength.

The sun's merciless heat bounced off the rocks and soaked into the land, until the earth itself seemed to burn.

The mid-afternoon sun burned like a furnace and everything in its path cowered and withered under its hammer blow.

As the sun rose, the temperature soared, until she was suffocating in the intolerable heat.

The forest was a hot, steamy, churning chaos; the heat clinging to the trees and drifting through the air in a misty haze.

SECTION 3 – AUTUMN

WORDS

Nouns	Ground, trees, branches, leaves, breeze
Adjectives	Red, scarlet, golden, green, yellow Crisp, fluffy
Verbs	Painted, decorated Danced, crackled, crunched Drifted, rushed

PHRASES – NOUNS AND ADJECTIVES

- ★ Crisp, golden leaves
- ★ Autumn's scarlet leaves
- ★ In their suits of red and gold
- ★ Brisk breeze
- ★ Clouds like fluffy cotton balls
- ★ Glorious rainbow

PHRASES – VERBS

- ★ Painted with autumn's crisp leaves
- ★ Danced in the brisk breeze
- ★ Rushed across the ground
- ★ Crunched under her feet
- ★ Drifted across the sky

SENTENCES

The branches were painted with autumn's crisp leaves of green and yellow, gold and red.

The leaves on the trees were dressed in their suits of red and gold.

The rays of sunlight burst through the storm and painted a glorious rainbow over the grey sky.

The trees danced in the brisk breeze, whilst their crackling leaves rushed across the ground.

Above her, clouds like fluffy cotton balls drifted across the sky and, below, autumn's crisp leaves crunched under her feet.

SECTION 4 – WINTER

WORDS

Nouns

Ice, frost, icicles, snow, flakes, crystals, showers, carpet

Horizon, fields, hills, hedges, trees, pine needles, leaves, grass, roads, buildings, roofs, windows

Adjectives

White, crystal, crisp, frosty

Sparkling, shimmering, delicate, fairytale

Cold, icy, bitter, frozen, freezing, deathly, savage, bone-crushing, ferocious, intense, dangerous, whirling, billowy, wind-whipped

Verbs

Fell, lay, hung, cloaked, heaped, sprinkled, surrounded, blanketed, buried

Frosted, shone, glittered

Bowed, lashed, trapped

Crunched, cracked, growled, muffled

Gnawed, burned, scalded

PHRASES – NOUNS AND ADJECTIVES

- Fairytale world
- Frosty, sparkling pavements
- Crystal patterns on the windows
- Icicles like crystal earrings
- Glittered like a diamond necklace
- Crisp carpet beneath her feet
- White and shimmering on the hills
- Delicate showers like tiny pieces of lace
- Smell of pine needles and cinnamon
- Freezing breath in clouds around them
- Bitter wind
- Savage, bone-crushing cold like the jaws of a vice
- No horizon to the white world
- Billowy, white ocean
- Bitter whirl of icy crystals
- Trees like ice sculptures

15 *Atmosphere: seasons*

PHRASES – VERBS

- Cloaked in snow
- Glittered with frost
- Hung from the trees
- Fell from the branches in delicate showers
- Sprinkled the ground like a white dust
- Lay white and shimmering
- Frosted the early morning windows
- Glittered like starlight on the roofs
- Breath smoked in the freezing air
- Savage cold took their breath away
- Scalded their skin like acid
- Sunk its teeth into his bones
- Gnawed away from the inside
- Heaped over the fields and buildings
- Blanketed the village
- Trapped in a white, whirling wall of flakes
- Bowed their heads and buried their feet
- Struggled to see in the wind-whipped snow
- Fell with a dull thump
- Created a thick, muffled silence
- Icicles fell like daggers
- Ice cracked and growled
- Split like a lightning bolt

SENTENCES

The snow lay white and shimmering on the distant hills.

They woke up to a fairytale world cloaked in snow.

The frost glittered like a diamond necklace on the spider's web.

Crystal patterns frosted the early morning windows and glittered like starlight on the roofs.

Snow fell like tiny pieces of lace and sprinkled the ground like a white dust.

Icicles hung from the trees like crystal earrings, whilst the snow made a crisp carpet beneath her feet.

As they passed underneath, the snow, too heavy for the branches, fell in delicate showers on their heads.

Their breath was in clouds around them.

The ferocity of the cold took their breath away.

There was no horizon to the white world. It was a billowy, white ocean blending into the sky.

The bitter wind rubbed against her ankles and scattered the leaves in front of her.

The snow created a thick, muffled silence and fell with a muted thump.

The savage, bone-crushing cold sank its teeth into his bones and gnawed away from the inside.

They were trapped in a white, whirling wall of flakes that bowed their heads and buried their feet.

The village looked wild and strange under the snow, which blanketed the fields and buildings and lay in piles on the dark road.

The trees were ice sculptures, with long icicles that fell like daggers.

They were surrounded by ice, which cracked and growled under their weight, until eventually it split like a lightning bolt.

16

Rain, mist and fog

SECTION 1 – RAIN

WORDS

Nouns	Sky, clouds, rain, sleet, hail
	Drops, spots, bullets, stream, waves, showers, downpour, curtain, blanket, shroud
	Forest, mountain, trees, bushes, leaves
	Street, roof, window
	Face, hands, neck
Adjectives	Dark, grey
	Icy, chilly, freezing, bitter, stinging
	Merciless, relentless
Verbs	Dripped, poured, crashed
	Beat, drummed, pelted, lashed, hammered, exploded, pummelled
	Rattled, hissed
	Scattered, spattered, danced, jumped, flinched, shivered

PHRASES – NOUNS AND ADJECTIVES

- ★ Layers of pregnant clouds
- ★ Drops the size of bullets
- ★ Cords of grey water
- ★ Curtain of icy rain
- ★ Stinging waves of rain
- ★ Like a steady downpour of tears
- ★ Freezing rain
- ★ Melting chips of ice

PHRASES – VERBS

- Clouds unleashed their heavy load
- Arched down in stinging waves
- Lashed sideways down the street
- Drawn by the wind into an icy curtain
- Pelted the trees and beat on the bushes
- Scattered showers of blossoms onto the ground
- Dripped from every fern and leaf like the tick of a very slow clock
- Grass shivered in the freezing rain
- Drove along the road like smoke
- Puddles jumped to life
- Exploded like spots of ink on the windowsill
- Hammered relentlessly at the windows
- Hissed around them
- Stung their face and hands
- Chilly stream poured down his neck

SENTENCES

The rain was relentless.

The first, heavy drops of rain had started to fall

Drops the size of bullets hammered at the windows.

Layers of pregnant clouds clung to the mountain and blanketed the forest.

The rain was hammering down and a chilly stream poured down his face.

The trees flinched and the grass shivered in the freezing rain.

Melting chips of ice hammered on his head and face, and streamed down the back of his neck.

The dancing hail hung in a cloud and drove along the road like smoke.

The rain was a steady downpour of tears, crashing to earth and spreading darkness and damp.

The puddles jumped to life as pellets of water drummed the surface.

The downpour had flooded the gutters. Even after the rain had stopped, water dripped like the tick of a very slow clock.

SECTION 2 – MIST AND FOG

WORDS

Nouns Mountain, forest, river, ground, grass, path, trees, hedges, house, street
Blanket, quilt, veil, shapes, coils, tentacles

16 *Atmosphere: rain, mist and fog*

Adjectives	Icy, damp, soggy Grey, yellow Swirling, ghostly, brooding
Verbs	Rose, drifted, floated, covered, blanketed, descended Crept, slid, spread, slipped, prowled, flicked, slithered

PHRASES – NOUNS AND ADJECTIVES

- Blanket of grey mist
- Coils of mist
- Slinky, grey arms
- Like a ghostly serpent
- Mist was like an icy breath
- Swirling, brooding mist
- Veil of stinging mist

PHRASES – VERBS

- Floated above the grass
- Hung over the park
- Descended from the mountain
- Blanketed everything like a padded quilt
- Crept up on the house
- Slid along the window
- Crept along the forest floor
- Flicked its tongue into every gap
- Prowled and slithered over their feet
- Covered his feet and muffled all sound
- Drifted up from the soggy soil
- Filled the air with its slinky, grey arms
- Twisted the trees into monstrous shapes
- Waited a moment and then slipped back along the path
- Hung like a stilled breath on everything that it touched

SENTENCES

There was a blanket of grey mist floating above the grass.

The mist rose and spread to fill the air with its slinky, grey arms.

The mist was like an icy breath descending from the mountain.

The fog blanketed everything like a padded quilt.

The wind moaned and howled like a ghostly spirit and dragged with it a veil of stinging mist from the river.

A brooding mist crept low along the ground, prowling around them, slithering over their feet.

Coils of mist drifted up from the soggy soil and hung like a stilled breath on everything they touched.

A damp, yellow fog hung over the park and twisted the trees into monstrous shapes.

The fog crept up on the house like a ghostly serpent, slid along the window, flicked its tongue into the corners of the house, waited a moment and then slipped back along the path.

17

Wind, thunder and lightning

SECTION 1 – WIND

WORDS

Nouns	Breeze, gust, storm Trees, branches, leaves House, windows, roof, chimney Head, face, hair
Adjectives	Warm, gentle, cool, welcome Chilly, bitter, fiery High, harsh, gritty, fierce, ferocious, colossal Shivering, stammering, billowing Ghostly, eerie, monstrous, demented
Verbs	Blew, stirred, teased, tickled, caressed, fluttered Rushed, tore, lashed, blustered Rocked, bent, arched, chased, shoved, pulled, tugged, whipped, stabbed, hammered Shuddered, quivered, shivered, staggered, struggled Whispered, whined, sighed, creaked, rustled, moaned, howled, raged, rattled, crashed, grated, roared, screeched, screamed

PHRASES – NOUNS AND ADJECTIVES

- Welcome breeze
- Breath of wind
- Warm, gentle breeze
- Like a tickling feather
- Ghostly night breeze

- High, eerie wind
- Fiery, swirling wind
- Stammering gusts
- Colossal rush of wind
- Billowing clouds of dust

PHRASES – VERBS

- Caressed their faces
- Stirred their hair
- Tickled his face
- Rustled the leaves
- Waved gently in the breeze
- Ghosted past him
- Bent the branches and stole their leaves
- Trunks arched in the wind
- Rushed through the grass and chased the leaves in circles
- Rattled the bare branches of the shivering trees
- Tore the clouds like a shredded veil
- Darkened the air with billowing clouds of dust
- Blustered around the house
- Lashed against the windows
- Hammered at the glass
- Beat like a fist against the roof
- Car rocked and shuddered
- Surged past her cheek
- Tore at his clothes with its invisible fingers
- Hunted her like a beast
- Struggled to stay on his feet
- Wind shoved, pulled, tugged at him ferociously
- Tried to lift the skin from his bones and the hair from his head
- Sighed and moaned across them
- Eerie wind sighed and whispered
- Whined through the trees
- Branches creaked eerily in the breeze
- Grated together like rusty hinges
- Roared in the chimney
- Screeched like a boiling kettle

SENTENCES

The gentle breeze tickled his face like a feather.

The leaves waved gently in the breeze.

A welcome breeze sprang up and brought relief from the burning heat.

The warm, gentle breeze stirred their hair and caressed their faces.

The stammering gusts tore the clouds like a shredded veil.

The car rocked and shuddered under the force of the wind.

The branches quivered as they were stabbed by the wind.

The wind was ferocious. It screamed over the house and beat like a fist against the roof.

The wind was lashing against the windows and hammering at the glass.

The wind whined through the trees and bent the tops of the branches.

A breath of wind ghosted past him, tickling his ear like a feather and making the skin at the back of his neck prickle with foreboding.

The trunks arched in the swirling wind, which bent their branches and stole their leaves.

The wind screamed like a boiling kettle as it blustered around the house.

He staggered back and forth, side to side, struggling to stay on his feet, as the wind shoved and tugged at him fiercely, hunting him like a beast.

SECTION 2 – THUNDER AND LIGHTNING

WORDS

Nouns	Air, echo, horizon, heavens Blade, arrow, spear, firework
Adjectives	Huge, torn, jagged Dazzling, dangerous, menacing, ominous
Verbs	Rumbled, crashed, howled, boomed, pulsed Tore, streaked, flickered Lit, flooded, blinded, illuminated

PHRASES – NOUNS AND ADJECTIVES

- Like an exploding firework
- Thunderous echo
- Jagged spears of lightning
- Dazzling arrows of lightning

PHRASES – VERBS

- Rumbled closer and closer
- Crashed and howled overhead
- Struggled and howled in fits and starts
- Boomed through the house
- Streaked across the horizon
- Flooded the land
- Tore the night sky apart and ripped its belly

- Blinded him as it flickered in and out
- Sky was set alight by . . .
- Streaked through the streets like an exploding firework

SENTENCES

Thunder rumbled ominously and then crashed and howled overhead.

The thunder rumbled closer and closer, the lightning followed almost immediately.

An immense guillotine blade of lightning streaked across the horizon and illuminated it with a stark blue-whiteness.

Thunder boomed through the house, shaking it to its core, and streaking through the streets like an exploding firework.

Lightning tore through the sky, blinding him as it flickered in and out.

Suddenly, dazzling arrows of lightning tore the night sky apart, ripping its belly and flooding the land.

It was as if the heavens were being torn apart by the jagged spears of lightning – the thunder howling their pain.

18

Smell and touch

SECTION 1 – SMELL

WORDS

Nouns	Smell, scent, aroma, fragrance, perfume
	Stink, stench, reek
	Jasmine, cinnamon, ginger, pine needles, apple, orange, lemon, honeysuckle, lavender, peach, lilac, eucalyptus, rose, spearmint, grass
	Leather, coffee, baking, polish, disinfectants
	Sweat, damp, mildew, fish, cat, meat, milk, petrol, smoke, urine, eggs, mushrooms, seaweed
	Flesh, pain, death, decay, rubbish, bin bags, termites
	Breath, throat, cough, nose, nostrils, vomit
Adjectives	Sweet, clean, fresh, fragrant, perfumed, aromatic
	Thick, heavy, warm, bitter, damp, dank, musty, salty
	Rotten, decaying, stinking, rancid, revolting, pungent, putrefying
Verbs	Smelt, scented
	Rose, wafted, drifted, released, seeped, dogged
	Mixed, blended, mingled
	Choked, coughed, churned, clenched, retched, vomited

PHRASES – NOUNS AND ADJECTIVES

- ★ Fresh and sweet
- ★ Aroma of barbecued food
- ★ Sweet smell of roasting vegetables
- ★ Warm, sweet, pungent smell of coffee

- Freshly baked bread
- Scent of fresh flowers
- Scent of orange and lemon blossoms
- Perfume of sweetly scented jasmine
- Flowers and spices from around the world
- Pine needles and cinnamon
- Scents of Christmas
- Smell of disinfectants and polish
- Dank, musty smell
- Sweaty socks
- Smell of pain and death
- Decaying flesh
- Sour, curdled milk
- Salty stink of seaweed
- Choking smoke
- Rotten eggs and decaying mushrooms
- Pungent smell of rotting rubbish
- Putrefying smell of rotting meat
- Thick, rancid smell of warm petrol
- Overwhelming smell of rotten fish and cat's urine

PHRASES – VERBS

- Smelt fresh and sweet
- Blended and mingled together
- Lingered in the air
- Scented with . . .
- Overcome by the smell of . . .
- Air was thick with the scent of . . .
- Wafted towards her
- Dogged the air
- Rose from his clothing
- Came from the rotting bin bags
- Lingered in the room
- Gave off a smell of rot and decaying corpses
- Seeped from the damp, mouldy curtains
- Stomach clenched and churned
- Stung his nostrils and eyes
- Took a deep breath
- Coughed and retched
- Caught in the back of her throat
- Covered their nose and mouth
- Attacked their senses

18 *Atmosphere: smell and touch*

SENTENCES

The air was thick with the scent of honeysuckle.

The warm air was scented with rosemary and orange blossom.

The lavender bush wafted its scent in through the open window.

They were surrounded by the perfume of the honeysuckle that clung to the oak tree.

It was as if all the flowers and spices of the world had been blended together and tossed in the air.

Wafting in the air was the sweet smell of roasting vegetables and chicken.

The fragrance of freshly mown grass and tree blossoms drifted towards her.

The kitchen was filled with the warm, sweet aroma of coffee brewing.

The smell of pine needles and cinnamon filled the room with the scents of Christmas.

She needed to leave the room to escape the smell of dust and mould.

A stench of rottenness and decay wafted up from the darkness and stung his nostrils.

Even the plants seemed to give off a smell of rot and decaying corpses.

As he opened the trunk, a dank, musty smell was released into the cold air.

Her stomach churned, as the revolting smell of rotten fish drifted towards her.

The thick, rancid smell of warm petrol dogged the air and caught in the back of their throats.

They covered their nose and mouth to block out the putrefying smell of rotting meat.

A pungent smell of rotting rubbish came from the bulging bin bags, rancid in the heat and crawling with termites.

Clutching her hand to her mouth, she bent over and retched violently.

She coughed and retched as the putrefying smell of decaying flesh wafted towards her.

SECTION 2 – TOUCH

WORDS

Nouns	Head, face, cheek, skin, nose, nostrils
	Body, bones, arms, hands, fingers, fist, legs, feet, ankles
	Glass, silk, cotton, satin, wool, feather, rubber, wax, leather, marble, stone, wood
	Breath, air, dust, wind, ice, crystals
	Ground, dust, mud, rocks
	Branches, twigs, thorns, brambles
	Moths, bats, fish, wings, claws
Adjectives	Smooth, soft, sleek, shiny, polished
	Hairy, furry
	Dry, stale, crusty, rough, coarse, bristly, cracked, brittle, wrinkled, shrivelled, withered

	Sharp, spiky, prickly, jagged, pointed, thorny, needle-sharp
	Wet, damp, slippery, dewy, mossy, mouldy, sticky, slimy, soggy, squelchy, oily, greasy, waxy
	Cold, icy, chilly, crisp, arctic, glacial, bitter, frosty, bone-crushing
	Warm, hot, fiery, boiling, savage, scorching, blistering, roasting, sizzling
Verbs	Felt, held, touched, caressed, tickled, brushed
	Slid, slithered, slipped
	Pushed, moved, nudged, gripped, trapped, tangled
	Tore, bit, clawed, scratched, pricked, pierced, stung, burnt, scalded, numbed
	Rippled, flickered, fluttered, swished

PHRASES – NOUNS AND ADJECTIVES

★ As smooth as silk
★ As shiny as satin
★ Like polished wood
★ As soft as velvet
★ Smooth, marble floor
★ Warm, woollen coat
★ Swish of wings
★ Furry bodies
★ Pointed, sharp twigs and thorns
★ Needle-sharp points
★ Jagged edges
★ Sharp with rust
★ Slimy water plants
★ Squelching mud
★ Slimy, like a dead fish
★ Icy breath against his face
★ Crisp night air
★ Savage, bone-crushing cold
★ Swirls of hard, icy crystals
★ Fiery wind
★ Stifling heat
★ Burning heat of the sun on her arms

PHRASES – VERBS

★ Tickled his ear
★ Flickered over her face
★ Hand that held his was . . .
★ Wrapped tightly around her

- Relief from the burning heat
- Brushed against his face
- Scratched at his skin
- Slithered over his shoe
- Tore at his face and hands
- Pricked his fingers
- Tangled in his clothes
- Clutched him in their thorny grasp
- Trapped his legs
- Slipped on the squelching mud
- Rubbed against her ankles
- Rolled over her face
- Stung her face
- Surged past his cheek
- Scalded her skin like acid
- Sank its teeth into her bones
- Gripped him like a clenched fist
- Burnt her nostrils
- Enveloped her like a damp towel
- Dripped from her skin

SENTENCES

The rock was as smooth as polished slate.

The hand that held his was as smooth as velvet.

A breath of wind, like rippling silk, tickled his ear.

As the wind rose, she wrapped the warm, woollen coat tightly around her.

The cold water of the pool was a welcome relief from the burning heat.

The coat was rough and scratched at his skin.

Her feet slipped on the squelching mud and she was sent tumbling into the murky water.

Something sleek and slimy slithered over his shoe and plucked at his ankle.

The jagged edges of the gate tore his hand as he pushed it open.

He ducked, as a swish of wings rushed through the air and the invisible predator brushed his head with its furry body.

The prickly spines tangled in his clothes, clutching him in their thorny grasp.

His hand touched something at the bottom of the bag; something slimy, like a dead fish.

He crashed through the trees on the shore of the lake, but was held by the creeping, slimy water plants that crawled down the hillside and trapped his legs.

The chill air rubbed at her legs.

The hot, wet air enveloped her like a damp towel.

The hot fingers of dust clawed all over them.

It was a savage, bone-crushing cold that scalded his skin like acid.

She felt the heat of the sun on her exposed arms – a burning, stinging heat.

Robert could feel the icy breath on the back of his neck. Shivers ran down his spine, as if he had been touched by acid.

As she inhaled, the dry air hurt her nose and burnt her nostrils.

19

Sound

SECTION 1 – CALM

WORDS

Nouns	Forest, wood, trees, leaves
	Birds, blackbirds, magpies, thrush, sparrow, starling, blue tit, crow, raven, wren, robin, nightingale, owl
	Insects, bees, dragonflies, crickets, butterflies
	Calves, lambs, frogs
	Water, stream, waves
	Breeze, wind
	Echo, song, chorus, lullaby
	Room, fire, wind chimes, fridge, washing machine, pipes
Adjectives	Bright, cheerful, joyous, beautiful, melodious
	Soft, quiet, gentle, lazy
Verbs	Whispered, murmured, sang, hummed, called, buzzed, whistled, warbled, chirruped, trilled, bawled, bleated, croaked
	Crackled, crunched, rustled
	Fluttered, whirred, hovered, darted
	Bubbled, trickled, gurgled, lapped, splashed

PHRASES – NOUNS AND ADJECTIVES

- Soft, murmuring sounds
- Whisper of a gentle breeze
- Rustle of nature
- Golden crunch of leaves
- Waking call of the songbirds
- Symphony of joyous birdsong

- Trill of blackbirds
- Melodious magpies
- Birds singing, insects humming, butterflies hovering
- Gentle rhythm of frogs and nocturnal insects
- Soft bubble of a stream
- Sound of lapping water
- Splash of the sea
- Gentle roll of the waves on the shore

PHRASES – VERBS

- Filled with the sound of . . .
- Air hummed with . . .
- Sounds of spring drifted through the air
- Whispered through the trees
- Frogs croaked and called
- Birds darted and fluttered
- Insects buzzed around the flowers
- Calves bawled for their mothers
- Lambs bleated
- Dragonflies darted
- Short, sudden fluttering of wings
- Wind chimes clinked in the breeze
- Crackling of the fire
- Hum of the fridge, whirr of the washing machine, gurgle of the pipes

SENTENCES

The air was full of soft, murmuring sounds.

The room was quiet except for the crackling of the fire.

The dusk birdsong was suddenly silenced and replaced by the gentle rhythm of frogs and nocturnal insects.

The garden was full of sound – birds singing, insects humming and dragonflies darting.

The air around him was bright and cheerful, filled with the sound of lapping water and a symphony of joyous birdsong.

The silence was broken by the whisper of a soft breeze through the trees and the rustle of nature creeping into the sun.

They sat in the shade of the majestic oak tree and lounged lazily to the sound of humming bees, sizzling grasshoppers and clicking crickets.

The familiar sounds of the house reassured him – the hum of the fridge, whirr of the washing machine and gurgle of pipes in the airing cupboard.

Everywhere, the sounds of spring pierced the air – calves bawling and lambs bleating, calling for their mothers.

In the distance he could hear the bubble and trickle of a stream as it danced down the slopes.

19 *Atmosphere: sound*

SECTION 2 – SILENCE

WORDS

Nouns	Gloom, echo, fog, anxiety, suspense
Adjectives	Quiet, silent, secretive Dark, misty, deathly, ghostly, eerie, sinister, threatening, brooding
Verbs	Beat, rang, thudded, throbbed Wrapped, pressed, coiled, surrounded Stopped, waited, stirred

PHRASES – NOUNS AND ADJECTIVES

- Eerily quiet
- Deathly quiet
- Silence as thick as fog
- A horrible, waiting silence
- Throbbing silence
- Like a thick blanket
- Like a throbbing heartbeat
- Old house was silent and secretive
- No sound, just a dark, eerie gloom
- Only her own gasping breath

PHRASES – VERBS

- Surrounded by a wall of silence
- Thudded in her ears
- Rang in her ears
- Coiled around them
- Wrapped around them like a thick blanket
- Nothing stirred
- As if time had stopped
- As if the world was holding its breath
- Quiet of something waiting in the dark
- Made them feel isolated from the rest of the world
- Moved in a silence of anxiety and suspense

SENTENCES

The room had gone very quiet. It was as if time had stopped.

The old house was silent and secretive. Nothing stirred. He was surrounded by a wall of silence.

There was a deep silence, as if they were in a padded room.

The house was quiet. The silence of something waiting in the dark, holding its breath.

When the echoes had died away, there was only silence thudding in her ears.

It was eerily quiet. A throbbing silence, which wrapped around them like a thick blanket.

There was no sound. No birds singing. No trees rustling. No voices murmuring. Just an eerie silence and her own gasping breath.

The silence came surging back, wrapping round them, making them feel isolated from the rest of the world.

SECTION 3 – QUIET NOISES

WORDS

Nouns
Whispers, sigh, moan, murmur, hiss, whine, groan, creak, rustle, echo
Wind, breeze, draught
Trees, branches, leaves
Floorboards, door, hinge, lock, key, window, light, chandelier
Creatures, rats, mice, mosquito
Ghosts, shadows

Adjectives
Small, weak, soft, dull, faint, distant, misty, wheezing
Old, ancient, rusty

Verbs
Sighed, whispered, hummed, whined, buzzed, groaned
Rustled, clicked, creaked, clinked, vibrated
Opened, closed, turned, moved, scuttled, scratched

PHRASES – NOUNS AND ADJECTIVES

- In the passage ahead of him . . .
- Out of the shadows . . .
- From behind the wall
- Somewhere at the back of the room
- Scratching sound
- Small rustle and scrape
- Leaves like dry, dead fingers
- Squeal, flutter, creak
- Rustle of a night hunter
- Tick of a beetle
- Whine of a mosquito
- Drip, drip of water like a leaking tap
- Rasping hiss
- Soft, misty voice
- Faint wheezing

19 *Atmosphere: sound*

- Ancient hinges
- Rusty lock
- Creaky floorboards
- Creaks and rustlings of the old house
- Distant rumble of thunder
- Whine of distant traffic

PHRASES – VERBS

- Moved closer to his hiding place
- Beneath the quiet he could hear . . .
- Silence teemed with noises
- Kept him awake
- Held her breath
- Heart raced
- Wind sighed in her ear
- Whispers rode on the wind through the empty branches
- Ghosts sighed and moaned
- Like a huge creature sucking in air
- Thud and click as the door creaked open
- Hinges groaned
- Scratching sound vibrated the floor

SENTENCES

A faint, wheezing noise came from the back of the room.

The crisp night breeze ruffled her hair, sighed into her ear and whispered through the trees.

It was a dark, desolate place, where ghosts sigh and moan on stormy nights.

The holly trees gave a prickly murmur. The whispers were not far behind, riding on the wind through the empty branches.

The quiet was broken by a thud and click and the key turned in the lock. The ancient hinges groaned as the door was edged open.

The noises seemed to be closing in on them – the tick of a beetle, the whine of a mosquito, the rustle of leaves, the snap of a twig.

As the bushes shivered, there was a drip, drip of water like the sound of a leaking tap.

As she moved through the trees, the leaves rustled and brushed her head like dry, dead fingers.

The silence was filled with noises from the draught blowing through the gap in the window – the swish of curtains, creak of a door and the clink of a light.

She held her breath as the floorboards creaked and he moved closer to her hiding place.

SECTION 4 – STARTLING NOISES

WORDS

Nouns

Echo, voices, call, shouts, roars, shriek, squeal, scream, screech, howl, moan, grunts

Footsteps, boots, stones, rocks, twigs, leaves, floorboards

Car, horn, tyres, traffic

Hunter, pursuer, predator, prey

Animals, creatures, monkeys, birds, owl, seagull, bats, insects

Waterfall, sea, waves

Rustle, swish, flutter

Adjectives

Secret, careful, eerie, sinister

Loud, shrill, desperate, throaty, rasping, piercing, deafening, monstrous, sickening, bloodcurdling, spine-chilling

Cold, threatening, ominous

Breathless, gasping, anxious

Verbs

Moved, crept, shuffled, ran, fled, slithered, thudded

Cracked, crunched, scraped, snapped, crashed, backfired, rumbled, boomed

Heard, broke, sliced, ripped, slashed, shattered, pierced, vibrated, echoed

Hissed, hummed, gasped, groaned, whined, hooted, wailed, screamed, screeched, roared

Hid, concealed, stalked, surrounded

PHRASES – NOUNS AND ADJECTIVES

- ★ Huge, slow, shuffling feet
- ★ Scuffling run
- ★ Clumsy scrapes
- ★ Squeak of a boot heel on the tiled floor
- ★ Thump and thud of pursuers' feet
- ★ Piercing screech
- ★ Loud gasping of a breathless man
- ★ Anxious shouts and panicked voices
- ★ Desperate howl of pain
- ★ A piercing, spine-chilling scream
- ★ Blare of a horn
- ★ Gunshot of a car backfiring
- ★ Grinding of gears
- ★ Screech of tyres

- Sound of ringing metal
- Shattering crash of breaking glass
- Sickening crack
- Grunts, rustles and roars
- Shrill click of crickets
- Eerie, mournful cry
- Scream of an owl
- Bloodcurdling scream
- Howls and shrieks of concealed creatures
- Invisible predators
- Deafening wind
- Whining, wailing wind
- Cascading rumble of a wave
- Roar of the waterfall

PHRASES – VERBS

- Shattered the silence
- Announced her presence
- Silence broken by . . .
- Echoed through the building
- Echoed like gunshots
- Noises died away in their own echoes
- Screamed all around them
- Ripped through the air
- Boomed through the deserted warehouse
- Screamed their warning of a predator
- Bushes rustled with secret scratching of invisible predators
- Crunched under her feet
- Rumbled closer until it filled her ears
- Rattled the windows as it wailed by
- Boomed ominously
- Roared in through the chimney
- Grinding, groaning crack as the ground was ripped apart
- Terrified of what was waiting for him in the shadows
- Made her heart race and hands tremble
- Echoed in his head like a monstrous ghost

SENTENCES

A desperate howl of pain echoed through the building.

The silence was suddenly broken by the squeak of a boot heel on the tiled floor.

Somewhere off in the distance, a hunting owl shrieked.

Something moved in the passage ahead of him. Something quick and scuttling like a rat.

Something huge was moving towards him. Its slow, shuffling feet shattered the silence with its echoes.

The silence was broken by the blare of the horn and a screech of tyres.

A piercing, spine-chilling scream ripped through the air and sent the birds crashing through the trees.

Beneath the quiet, there was a trembling among the leaves and then the snap of a twig resounded like a gunshot.

The dried brown leaves crunched under her feet, growing louder and louder, becoming snapping thuds as she broke into a run.

The deafening wind echoed like a horn and rattled the windows as it wailed by.

There was a sickening crack that made the walls shake. Then, the shattering crash of breaking glass and splintering woodwork, as the walls collapsed.

As she tried to creep past the building, the stones crunched under her feet and announced her presence.

A piercing screech tore through the deserted warehouse, as the metal shutter opened into the silent darkness.

Suddenly, she heard the rustle of a night hunter. She was frozen to the spot, afraid to move, terrified of what was waiting in the shadows.

The silence was pierced by the screech of a gull – a sound like a cold omen that sent a chill down his spine.

A shriek slashed the air as the monkeys swung through the trees, screaming their warning of the predator rustling through the undergrowth below.

Part 2
Characters

Appearance

20

Age, height and shape

SECTION 1 – AGE

WORDS

Nouns	Baby, infant, toddler, child, teenager, teens, youth, juvenile, adolescent, thirties, seventies
Adjectives	Young, middle-aged, old, elderly, aged, wizened

PHRASES – NOUNS AND ADJECTIVES

- ★ Eleven years old
- ★ Man in his thirties
- ★ Middle-aged woman
- ★ Little, wizened old man
- ★ About ten

SENTENCES

He was eleven years old, tall and had curly brown hair.

The man was middle-aged and had a sly, crumpled face.

Even though he must have been in his seventies, he was still running five miles a day.

SECTION 2 – HEIGHT

WORDS

Adjectives	Short, small, little, tiny, elfin Average, medium Tall, big, large, lanky Huge, massive, enormous, gigantic

20 *Appearance: age, height and shape*

PHRASES – NOUNS AND ADJECTIVES

- Short, squat and as broad as a bull
- Small man with stumpy little legs
- Small, delicate boy
- Tiny, elfin girl
- Girl of average height
- Tall, lanky teenager
- Big for his age
- An enormous giant of a man
- Like a human pyramid
- Legs like tree trunks

SENTENCES

John was short, squat and as broad as a bull.

A small man, with stumpy little legs, shuffled towards them.

The girl was elfin, but surprisingly strong for someone so small.

Ann was of average height and had a lean, athletic build.

He was big for his age, with broad, muscular shoulders.

The tall, lanky teenager used his long legs to intercept the ball.

The doorway was blocked by an enormous giant of a man, with huge, powerful shoulders and legs like tree trunks.

He shivered as he looked up at the human pyramid towering over him.

SECTION 3 – SHAPE

WORDS

Nouns

Body, build, legs, shoulders, chest, stomach, belly, arms

Chin, neck, face

Skin, pouch, folds, muscles

China doll, rake, stick, skeleton

Bull, ox, wrestler, rugby forward

Adjectives

Huge, enormous, massive

Chubby, plump, pot-bellied, flabby, fleshy, obese

Slim, slender, slight, petite, elfin

Bony, skinny, weedy, scrawny, spindly, skeletal, gaunt, emaciated, haggard

Broad, square, burly, strong, powerful, muscular

Athletic, dainty, graceful

Stooped, hunched, crooked

Upright, straight-backed, erect

Verbs
Stood, walked, moved, ran, shuffled, hobbled
Hung, wobbled, flapped, slumped
Hunched

PHRASES – NOUNS AND ADJECTIVES

- Jolly, pot-bellied man
- Small and dumpy
- Short and plump
- Like a well-padded cushion
- Huge pot-belly
- Massive, puckered folds
- Like an enormous skin pouch
- Loose skin like huge, fleshy wings on her arms
- Tall and slender
- Slim and dainty
- Like a ballet dancer
- Small, slight body
- Petite, dainty woman
- Tiny, fragile boy
- Like a china doll
- Thin as a rake
- Tall and scrawny
- Weedy boy
- Painfully thin
- Tall, thin stick of a man
- Scrawny like a plucked chicken
- Legs and arms like sticks
- Spindly arms and legs
- Emaciated and gaunt-looking
- As broad as a bull
- Square shoulders
- Burly like a rugby forward
- Built like a wrestler
- Strong and muscular
- As strong as an ox
- Powerful, with broad, muscular shoulders
- Slim body with muscular arms and legs
- Heavily muscled arms and legs
- Athletic build
- Crooked as a walking stick
- Old and stooped
- Hunched like a question mark
- Straight-backed like a soldier

20 *Appearance: age, height and shape*

PHRASES – VERBS

- Wobbled when he walked
- Hung over his trousers
- Slumped onto his chest
- Built for speed
- Ran with a natural rhythm
- Walked gracefully
- Looked like a walking skeleton
- Looked as if a gust of wind would bend him in half
- Hips stood out like tusks
- Skin hung in folds
- Looked as if he had shrunk inside his skin
- Stooped badly
- Could only walk with the aid of a walking stick
- Stood straight-backed
- Stood erect

SENTENCES

Santa Claus is a jolly, pot-bellied man with a white beard.

Her huge pot-belly hung over her trousers like an enormous skin pouch.

She was short and plump, and cosy like a well-padded cushion.

The skin on her arms was loose and flapped like huge, fleshy wings.

His chins hung in massive folds, covering his neck and slumping onto his chest.

He was short, fat and so flabby his stomach wobbled when he walked.

For someone so short and dumpy, he was very fast on his feet.

The gymnast was a petite, dainty woman.

She was slim and dainty and walked gracefully like a ballet dancer.

The girl was tiny and delicate like a china doll.

The fragile boy looked as if a gust of wind would bend him in half.

He was a tall, scrawny boy with a face like a weasel.

He was so emaciated he looked like a walking skeleton.

Robert was a tall, thin stick of a man, with hips that stood out like two tusks.

She was old, stooped and painfully thin. Every step, every painful shuffle, took every ounce of her strength.

He was tall and scrawny like a plucked chicken, with horrid, bony hands and long, clawed fingers.

Her skin hung in creased folds around her neck and arms, as if she had shrunk inside it.

His father was as broad as a bull and burly like a rugby forward.

Robert may have had a slim body, but he had broad, powerful shoulders and muscular arms and legs.

Slim and athletic, Kitty ran with a natural rhythm.

Robert was old and stooped and could only walk with the aid of a walking stick.

An old tramp hobbled towards the bench. He was frail, crumpled and hunched like a question mark.

He was tall and thin and stood straight-backed like a soldier.

She stood erect, her head held high, with the air of someone who was used to being obeyed.

21

Face

SECTION 1 – SHAPE

WORDS

Nouns	Forehead, brow, cheeks, cheekbones
Adjectives	Oval, round, square, rectangular, heart-shaped
	Wide, broad, full, plump, fleshy
	Narrow, long, thin, lean, bony, sunken, hollow
	Pointed, sharp, angular
	Drooping, sagging

PHRASES – NOUNS AND ADJECTIVES

- Narrow, pointed face
- Oval, bony face
- Thin, sunken face
- Hollow cheeks
- High cheekbones
- Sharp, angular cheekbones
- Broad, round face
- Plump hamster cheeks
- Wide, heart-shaped face
- Round-faced woman
- Square, wrinkly face
- Rectangular-shaped face with a high, bald forehead

SENTENCES

- ★ She had a long, pointed face like a bird.
- ★ His once full cheeks were droopy and grey.
- ★ Her wide, round face was framed by a mass of curly black hair.
- ★ He had a very round face and plump hamster cheeks.
- ★ His face was oval-shaped and he had a high, bald forehead.
- ★ The little girl looked like a cherub with her plump, heart-shaped face and angelic smile.
- ★ Her cheeks looked hollow and the flesh was wrinkled and sagging.
- ★ Her cheekbones were so high, they formed two slashes across her face.
- ★ Bald, with a thin, angular face, his high, sharp cheekbones gave him a haunted look.

SECTION 2 – COLOUR AND TEXTURE

WORDS

Nouns	Freckles, veins, shadows, bags, circles
	Wrinkles, folds, lines, slashes
Adjectives	Pale, grey, ashen, pallid, deathly, colourless, translucent
	Black, brown, olive-skinned
	Red, pink, ruddy, bronze-coloured, sunburned, tanned, leathery
	Smooth, shiny, glowing
	Deep, sharp, vertical
Verbs	Scrubbed, glowed
	Lined, creased, wrinkled, crumpled
	Hung, sagged, drooped
	Stretched, bulged

PHRASES – NOUNS AND ADJECTIVES

- ★ Pale like a porcelain doll
- ★ Deathly pale
- ★ Pale, almost colourless skin
- ★ Pallid, deathly, grey colour
- ★ Smooth, brown skin
- ★ Ruddy, glowing face
- ★ Like beaten leather
- ★ Round, pinkish look of a prize pig
- ★ Dark circles
- ★ Purple shadows
- ★ Bags like giant, purple suitcases

21 *Appearance: face*

- Deep laughter lines in the corners of his eyes and mouth
- Sharp, vertical lines
- Face like thin, crumpled paper
- Like the skin of a lizard

PHRASES – VERBS

- Crumpled and unshaven
- Sagged with wrinkles beneath her eyes
- Hung in wrinkled folds
- Stretched tight over his face
- Gave him a skull-like appearance
- Scrubbed until it glowed
- Laughter lines burnt into her skin
- Lines drew together when he smiled
- Deeply lined with age
- Covered in wrinkles
- Wrinkles looked like cruel slashes
- Eyes were lost within their wrinkles
- Lines burrowed between his brows
- Gave him a permanent frown

SENTENCES

He was painfully thin and his face deathly pale.

His face was ashen and twisted with pain.

Her skin was a sickly, grey colour and hung in wrinkled folds.

He had a ruddy face that had been scrubbed until it glowed.

His face was crumpled, unshaven and grey with anxiety.

He looked like a walrus, with huge folds of sagging skin drooping from his face.

Her pale skin was translucent. It was almost purple under her eyes and limp and sagging with wrinkles.

He had a sallow, scarred face and the haunted look of someone who had seen many battles.

With her pale, almost colourless skin, she looked like a fragile china doll.

His colourless skin was stretched tight over his face and gave him a skull-like appearance.

There were shadows and bags like giant, purple suitcases under her eyes.

Sharp, vertical lines burrowed between his brows and gave him a permanent frown.

Laughter lines surrounded her eyes and mouth, burnt by the sun and wind during the hours spent outside with the animals.

The years had not been kind to her and decay was obvious in a face covered in wrinkles like thin, crumpled paper.

SECTION 3 – WOUNDS AND SCARS

WORDS

Nouns	Skull, face, jaw, cheeks, mouth, lip, eye, eyebrows
	Skin, flesh, tissue, folds, lumps, patches
	Sores, blisters, burns, bruise, wound, scabs
	Scar, mole, wart
	Width, length
Adjectives	Red, pink, black, purple, brown, green, yellow, creamy
	Wide, thin, huge, small
	Jagged, gnarled
	Ugly, horrible, grotesque, hideous
	Angry, swollen, festering
	Peeling, flaking, blotchy
Verbs	Scarred, scabbed, burnt, blistered
	Ran, covered, stretched, oozed, sprouted
	Pulled, dragged, closed, twisted, puckered, disfigured
	Scorched, singed, seared, shrivelled

PHRASES – NOUNS AND ADJECTIVES

- ★ Black eye
- ★ Purple bruise
- ★ Flaking skin
- ★ Swollen, red blisters
- ★ Mass of angry sores around his lips
- ★ Festering, green wound
- ★ Creamy pus
- ★ Huge, pink mole
- ★ Enormous, wrinkled warts on her lip
- ★ Thin, jagged scar
- ★ Ugly, wide scar
- ★ Singed hair and eyebrows
- ★ Mass of seared, scarred skin
- ★ Blotched, horribly stretched skin
- ★ Puckered, fleshy folds
- ★ Gnarled lump of flesh
- ★ Scar above his left eyebrow
- ★ Scarred and twisted lip

21 *Appearance: face*

PHRASES – VERBS

- Had a battle-scarred face
- Disfigured by fire
- Sprouted two gristly hairs
- Oozed creamy pus
- Puckered around the wound
- Scorched into huge, pink patches
- Shrivelled into a twisted lump of flesh
- Stretched the width of his jaw
- Ran the length of one side of his face
- Just visible above left eyebrow
- Covered his face and skull
- Pulled into a permanent snarl
- Eye closed in the puckered folds of a scar
- Pulled his eye into a curious squint
- Twisted his lips
- Dragged his lip to meet his nostril

SENTENCES

His face was a mass of sores and peeling skin.

The swollen, red blisters twisted his lips into a grimace.

The skin on his face and bald skull was scarred and scabbed.

He had a black eye and an angry, purple bruise on his cheek.

A thin, jagged scar was just visible above his left eyebrow.

One of his cheeks was dragged downwards by an ugly scar.

The scars on his skull were clearly visible through his closely shaved hair.

One side of his face was a pocked mass of scars and seared skin.

The huge pink mole on her upper lip sprouted two long, gristly hairs.

The left side of his face was terribly burned. It was a mass of seared skin and scorched in huge, pink patches.

The skin was bunched up around the festering, green wound and oozing pus.

The skin around one eye had been pulled out of shape and gave her a curious squint.

He had a scarred and twisted lip, which was pulled up to meet his nostril.

His face had been disfigured by fire. His eyebrows were singed and sprouted at odd angles, and his ear was a shrivelled, gnarled lump.

His face was disfigured by a hideous scar that ran the length of one side of his face and pulled his mouth into a permanent snarl.

His face was a mass of scar tissue that almost closed one eye in its puckered folds.

22

Eyes

SECTION 1 – COLOUR

WORDS

Adjectives	Blue, grey, green, brown, hazel, black, yellow, bloodshot, pink-rimmed Dark, pale, transparent Sapphires, emeralds, diamonds, charcoal, slate, velvet Beautiful, brilliant, sparkling, gleaming, twinkling Soft, gentle, calm Laughing, impish, mischievous Cold, icy, steely, piercing, flinty, dangerous, mysterious
Verbs	Lit, shone, beamed, danced, sparkled, gleamed Burned, glinted, stared, drilled, pierced, bulged

PHRASES – NOUNS AND ADJECTIVES

- Pale, sapphire blue
- Emerald green
- As black as coal
- Velvet brown
- Flinty grey
- Slate grey
- Enormous mud brown eyes
- Marsh brown
- Yellow wolf's eyes
- Eyes like a hawk
- Beautiful blue eyes
- Eyes like sparkling diamonds
- Twinkling, grey

22 *Appearance: eyes*

- Like candles in the dark
- Icy blue
- Steely blue
- Piercing grey
- Yellow and unblinking
- Staring, bright green eyes
- Cold and almost transparent
- Brown, deep and mysterious
- Cold and dangerous

PHRASES – VERBS

- Danced with laughter
- Lit up his face
- Beamed with warmth
- Sparkled impishly
- Peered at her from beneath long lashes
- Glinted like frost
- Burned with a cruel light
- Drilled into him
- Burned with anger
- Bulged like a frog
- Filled with sadness
- Swollen and bloodshot from weeping
- Rimmed with bulging, blue veins
- Hidden beneath huge, bushy eyebrows
- Took in every detail, every move

SENTENCES

His emerald green eyes sparkled impishly.

Curly, ink-black eyelashes feathered her beautiful sapphire blue eyes.

Her eyes were mud brown and as big as saucers.

Kitty's eyes were like sparkling blue diamonds and always seemed to dance with laughter.

Her eyes were velvet-brown and beamed with warmth like candles in the dark.

Robert's mouth was set in a firm line, but his twinkling grey eyes lit up his face.

Eyes that were as black as coal peered at her from beneath curly black lashes.

His steely blue eyes glinted like frost.

His large, staring eyes were an icy grey.

His bright green eyes burned with a cruel light.

Her eyes were an icy blue – cold and dangerous.

His eyes were a slate grey and bulging like a frog.

His eyes were as black as coal and hidden beneath huge bushy eyebrows.

His flinty, narrowed eyes were cold and rimmed with bulging blue veins.

Like a hawk, her eyes were yellow and unblinking and took in every detail, every move.

Her cold blue eyes were almost transparent and made Robert shiver as they drilled into him.

SECTION 2 – SIZE

WORDS

Nouns	Saucers, frog
	Slits, folds
Adjectives	Big, wide, bulging, gaping
	Small, little, beady, oval, narrow
	Buggy, puffy, sunken
	Staring, unblinking
Verbs	Stared, glared, darted

PHRASES – NOUNS AND ADJECTIVES

- Wide, bulging eyes like a frog
- Big, staring eyes
- As big as saucers
- Long, narrow eyes
- Like dangerous slits
- Small, buggy eyes
- Little, puffy brown eyes

PHRASES – VERBS

- Stared as if he was in a trance
- Glared unblinking
- Darted rapidly
- Hidden in drooping skin

SENTENCES

His narrow, flint grey eyes were like dangerous slits.

Her eyes were as big as saucers and twinkled with laughter.

Her small, pig-like eyes were hidden in the folds of her wrinkled, drooping skin.

He had wide, bulging eyes like a frog, that stared as if he was in a trance.

Kitty watched as his small, buggy eyes darted rapidly from one to the other.

22 *Appearance: eyes*

SECTION 3 – EYEBROWS

WORDS

Adjectives	Dark, black, heavy, bushy, thin Arched, straight, rectangular
Verbs	Stuck, sprouted, met, shadowed, curtained

PHRASES – NOUNS AND ADJECTIVES

- ★ Bushy eyebrows
- ★ Heavy black eyebrows
- ★ Rectangular eyebrows
- ★ Gnarled brow
- ★ Thinly plucked, arched eyebrows

PHRASES – VERBS

- ★ Shadowed by a gnarled brow
- ★ Stuck out fiercely at odd angles
- ★ Met in the middle
- ★ Curtained her eyes
- ★ Gave her a constant look of surprise

SENTENCES

Her eyes were curtained by heavy black eyebrows.

Her thinly plucked, arched eyebrows made her look permanently surprised.

His bushy eyebrows met in the middle and stuck out fiercely at odd angles.

He had deep-set eyes, which were shadowed by a gnarled brow.

23

Mouth, teeth, nose and ears

SECTION 1 – MOUTH

WORDS

Adjectives	Narrow, thin, tight
	Wide, thick, full, fleshy, flabby, plump, big-lipped
	Wrinkled, dry, flaking, drooping
	Beaming, excited, impish
	Stern, menacing, sneering, reptilian
Verbs	Rose, curved
	Pressed, pursed, pinched, puckered

PHRASES – NOUNS AND ADJECTIVES

- Wide, full mouth
- Wide mouth and thick lips
- Tiny rosebud mouth
- Narrow mouth and thin, pursed lips
- Wrinkled, puckered mouth
- Plump lips
- Thick, fleshy, drooping lips
- Thin, stern lips
- Dry, flaking lips
- Pinched lips
- Reptilian smirk
- Impish grin
- Excited grin
- Beaming smile

23 *Appearance: mouth, teeth, nose and ears*

PHRASES – VERBS

- Rose in a perfect curve
- Curved upwards into a wide, beaming smile
- Pressed into a tight, thin line
- Stuck in a sneering smile
- Stuck in a permanent pucker
- Turned down at the corners in a permanent sulk

SENTENCES

She had a tiny rosebud mouth.

Her mouth and plump lips rose in a perfect curve.

He was big-lipped and gap-toothed.

Her lips were pale and pressed into a tight, thin line.

Saliva dribbled onto his chin from his limp, drooping lip.

He had a wide, full mouth that seemed stuck in a sneering smile.

Her lips looked like they had been blown up by a bicycle pump and stuck in a permanent pucker.

She had a wide mouth and thick lips, which curved upwards into a broad, beaming smile.

SECTION 2 – TEETH

WORDS

Nouns	Molars, fangs, stumps, tombstones, false teeth, pearls
Adjectives	Toothless, gap-toothed Straight, crooked, jagged Rotting, crumbling White, brown, yellow, grey, gold-capped Sparkling, polished, stained
Verbs	Chipped, jutted, protruded

PHRASES – NOUNS AND ADJECTIVES

- Teeth like polished pearls
- Great sheet of white, polished teeth
- Toothless smile
- Two jagged rows of rotting, brown teeth
- Like crumbling tombstones
- Stained, chipped teeth
- Mouth full of yellow teeth
- Crooked teeth and cracked, flaky lips

PHRASES – VERBS

- Jutted out like fangs
- Chipped diagonally in half
- Worn to yellowing stumps
- Clicked when she moved her lips
- Curved down over his lower lip
- Teeth bared in a reptilian leer

SENTENCES

Her teeth were like polished pearls.

He had a great sheet of polished, white teeth and a warm smile.

Her false teeth clicked when she moved her lips.

A gold-capped molar glinted when he opened his mouth.

His teeth jutted out like fangs and curved down over his lower lip.

His teeth had worn away into yellowing stumps that looked like crumbling tombstones.

Behind the thick fleshy lips, she could see his stained and crooked teeth.

When he snarled, he revealed two jagged rows of brown, rotting teeth.

SECTION 3 – NOSE

WORDS

Nouns	Nose, nostrils, freckles, veins, hairs
	Boxer, hawk, eagle
Adjectives	Large, small, long, short
	Thin, narrow, wide, broad
	Straight, flattened, pointed, curved, turned up, hooked, broken, crooked
	Pug, button, snub, triangle, beak-like
Verbs	Covered, spread, stretched
	Flared, pinched

PHRASES – NOUNS AND ADJECTIVES

- Small pug nose
- Tiny, triangular nose
- Long, narrow and pointed
- Thick and broad
- Large, hooked nose
- Broken nose

- Crooked nose
- Flattened nose of a boxer
- Perfectly straight
- Large bulbous nose
- Narrow pinched nostrils
- Wide flared nostrils
- Thick tufts of sprouting hair

PHRASES – VERBS

- Covered in swollen red veins
- Covered in freckles
- Sprouted from his nostrils
- Spread across his cheek
- Made him look stern and arrogant
- Flared with every breath

SENTENCES

He had the flattened nose of a boxer.

Her small, upturned nose was covered in freckles.

She was a petite woman with a thin, perfectly straight nose.

His eagle beak of a nose made him look stern and arrogant.

His wide nostrils flared with every breath like an angry bull.

His bulbous nose was covered in swollen red veins and had clumps of dark wiry hair sprouting from the nostrils.

He had a thin, scarred face and a nose that had been broken so many times it seemed to spreading across his right cheek.

He looked at them over his glasses, which were perched on the end of his large, hooked nose.

She glanced down at him over her narrow pinched nostrils, as if he was a nasty smell under her nose.

SECTION 4 – EARS

WORDS

Nouns	Cauliflower, cabbage, bat, basset hound, satellite dish Earlobes, earrings
Adjectives	Big, large, huge, enormous, small, tiny Droopy, dangling, prominent, protruding
Verbs	Jutted, stretched, veined

PHRASES – NOUNS AND ADJECTIVES

- Big, droopy ears
- Huge cauliflower ears
- Like a basset hound
- Like mini satellite dishes
- Small, bat-like ears
- Enormous, heavy, dangling earrings

PHRASES – VERBS

- Jutted out on either side of his head
- Attached to his head
- Veined like a cabbage leaf
- Earlobes stretched into long, narrow ovals

SENTENCES

His huge, cauliflower ears jutted out on either side of his head.

His ears were large and veined like a cabbage leaf.

Her earlobes were stretched into long narrow ovals by enormous, dangling earrings.

His ears were so big it looked like he had two mini satellite dishes attached to either side of his head.

24

Hands and fingers

WORDS

Nouns	Nails, claws, talons Veins, spots, dirt, grime
Adjectives	Bony, skeletal, shovel-like, long-fingered Wrinkled, swollen, lumpy Black, sharp, dirty
Verbs	Covered, blackened, encrusted Chipped, burnt, twisted Felt, shook, held Drummed, grabbed, grasped, lunged

PHRASES – NOUNS AND ADJECTIVES

- Wrinkled hands
- Burnt, twisted claw
- Bony, long-fingered hands
- Shovel-like hands
- Nails like claws
- Black talons
- Dangerous weapons
- Swollen, lumpy veins
- Veins like rivers on a map
- Filthy with dirt and grime

Appearance: hands and fingers 24

PHRASES – VERBS

- Sharpened to points
- Chipped and encrusted with dirt
- Felt as cold as a skeleton
- Shook his hand
- Held out a bony hand
- Backed away from the claw-like hand
- Grabbed her by the wrist
- Grasped at the air in front of him
- Lunged at him
- Drummed on the table impatiently

SENTENCES

His nails were chipped and encrusted with dirt.

Two enormous shovel-like hands lunged at him.

She drummed her long, bony fingers on the table impatiently.

His hand was a burnt, twisted claw, with blackened talons for nails.

Her old hands were swollen and covered in lumpy blue veins like rivers on a map.

He backed away from the claw-like hand that was grasping at the air in front of him.

Her nails were like claws, sharpened to points and dangerous weapons.

She held out a bony hand, which felt as cold as a skeleton when Robert shook it.

25

Hair and facial hair

SECTION 1 – COLOUR

WORDS

Adjectives	Black, dark, jet black, raven black
	Grey, silver, white
	Blond, yellow, straw-coloured, fair, golden, sandy, honey, bleached
	Red, copper, ginger, orange, carrot-coloured
	Brown, chestnut, auburn, dark, light
	Bald
Verbs	Cut, dyed, streaked, receded

PHRASES – NOUNS AND ADJECTIVES

- Raven black
- Jet black hair
- Auburn hair like liquid copper
- Thick and chestnut-coloured
- Light brown hair
- Unruly orange hair
- Silver tufts on either side of his round head
- Hair as white and fluffy as cotton wool
- Shaggy, grey-streaked hair like a wolf
- Thin strip down the centre of his forehead
- Few tufts of grizzled, black hair
- Completely bald

PHRASES – VERBS

- Cut short like a hedgehog
- Dyed a fierce red
- Cut in a bob
- Fluffed out like a dandelion
- Scalp gleamed like polished bone
- Losing his hair
- Strands combed from one side to the other
- Receding at the temples

SENTENCES

Her unruly orange hair looked like flames blazing around her head.

His blond hair fluffed out from his head like a dandelion.

Her long white hair hung in thin, limp strands on her shrunken head.

Her scalp gleamed like polished bone through her white, sparse hair.

He had jet black hair, cut short and spiked like a hedgehog.

She had shiny black hair that fell in a sheet down her back and fanned across her shoulders.

Her short hair was still thick and dark, but streaked with lines of pure white.

She had a head of tamed, reddish curls that cascaded down her back.

He was losing his hair and combed the remaining strands from one side to the other, then greased them heavily in place.

SECTION 2 – STYLE (LONG)

WORDS

Nouns	Ponytail, pigtail, plaits, bun
Adjectives	Long, shoulder length Curly, frizzy, wavy, straight
Verbs	Fell, flowed, streamed, cascaded, swung Tied, held, pulled, dragged, gathered, fastened

PHRASES – NOUNS AND ADJECTIVES

- Heavy rope of black hair
- Loose ponytail
- Two long pigtails
- Tight bun on top of her head

25 *Appearance: hair and facial hair*

PHRASES – VERBS

- Fell in a sheet down her back
- Flowed over her shoulders
- Cascaded down her back
- Swung rhythmically from side to side
- Fell around her face like a curtain
- Gathered in a loose ponytail
- Tied in plaits
- Hung down in two long pigtails
- Hung behind her like a tail
- Streamed back from her face
- Pulled tightly into a bun
- Held back by a silver headband
- Fastened at the back with a wooden spike

SENTENCES

Her hair hung down in two long pigtails.

Her long black hair fell around her face like a curtain.

Her sandy hair was held back from her face by a silver headband.

Her dark hair was pulled back tight to her head and fastened at the back with an enormous wooden spike.

She had a head of reddish curls, which cascaded down her back.

She had shiny black hair, which fell in a sheet down her back and fanned across her shoulders.

Her hair was gathered on top of her head and held in place by diamond pins that had turned her hair into a sparkling tiara.

Her shiny brown hair swung rhythmically from side to side as she walked.

SECTION 3 – STYLE (SHORT)

WORDS

Nouns	Bob, crew cut, quiff, tuft, spikes
Adjectives	Short, curly, frizzy, wavy, straight, spiky, scalp-hugging
Verbs	Wore, combed, styled
	Cut, cropped, shaved
	Spiked, stuck up, sleeked, gelled

PHRASES – NOUNS AND ADJECTIVES

- ★ Stylish, sleek bob
- ★ Military, scalp-hugging crop
- ★ Short to the nape of her neck

PHRASES – VERBS

- ★ Wore her hair short
- ★ Cropped stylishly in a bob
- ★ Sleeked back
- ★ Stuck up in a tuft at the front
- ★ Swept back behind her ears
- ★ Combed back from his face
- ★ Cropped tight to his head
- ★ Spiked like a hedgehog
- ★ Sticky and spiked with gel
- ★ Gelled in an oily quiff
- ★ Hung down to hide his face

SENTENCES

Her blonde hair was cropped stylishly in a sleek bob.

She wore her hair short and swept behind her ears.

His thick fair hair stuck up in a tuft at the front.

He had jet black hair, which was cut short and spiked like a hedgehog.

He had curly black hair that was cut close to his head.

His hair had been shaved into a military, scalp-hugging crop.

She had white hair cropped short to the nape of her neck.

SECTION 4 – UNTIDY

WORDS

Nouns	Dreadlocks, mane, strands
Adjectives	Thick, bushy, shaggy, unruly Straggly, stiff, limp, knotted, tangled, twisted Dry, greasy
Verbs	Hung, fell, tousled, stuck up

25 *Appearance: hair and facial hair*

PHRASES – NOUNS AND ADJECTIVES

- Limp red hair
- Long, greasy black hair
- Unruly orange hair
- Shaggy mane of blond hair
- Hair was a tangled, wild stack
- Like great, twisted roots

PHRASES – VERBS

- Fell into his eyes
- Hung in thin, limp strands
- Sprawled over her face
- Stuck up madly in all directions
- Grew at odd angles out of her head
- Fluffed out from his head
- As if he had had an electric shock
- Looked as if it had been cut by a pair of garden shears
- Combed by the fingers of the wind

SENTENCES

Her hair was dry and a tangled wild stack.

Her long, grey hair sprawled over her shrivelled face.

He had a mop of dreadlocked hair like great, twisted roots.

His black hair was long and greasy and combed back from his face.

His thick, black hair stuck up in all directions and looked as if it had been cut by a pair of garden shears.

Her hair had been combed and knotted by the fingers of the wind.

SECTION 5 – FACIAL HAIR

WORDS

Nouns	Stubble, shadow, tufts
	Beard, moustache, whiskers, sideburns
Adjectives	Stubbly, unshaven
	Thin, little, narrow, pencil, goatee
	Enormous, heavy, bushy, drooping
	Dark, black
	Scruffy, grimy, tangled, grizzled, unkempt
	Neat, trim

Verbs Grew, sprouted, poked
Curved, drooped
Spread, crept, covered
Cut, trimmed

PHRASES – NOUNS AND ADJECTIVES

- Dark stubble
- Grizzled tufts of hair
- Thin little moustache
- Enormous, heavy moustache
- Dark moustache on her upper lip
- Bushy sideburns
- Goatee beard
- Tangled and grimy with food

PHRASES – VERBS

- Spread across his cheeks and chin
- Crept down his neck
- Covered most of his face
- Poked out from her chin
- Grew in grizzled tufts from ears and nostrils
- Twisted fiercely upwards
- Curved around his face
- Drooped over his upper lip and into his mouth
- Sprouted in all directions
- Looked like a clothes brush
- Looked as if it had been cut by a hedge trimmer
- Gave him a rugged look
- Made him look slightly eccentric

SENTENCES

His black, carelessly trimmed beard looked as if it had been cut by a hedge trimmer.

His goatee beard and thick glasses made him look slightly eccentric.

Grizzled hair sprouted in all directions from his unkempt, bushy sideburns.

Dark stubble was spreading across his cheeks and chin, and creeping down his neck.

His beard covered so much of his face that only his nose and black eyes were visible.

His beard was tangled and grimy with food, which had dribbled when he was eating.

26

Clothes

WORDS

Nouns	Coat, jacket, parka, duffle, bomber, blazer, trench, suit
	Trousers, chinos, jeans, leggings, tracksuit bottoms, shorts
	Blouse, smock, shirt, t-shirt, vest, sweatshirt, jumper, sweater, fleece
	Dress, gown
	Shoes, sandals, boots, trainers
	Rags
Adjectives	Black, brown, beige, khaki, purple, green, blue, turquoise, grey, yellow, orange, red, pink, white, cream
	Floral, striped, spotted, patterned, psychedelic, pin-striped
	Linen, cotton, nylon, denim, leather, woollen, down, tweed, corduroy, silk, jersey
	Loose, baggy, shapeless, tight, fitted, tailored
	Straight, flared, wide-legged
	Long, flowing, short, mini, cropped
	Trendy, designer, new, old, battered, faded
	Polo, rugby, football
	Bermuda, skater, combat
	Long-sleeved, short-sleeved
	Hooded, open-necked, v-neck, roll-neck
Verbs	Dressed, wore, wrapped, hung, draped, buttoned
	Ripped, torn, crumpled, creased

PHRASES – NOUNS AND ADJECTIVES

- Black trench coat
- Green nylon parka

- Pink, hooded bolero
- Denim jacket
- Pilot's bomber jacket
- Grey pin-striped suit
- Linen suit
- Loose, faded jeans
- Designer skinny jeans
- Cropped leggings
- Blue, wide-legged trousers
- Khaki Bermuda shorts
- Loose skater shorts
- White polo shirt
- Striped rugby shirt
- Psychedelic smock top
- Layered skateboard shirt
- Long-sleeved t-shirt
- Cropped vest top
- Baggy sweatshirt
- Hooded fleece
- Red silk blouse
- Floral cotton shirt
- Open-necked shirt
- Long black dress
- Linen sundress
- Blue cotton shirt dress
- Shapeless brown dress
- Turquoise silk gown
- Beige miniskirt
- Flared denim skirt
- Canvas sandals
- Black suede boots
- Sturdy, black lace-up shoes
- Navy high-heeled shoes
- Purple platform shoes
- Walking boots
- Worn, filthy clothes
- Like rags on a scarecrow
- Shoes with flapping soles
- Filthy, tattered jeans

PHRASES – VERBS

- Wrapped in a heavy winter coat
- Wearing a denim jacket

- Draped casually around his shoulders
- Dressed in loose, faded jeans
- Hung loosely on his hips
- Dragged along the floor
- Casually dressed
- Smartly dressed
- Tucked in loosely
- Fastened by a brooch
- Fastened to the neck
- Left her midriff bare
- Dressed in rags
- Collar torn off his shirt
- Shirt hung outside his trousers
- Sleeves rolled to the elbows
- Wore jumper inside out and back to front
- Trousers ripped at the knees

SENTENCES

Her gown was a beautiful turquoise silk.

Her black trench coat was draped casually around her shoulders.

He was casually dressed in skater shorts and sandals.

She was wearing a blue linen blazer and white, wide-legged trousers.

He was casual in designer jeans and a pilot's bomber jacket.

A plump woman, in a shapeless black dress, sat down beside her.

It was freezing cold, but she was warm and snug in her white down jacket.

He was wrapped in a heavy winter overcoat and his face hidden by a scarf.

She was dressed in a striped shirt and tight, faded jeans.

He looked out of his place in his rugby shirt, jeans and denim jacket.

His loose, shapeless jeans hung loosely on his hips and dragged along the floor.

He was wearing a layered skateboard t-shirt, torn tracksuit bottoms and muddy trainers.

She was elegantly dressed in a long black dress, with a shimmering silver scarf draped over her shoulders.

She was smartly dressed in a navy skirt and matching jacket, with a cream blouse fastened with a brooch.

Her cotton miniskirt and cropped top left her midriff bare.

She looked stern, but professional, in a black tailored suit, and a red silk blouse fastened to the neck.

He felt casual, but smart, in his linen suit and t-shirt.

She had changed into a white, chic blouse, tailored black trousers and expensive, black, high-heeled boots.

She was dirty and dressed in rags.

His worn clothes hung on him like rags on a scarecrow.

The soles of her shoes flapped as she walked.

He looked like a tramp in his filthy, tattered jeans and ripped, shapeless t-shirt.

The collar of his shirt was torn and hanging loose on his shoulder.

His shirt was hanging outside his trousers and his long sleeves were rolled to the elbows.

His trousers were ripped at the knees, his t-shirt torn and blood soaked through both in dark, damp patches.

27 *Voice*

WORDS

Nouns	Whisper, murmur, wheeze, rattle Scream, yell, shriek
Adjectives	Loud, big, strong, booming, thunderous, deafening, piercing, theatrical Quiet, soft, gentle, mild, calm Low, low-pitched, deep High, squeaky, shrill, high-pitched, harsh Dry, rough, hoarse, husky, croaky, scratchy, throaty Smooth, sweet, musical, lilting, chirpy, sing-song Bossy, whining, smug, mocking, wheedling, simpering, monotonous Pleasant, silky, creamy, sweet, syrupy Educated, cultured, drawling
Verbs	Echoed, vibrated, drilled, droned Cracked, croaked, clicked, gurgled, rasped Shouted, snarled, barked, growled Yelled, boomed, thundered, bellowed Hissed, whispered, muttered, mumbled, murmured Whined, whimpered, simpered, bleated

PHRASES – NOUNS AND ADJECTIVES

- Big, booming voice
- Thunderous voice
- Rich, theatrical voice
- Calm, deep voice
- Quiet, low-pitched voice
- As smooth as silk

- Dry rattle in his voice
- Cracked, old voice
- Throaty wheeze
- Husky murmur
- Croaky whisper
- Loud, rasping rattle
- Voice clicked in an odd way
- Gruff voice with a thick accent
- High-pitched, whining voice
- Squeaky, rasping voice
- Shrill and harsh like the shriek of a seagull
- Low, droning voice
- High-pitched whimper
- Wheedling tone
- Thick, drawling accent
- Smooth like polished glass
- As sweet as syrup
- Quiet and soft
- Chirpy, sing-song voice
- Lilting and musical
- Soft, feathery whisper
- Pleasant, educated accent

PHRASES – VERBS

- Echoed around the room
- Like he was speaking through a loudspeaker
- As if he was acting on stage
- Seemed to vibrate in his chest
- Spoke in a wheedling tone
- Protested in a shrill voice
- Words floated out of her mouth
- As if she was speaking through velvet
- Made the words dance in his ears
- Spoke without a trace of an accent
- Difficult to know where he was from
- Difficult to understand
- Unable to listen to her whining
- Difficult to pay attention to . . .
- Found himself drifting off to sleep
- He closed his eyes to block out . . .
- Drove him mad
- Bored into him like a drill
- Had a calming effect

27 *Appearance: voice*

SENTENCES

'Don't move,' he urged in a croaky whisper.

'I didn't do it,' she screamed in a high-pitched, whining voice.

His voice was thunderous and seemed to vibrate in his chest.

Robert found it difficult to pay attention to her low, droning voice and drifted off to sleep.

He closed his eyes and tried to block out her squeaky whimper.

He had a thick, drawling accent that made it difficult to understand what he wanted her to do.

He had a big, booming voice, which echoed around the room as if he was speaking through a loudspeaker.

He spoke in a rich, theatrical voice, as if he was acting on a stage.

He turned and stomped out of the room, unable to listen to her simpering voice any longer.

When she yelled, her voice was high and harsh, like the shriek of a seagull.

The words floated out of her mouth as a soft, feathery whisper.

Her voice was as quiet and soft as velvet.

He spoke in a deep voice that was calm and as smooth as silk.

He had a pleasant, educated accent that inspired trust.

Kitty had a lilting, musical voice, which made the words dance in his ears.

It was difficult to know where he was from, as he spoke without a trace of an accent.

Emotions and personality

28

Excited, happy

SECTION 1 – EMOTIONS

WORDS

Nouns	Happiness, joy, delight, elation Excitement, eagerness, anticipation Heart, pulse
Adjectives	Happy, jolly, pleased, delighted, thrilled, overjoyed, elated, ecstatic Bubbly, fizzy, lively, buzzing, animated, radiant Eager, excited, enthusiastic
Verbs	Beat, raced, pounded, throbbed Tingled, shook, trembled, shivered

PHRASES – NOUNS AND ADJECTIVES

- ★ On top of the world
- ★ Over the moon
- ★ Bubbly like a fizzy drink
- ★ Buzzing with excitement
- ★ Glow of happiness
- ★ Sense of elation
- ★ Unbearable gurgle in his stomach

PHRASES – VERBS

- ★ Heart pounded
- ★ Pulse raced

- Shivered with eagerness
- Body tingled with excitement
- Hands shook with anticipation
- Could hardly contain his excitement

SENTENCES

His elation was an almost unbearable gurgle in his stomach.

He was buzzing with excitement and couldn't help breaking into a wide grin.

She felt as if she was on top of the world and a glow of happiness spread through her.

His pulse was racing and he took a deep and loudly enthusiastic breath.

With heart pounding and hands shaking, she tore open the envelope.

SECTION 2 – EXPRESSIONS

WORDS

Nouns	Look, grin, smile, laughter Mouth, lip, laughter lines
Adjectives	Wide, broad, huge, eager Toothy, cheeky, impish, comical, humorous
Verbs	Grinned, smiled, laughed, gazed Lit, shone, glowed Broke, flashed, flickered
Adverbs	Happily, comically Eagerly, excitedly, enthusiastically

PHRASES – NOUNS AND ADJECTIVES

- Broad grin
- Toothy grin
- Impish grin
- Wide, excited grin
- Grin as broad as his face
- Beaming smile
- Wide, gap-toothed smile
- Wide, eager smile
- Amused expression
- Eager expression
- Look of eager anticipation

PHRASES – VERBS

- Cheeks glowed
- Gazed eagerly
- Laughter shone in his face
- Face lit up in a wide smile
- Grinned like a Cheshire cat
- Broke into a broad grin
- Flashed her a warm smile
- Flickered across his face
- Waggled his eyebrows comically
- Nibbled at her lower lip to hold back a smile
- Laughter lines at the edge of her eyes deepened

SENTENCES

She looked up with an amused expression on her face.

His face was lit up by a huge smile as broad as his face.

She was thrilled to be chosen. Her cheeks glowed with excitement and her face broke into a wide, beaming smile.

With an impish grin, he gazed eagerly up at his mother.

He nibbled at his lower lip to hold back the laughter that was threatening to erupt.

As her face lit up in a wide grin, her eyes disappeared in deep wrinkles.

SECTION 3 – EYES

WORDS

Nouns	Humour, joy, delight, laughter, amusement Interest, eagerness, excitement Gleam, glint
Adjectives	Wide, bright, glittering
Verbs	Shone, beamed Laughed, danced, sparkled, twinkled

PHRASES – NOUNS AND ADJECTIVES

- Bright, twinkling eyes
- Wide with excitement
- Bright with interest and excitement
- Gleam of humour in her eyes

28 *Emotions: excited, happy*

PHRASES – VERBS

- ★ Danced with laughter
- ★ Twinkled with amusement
- ★ Laughter shone in her eyes
- ★ Shone like beams from a torch
- ★ Burned with excitement
- ★ Sparkled with eagerness

SENTENCES

Her bright eyes danced with laughter.

She looked down at him with laughter shining in her eyes.

She leaned forward, her blue eyes bright with interest and excitement.

His eyes burned with excitement and he kept shifting from one foot to the other.

The delight shone from his eyes like beams from a torch and he clenched his fist and punched the air.

As he burst into the room, his eyes were wide with excitement.

Even though she was not smiling, there was a glint of humour in her eyes.

SECTION 4 – VOICE

WORDS

Nouns	Laugh, giggle, chuckle, squeal, snort, gurgle Shriek, guffaw, roar
Adjectives	Low, little, big, loud, high-pitched Hearty, manic, raucous, devilish
Verbs	Giggled, chortled, snorted, laughed Shook, trembled, cracked Let out, stifled, blurted, exploded

PHRASES – NOUNS AND ADJECTIVES

- ★ Big, hearty laugh
- ★ Loud, raucous laughter
- ★ Piercing shriek
- ★ Devilish roar of glee
- ★ Squeal of delight
- ★ Stifled snort
- ★ Low, wheezing chuckle
- ★ Excited gasps

PHRASES – VERBS

- ★ Shook with laughter
- ★ Giggles bubbled at the back of her throat
- ★ Blurted out a little laugh
- ★ Chortled at the look on her face
- ★ Let out a peel of manic laughter
- ★ Exploded into loud guffaws
- ★ Rose with excitement into a piercing squeal
- ★ Words tumbled over each other in a high-pitched gabble
- ★ Words came in excited gasps

SENTENCES

He laughed a big, hearty laugh that echoed around the room.

She let out a squeal of delight and hopped up and down on the spot.

He threw back his head and exploded into loud guffaws of laughter.

Kitty tried to smother her laughter, but it exploded as a snort.

His voice cracked with loud, raucous laughter and tears poured down his cheeks.

She pressed her lips tightly together to smother the giggles that were bubbling in the back of her throat.

Robert let out a peel of manic laughter and held his sides.

As the laughter exploded in his throat, his shoulders shook and his body convulsed helplessly.

SECTION 5 – MOVEMENT

WORDS

Nouns	Arms, hands, palms, fist
Verbs	Skipped, hopped, jigged, pranced, danced Leapt, sprung, jumped, bounced Rubbed, clapped, pumped, punched, clenched Hugged

PHRASES – VERBS

- ★ Walked with a bounce in her step
- ★ Jumped up and down
- ★ Leapt in the air, screaming with excitement
- ★ Hopped up and down on the spot
- ★ Skipped along the pavement

28 *Emotions: excited, happy*

- Jigged around the room
- Threw her arms around his neck
- Clenched his fist and punched the air
- Rubbed palms together with excitement
- Clapped hands and squealed with delight
- Pumped each other's hands frantically

SENTENCES

She threw her arms around his neck and shrieked with joy.

She dropped the phone and leapt into the air. Screaming, she pumped the air with her fist.

He walked with a bounce in his step and a wide, eager grin on his face.

She skipped along the pavement, grinning from ear to ear.

He burst into the room, laughing madly and clapping his hands with delight.

They were shivering with excitement and pumped each other's hands enthusiastically.

His whole body tingled with anticipation and he kept patting his plump hands together like an excited child.

29

Concentrating, determined

SECTION 1 – EMOTIONS

WORDS

Nouns	Thoughts, concentration, determination
Verbs	Felt, tried, resolved, determined Heard, remembered

PHRASES – VERBS

- Deep in thought
- Lost in her own thoughts
- Tried desperately to remember
- Heard little of what was being said around her
- Nothing was going to stop him now
- Felt a hard ball of determination tightening in his stomach

SENTENCES

She tried desperately to remember where she had seen him before.

She was deep in thought and heard little of what was being said around her.

He shuddered and tensed, as a hard ball of determination tightened in his stomach.

29 *Emotions: concentrating, determined*

SECTION 2 – EXPRESSIONS

WORDS

Nouns	Face, chin, mouth, teeth, forehead, brow
Adjectives	Silent, stony-faced, firm
Verbs	Jutted, clenched, gritted Creased, scrunched, squinted, furrowed

PHRASES – NOUNS AND ADJECTIVES

- ★ Silent and stony-faced
- ★ Mask of determination

PHRASES – VERBS

- ★ Chin jutted out
- ★ Mouth set in a firm line
- ★ Clenched his teeth
- ★ Forehead creased
- ★ Brow furrowed with concentration
- ★ Scrunched his face
- ★ Squinted at the page

SENTENCES

He was silent and stony-faced. With his chin jutting out, he paced backwards and forwards across the room, deep in thought.

His face was a mask of determination, as he clenched his teeth and looked over the edge.

SECTION 3 – EYES

WORDS

Nouns	Trance, daze, dream
Adjectives	Steady, unblinking
Verbs	Narrowed, stared, peered

PHRASES – NOUNS AND ADJECTIVES

- ★ Steady and unblinking
- ★ As if in a trance

PHRASES – VERBS

- Narrowed eyes
- Stared off into the distance

SENTENCES

Kitty's forehead creased and her eyes narrowed, as she tried desperately to remember where she had seen him before.

He stared off into the distance, his eyes steady and unblinking.

SECTION 4 – VOICE

WORDS

Nouns	Tone, authority
Adjectives	Crisp, defiant, challenging Urgent, firm, forceful
Verbs	Spoke, insisted, commanded

PHRASES – NOUNS AND ADJECTIVES

- Urgent voice
- Crisp authority
- Tone was defiant and challenging

PHRASES – VERBS

- Answered in a firm tone
- Spoke in a tone that assumed no possibility of disagreement
- Demanded agreement
- Insisted forcefully

SENTENCES

Her gentle voice was urgent and demanded agreement.

He answered in a tone that was respectful, but firm.

He spoke in a tone that assumed no possibility of disagreement.

29 *Emotions: concentrating, determined*

SECTION 5 – MOVEMENT

WORDS

Nouns	Head, cheek, nose, lips, teeth, chin Arms, hands, palms
Adjectives	Silent, corpse-like, backwards, forwards
Verbs	Sat, stood, tilted, paced Tensed, braced Stroked, wound, chewed, pinched

PHRASES – VERBS

- ★ Wound a strand of her hair round and round her finger
- ★ Stroked chin absently
- ★ Pressed palms together
- ★ Tilted head
- ★ Caught lip between his teeth
- ★ Chewed inside of her cheek
- ★ Pinched bridge of her nose
- ★ Sat corpse-like
- ★ Shuddered and tensed
- ★ Stood silently, head bowed
- ★ Braced his feet
- ★ Stood with arms crossed and hands on hips
- ★ Stood with weight on one leg
- ★ Paced backwards and forwards

SENTENCES

He pressed the palms of his hands against his chin and gazed into the distance.

He stuffed both hands deep into his front pockets and looked intently at something in the distance.

She listened carefully, her head tilted and her brow furrowed with concentration.

As she listened to what he was saying, Kitty absent-mindedly wound a strand of hair round her finger.

She sat corpse-like, lost in her own thoughts, hearing little of what was being said around her.

30

Sympathetic, caring

SECTION 1 – EXPRESSIONS

WORDS

Nouns	Face, mouth, smile, eyebrows Concern, sympathy, comfort, warmth
Adjectives	Soft, warm, calm, sympathetic, comforting
Verbs	Gave, flashed Drew, turned

PHRASES – VERBS

- ★ Face turned soft and sympathetic
- ★ Gave her a look of concern
- ★ Drew her eyebrows together
- ★ Mouth turned down at the corners
- ★ Flashed a comforting smile

SENTENCES

His face turned soft and sympathetic and his voice sank to a murmur.

She drew her eyebrows together and turned her mouth down in a look of concern.

SECTION 2 – EYES

WORDS

Adjectives	Calm, patient, comforting Soft, warm

Verbs	Gazed, looked Shone, beamed

PHRASES – NOUNS AND ADJECTIVES

- ★ Calm and comforting
- ★ As soft as velvet
- ★ Beamed with warmth, like candles in the dark

SENTENCES

Her brown eyes were like velvet – warm and comforting.

As she looked down on him, her eyes beamed with warmth, like candles in the dark.

SECTION 3 – VOICE

WORDS

Nouns	Sigh, whisper, murmur
Adjectives	Soft, warm, low, silky, mild Gentle, calm, patient, comforting
Verbs	Whispered, sighed Sank, trailed off Comforted, reassured

PHRASES – NOUNS AND ADJECTIVES

- ★ Low sigh
- ★ No more than a whisper
- ★ Silky and soft, like a feathery whisper
- ★ Mild, patient voice
- ★ Words were gentle and comforting

PHRASES – VERBS

- ★ Whispered in his ear
- ★ Sighed gently
- ★ Made soothing noises
- ★ Voice turned soft and low
- ★ Trailed off to a low sigh

SENTENCES

Her voice was silky and soft, like a feathery whisper.

She held him close and murmured soothingly.

Her voice was low and soft and her words gentle and comforting.

SECTION 4 – MOVEMENT

WORDS

Nouns	Arm, hand, hair, head Gesture, squeeze, support
Adjectives	Gentle, mild
Verbs	Slid, wrapped Held, stroked, squeezed
Adverbs	Tightly, kindly, tenderly, calmly, reassuringly

PHRASES AND ADJECTIVES

- Gentle squeeze
- Gesture of support

PHRASES – VERBS

- Slid her arm around his shoulder
- Gave her a gentle squeeze
- Stroked his hair
- Tilted his head forwards
- Held her to his stomach
- Wrapped arms tightly around him
- Squeezed his arm in a gesture of support

SENTENCES

She gave him a loving look and hugged him tightly to her.

He tilted his head forward and flashed a comforting smile.

She held John to her stomach and wrapped her arms around him.

She slid her arm around Kitty's shoulder, gave her a gentle squeeze and whispered in her ear.

Her voice trailed off into a low sigh and she squeezed Robert's arm in a gesture of support.

31

Relieved

SECTION 1 – EMOTIONS

WORDS

Nouns	Heart, pulse, blood Chest, head, brow, scalp, sweat
Adjectives	Calm, grateful
Verbs	Eased, slowed, calmed, released Tingled, prickled, ached

PHRASES – VERBS

- ★ Pounding eased in her chest
- ★ Breathing slowed
- ★ Rapid beat of her heart became calmer
- ★ Scalp prickled with relief
- ★ Sweat dried on her brow
- ★ Blood surged round her body
- ★ Released the tension in her body
- ★ Grateful for his narrow escape

SENTENCES

She began to calm down and her heart started to slow, but the panic had left an ache in her head and a ringing in her ears.

Slowly, the pounding eased in her chest and the sweat dried on her brow.

She could feel the blood surging round her body and releasing the tension.

Her breathing grew slower, as a new calm settled over her.

SECTION 2 – EXPRESSIONS, EYES, VOICE AND MOVEMENT

WORDS

Nouns	Cheeks, eyes, shoulders, sigh
Adjectives	Pale, heartfelt
Verbs	Blew, uttered Closed, lowered, relaxed

PHRASES – VERBS

- ★ Blew out her cheeks
- ★ Closed her eyes
- ★ Lowered her shoulders
- ★ Uttered a heartfelt sigh

SENTENCES

Slowly, the rapid beat of her heart became calmer and her pale face relaxed, as the tension in her body eased.

She blew out her cheeks and closed her eyes, hardly daring to believe that she had escaped without any injuries.

As the tension left her body, she lowered her shoulders and uttered a heartfelt sigh.

32

Angry, aggressive, irritated, impatient

SECTION 1 – EMOTIONS

WORDS

Nouns	Heart, pulse, breath, throat
	Anger, rage, fury, temper, wrath, disgust, contempt, resentment
Adjectives	Cross, furious, raging
	Jealous, envious, resentful
	Irritating, frustrating
	Bitter, vicious, poisonous
	Breathless, sweating
Verbs	Swept, poured, simmered, smouldered
	Pounded, exploded, erupted
	Shook, trembled, writhed
	Raced, hammered
	Clenched, gripped

PHRASES – NOUNS AND ADJECTIVES

- Fog of rage
- Red mist
- Spitting bundle of rage
- Vicious flash of temper
- Simmering fury
- Hard lump at the back of her throat

PHRASES – VERBS

- Left him breathless
- Made his heart race
- Hammered in his head
- Swept through him like a tidal wave
- Burning with rage
- Wrath exploded like a volcano
- Poured from her like an acid
- Surrounded him like a foul stench
- Poisoned the air around him

SENTENCES

He was sweating and burning with rage.

She saw his face through narrowed eyes and a fog of rage.

Her reply fuelled his anger and he erupted like a volcano.

The anger had returned like a hard lump at the back of her throat.

His fury knew no limits – one vicious flash of temper after another.

Her rage swept through her like a tidal wave, surrounding her like a foul stench.

SECTION 2 – EXPRESSIONS

WORDS

Nouns	Look, glance, stare, gaze
	Snarl, grimace, leer
	Expression, mask, demeanour, countenance
Adjectives	Nasty, sharp, sour, fierce, hostile, livid, vengeful, volatile, malicious, murderous
	Scary, threatening, monstrous, venomous, reptilian, inhuman
Verbs	Looked, glanced, gazed, stared, glared, glowered
	Grinned, grimaced, leered
	Twisted, clenched, jutted
	Flushed, flared

PHRASES – NOUNS AND ADJECTIVES

- Evil look
- Venomous stare
- Murderous gaze
- Monstrous grimace

- Grimace like a hissing cat
- Reptilian snarl
- Nasty sneer
- Malicious expression
- Hostile demeanour
- Fierce countenance
- Expression of utter disbelief
- Pulsing, purple face
- Patches of red on his cheeks

PHRASES – VERBS

- Jaw tightened
- Chin jutted out angrily
- Teeth clenched
- Ground teeth together
- Arched her eyebrows
- Nostrils flared like an angry bull
- Lips curled back in a reptilian snarl
- Sucked his lips into his mouth
- Pressed lips tightly together into a thin line
- Lips were drawn into a sneer
- Twisted into a venomous snarl
- Paled with anger
- Flushed an angry red
- Veins pulsed furiously in her neck
- Exploded in a burning heat

SENTENCES

A burst of fury made his cheeks burn.

The man strode towards Kitty, wearing an angry expression.

It was as if her brain was flooding with boiling blood and her face exploding in a burning heat.

His reddening face was twisted into a venomous snarl and the veins in his neck pulsed furiously.

He made a fist and scowled at Kitty with malicious little eyes and a murderous gaze.

Kitty saw the veins pulsing in his neck and a flash of anger burning in his eyes.

There were patches of red on Robert's usually pale cheeks. Sweat glistened on his forehead and his face was thunderous.

Her face was twisted with fury, her eyes menacing slits, her mouth a nasty sneer.

His face twisted like a tribal mask – his eyes bulging and livid and his lips drawn back in a hideous sneer.

His foaming lips curled back in a malicious smirk, spraying spittle as he spat out the words.

Nostrils flaring like an angry bull, she curled back her lip in a reptilian snarl.

Eyes narrowed and teeth clenched, she stared at Robert with an expression of utter disbelief.

SECTION 3 – EYES

WORDS

Nouns	Glare, stare, scowl, squint
	Raisins, slits, razors
Adjectives	Hard, cold, steely, staring, unblinking, demon-haunted
	Cruel, fierce, hostile, piercing, withering, menacing, threatening, dangerous, malicious
	Bulging, buggy, feverish
Verbs	Glinted, glittered, darkened, burned, blazed
	Narrowed, bulged, rolled, flickered
	Drilled, blasted

PHRASES – NOUNS AND ADJECTIVES

- ★ Small and hard as raisins
- ★ Hard and narrowed
- ★ Cold, staring eyes
- ★ Steely, menacing eyes
- ★ Piercing like razors
- ★ Slits of fury
- ★ Fierce little eyes in a skull-like face
- ★ Full of hatred and anger
- ★ Bulging and fierce in his twisted face

PHRASES – VERBS

- ★ Glittered evilly
- ★ Drilled into her
- ★ Burned with a cruel light
- ★ Blasted her with a fierce stare
- ★ Glared at him through narrowed eyes
- ★ Darkened warningly
- ★ Burned like furnaces
- ★ Rolled eyes to heaven
- ★ Put head back and closed his eyes
- ★ Screwed eyes into narrow slits

32 *Emotions: angry, aggressive, irritated, impatient*

SENTENCES

His steely grey eyes were as piercing as razors.

Her eyes burned with a cruel light in her skull-like face.

His eyes were as dark and hard as raisins, and full of hatred and anger.

He squinted at her fiercely and snarled with frustration.

Her eyes were slits of fury; her voice full of ice cold venom.

His cold, staring eyes bulged in his twisted face and drilled into Kitty as if they would pierce her.

She drummed her fingers on the table impatiently and screwed her eyes into narrow slits.

Eyes bulging in her beak-like face, her voice rose to a harsh, shrill shriek.

Scowling, Robert rolled his eyes to heaven and blasted her with a fierce stare.

SECTION 4 – VOICE

WORDS

Nouns	Tone, hiss, growl, cry, yell, shout, snarl, scream, shriek, howl
Adjectives	Fierce, harsh, furious, hostile, savage, aggressive
	Shrill, rasping
Verbs	Hissed, muttered, snapped
	Shouted, yelled, barked, growled, snarled
	Roared, ranted, boomed, screamed, howled, shrieked, bellowed, stormed, thundered
	Shrugged, gasped, spat
Adverbs	Nastily, angrily, heatedly, fiercely, furiously
	Spitefully, viciously, impatiently

PHRASES – NOUNS AND ADJECTIVES

★ Raised voice
★ Menacing tone
★ Like a vicious dog

PHRASES – VERBS

★ Shouted nastily
★ Snapped furiously
★ Snarled impatiently
★ Yelled heatedly
★ Hissed angrily
★ Replied through clenched teeth

- Growled like a bear
- Demanded in a low, vicious tone
- Boomed viciously
- Shrieked at him
- Snarled with frustration
- Sighed bitterly
- Muttered under her breath
- Hissed at Kitty out of the side of his mouth
- Voice shook
- Gasped for breath
- Sucked air through his teeth
- Clicked tongue impatiently
- Sprayed spittle as he spat out the words
- Too choked with frustration to talk

SENTENCES

She snarled at him like a vicious dog.

Kitty's voice shook with anger and she glared at him through narrowed eyes.

He clicked his tongue impatiently and shrugged his shoulders. Muttering under his breath, he stomped out of the room.

Robert folded his arms across his chest and started speaking over her in a raised voice.

Rolling her eyes to heaven, Kitty sucked air through her teeth and hissed at him.

Eyes ablaze, fists clenched, he hissed at Kitty out of the side of his mouth, spraying spittle as he spat out the words.

She was a spitting bundle of rage. Waving her arms wildly in the air, she shrieked at him and advanced, with eyes bulging eyes in her twisted face.

SECTION 5 – MOVEMENT

WORDS

Nouns	Feet, hips, chest, shoulders, arms, hands, fist, palms, knuckles, fingers, nails, scalp, hair
Adjectives	Tense, rigid Quick, jerky, wild, furious, frantic, feverish
Verbs	Gripped, curled, crushed, clenched, balled Tapped, drummed, thumped, pounded Folded, crossed, raised, pointed, shook, waved Rubbed, twisted, tugged, pressed, buried Hunched, shrugged, braced Rocked, swayed, paced

Walked, moved, strode, marched, advanced
Ran, sprinted, bounded, hurtled
Slammed, barged, barrelled, clattered

PHRASES – NOUNS AND ADJECTIVES

- Rigid with fury
- Frantic, jerky movements
- As quick as a panther
- Like an uncoiled spring
- Feverish pace

PHRASES – VERBS

- Pounded on the table with his fist
- Thumped forehead with her fist
- Drummed fingers on the table impatiently
- Clenched fists
- Curled hand into a fist
- Raised hand with palm upwards
- Pointed index finger
- Waved hands wildly before him
- Gripped knuckles until they turned white
- Dug nails deep into the skin of her palms
- Pressed hands into eyes
- Buried head in hands
- Rubbed fingers into scalp
- Twisted and tugged at hair
- Braced his feet
- Hunched shoulders
- Stood with arms crossed and hands on hips
- Rocked back and forth
- Swayed on his feet
- Paced backwards and forwards
- Strode across the room
- Marched out of the room
- Advanced on him grimly
- Pounded down the street
- Bounded like an uncoiled spring
- Hurtled headlong . . .
- Barrelled forward . . .
- Slammed into . . .
- Barged through . . .
- Thudded into . . .

- Shot past . . .
- Fought his way through . . .
- Hurtled full pelt towards . . .

SENTENCES

She dismissed him with an impatient wave of her hand.

He bounded towards them like an uncoiled spring.

He pounded on the table with his fist and glared at her furiously.

He dug his fingers into his scalp and tugged at his hair, until it stood up in wild tufts.

He exhaled once, a long hard gust, put his hands on his hips and spoke very slowly.

She strode into the room, muttering under her breath, and then turned briskly and marched out again, with a stiff back and her head held high in the air.

Throwing his head back, he exhaled deeply and closed his eyes.

With a howl of rage, he buried his head in his hands and pressed them into his eyes.

Speechless with rage, she curled her fist and dug her fingers deep into her palms.

Kitty opened her mouth to speak, but before she could utter a word, Robert silenced her by putting his hand, palm upwards, in the air in front of her.

33

Cold, evil, sly, arrogant

SECTION 1 – EXPRESSIONS

WORDS

Nouns	Look, expression, gaze
	Grin, leer, sneer, smirk
Adjectives	Cold, chilly, icy, empty, expressionless
	Nasty, cruel, evil, spiteful, vicious, venomous, callous, vengeful, malicious
	Creepy, scary, hideous, monstrous, ghastly, demonic, moronic
	Sly, cunning, furtive, sinister
	Arrogant, sarcastic
Verbs	Stared, glared, glanced
	Grinned, grimaced, sneered

PHRASES – NOUNS AND ADJECTIVES

- ★ Smile as empty as a carcass
- ★ Like a grinning snake
- ★ Vicious smile
- ★ Unpleasant, sarcastic smile
- ★ Slow, demonic leer
- ★ Reptilian sneer
- ★ Leering smile
- ★ Cold, sinister look
- ★ Furtive, viperish expression
- ★ Cold, arrogant expression
- ★ Amused, callous look
- ★ Ghastly smile of pretended sympathy
- ★ Dramatic expression of mock concern and sympathy

PHRASES – VERBS

- Lips twisted briefly
- Face split into a nasty, demonic grin
- Twisted in a malicious smirk
- Mouth stretched in a hideous sneer
- Bared teeth
- Stretched his mouth into a grisly smile
- Face wrinkled with disgust
- Shot him a withering look
- Directed look of purest venom
- Features tightened with contempt
- Trained his steely gaze on her

SENTENCES

His pale, skull-like face split into an evil grin.

He curled his lips into a savage sneer.

She directed a look of pure venom at his retreating back.

His smile was as empty as a carcass.

Her expression suddenly changed to a dramatic look of mock concern and sympathy.

She took aim with an invisible gun and gave him a slow, demonic leer.

His mouth twisted into a smirk and his icy blue eyes narrowed to slits.

Robert trained his steely gaze on her and stretched his mouth into a grisly smile.

He raised his eyebrows and glanced at her with a cold, arrogant expression.

He had an amused, callous look on his face, as he watched Kitty writhing on the floor.

As he opened the door for them to leave, his mouth twisted into a knowing grin.

Snorting with contempt, he bared his yellow teeth in a reptilian sneer.

His mouth curled with revulsion, as she made a despairing lunge at his arm.

SECTION 2 – EYES

WORDS

Nouns	Look, stare, glare, slits
Adjectives	Small, little, beady, buggy, staring, unblinking Hard, cold, ice cold, frosty, steely Sharp, evil, cruel, piercing, withering Ghostly, monstrous, feverish, demon-haunted
Verbs	Stared, squinted, narrowed, bulged, flickered, drilled, blasted Darkened, burned, blazed, glinted, sparkled

33 *Emotions: cold, evil, sly, arrogant*

PHRASES – NOUNS AND ADJECTIVES

- Cold, steely eyes
- Small and hard as raisins
- Buggy little eyes
- Piercing like razors
- Frosty and narrowed
- Crafty look
- Demon-haunted expression

PHRASES – VERBS

- Glinted evilly
- Sparkled like frost – cold and dangerous
- Burned with a cruel light
- Drilled into her

SENTENCES

His small eyes were as dark and hard as raisins and had a demon-haunted expression.

She stared at Kitty for a moment and then a crafty look flickered in her buggy little eyes.

He stared with unblinking eyes, but his lips twisted in a sneer.

His feverish, staring eyes bulged in his monstrous face.

She stared with eyes that sparkled like frost – cold and dangerous.

SECTION 3 – VOICE

WORDS

Nouns	Tone, hiss, whisper, snort, giggle Snarl, shout, screech, shriek, laughter
Adjectives	Cold, icy, chilly, frosty, harsh, cruel, sharp Mocking, spiteful, vicious, threatening, venomous
Verbs	Sneered, sniggered, snorted, jeered

PHRASES – NOUNS AND ADJECTIVES

- Frosty voice
- Tone was firm and chilly
- Tone was chiselled with menace
- Voice was cold and cruel
- Voice of ice cold venom
- Splinter of ice in her voice

- ★ Voice was low, cold and full of menace
- ★ Stifled snort
- ★ Scornful giggle
- ★ Sneering shout
- ★ Screech like a seagull
- ★ Threatening, venomous hiss
- ★ Ghostly whisper
- ★ Manic laughter
- ★ Snort of mocking laughter
- ★ Voice was full of malicious laughter

PHRASES – VERBS

- ★ Responded coldly
- ★ Added nastily
- ★ Said in a low, vicious tone
- ★ Ordered with a sneer of cold command
- ★ Snorted with disgust
- ★ Snarled like a vicious dog
- ★ Laughed scornfully
- ★ Bored into her like a drill
- ★ Chilled her to the bone
- ★ Sharp words slashed the air

SENTENCES

Every word he spoke dripped with venom and hate.

She drew in her breath in a venomous hiss.

His hard, cold eyes and frosty voice chilled Kitty to the bone.

She threw back her head and laughed like a screeching seagull.

Her eyes narrowed dangerously and then she laughed scornfully.

It was a haunting voice, and one that visited her nightly in her dreams – a voice of ice-cold venom.

He was used to giving orders; his tone was firm and cold and one that expected to be obeyed without question.

His tone was so sharp that the words seemed to slash the air.

SECTION 4 – MOVEMENT

WORDS

Nouns

Snake, cobra, lizard, panther, peacock, cat
Shadow, ghost
Predator, prey

33 *Emotions: cold, evil, sly, arrogant*

Adjectives	Dark, quiet, silent Still, motionless, invisible Quick, deft, pecking, scuttling
Verbs	Moved, glided, ran, strutted Pointed, jerked, flexed Dismissed, beckoned

PHRASES – NOUNS AND ADJECTIVES

- ★ Like a dark ghost
- ★ Like a scuttling lizard
- ★ Like a figure carved from stone
- ★ Silent and motionless
- ★ Like a predator scenting its prey
- ★ Like a panther waiting to pounce
- ★ As silent as a shadow

PHRASES – VERBS

- ★ Raised to his full height
- ★ Broadened shoulders
- ★ Leaned forward menacingly
- ★ Poised on the balls of his feet
- ★ Crouched on the edge
- ★ Landed quietly like a cat
- ★ Advanced slowly
- ★ Strutted like a peacock
- ★ Glided like a shadow
- ★ Moved stealthily
- ★ Glided noiselessly like a dark ghost
- ★ Ran in pecking strides
- ★ Flexed his fingers and formed them into a fist
- ★ Beckoned them to come to him
- ★ Dismissed them with a wave of her hand

SENTENCES

He landed quietly like a cat.

He was crouched on the edge, like a panther waiting to pounce.

He beckoned them to him with a tense jerk of his fingers.

She dismissed them with a wave of her hand.

He was as silent and motionless as a figure carved from stone.

He stood still and poised, like a cobra about to strike.

Kitty leaned forward and grimaced at him malevolently.

He was tensed, poised on the balls of his feet, like a predator scenting its prey.

He flexed his fingers, formed them into a fist and advanced menacingly.

Gliding smoothly, noiselessly in the shadows, she was like a dark ghost.

34

Scared, frightened, timid

SECTION 1 – EMOTIONS

WORDS

Nouns	Fear, dread, panic, terror, horror, turmoil Thoughts, instinct Heart, chest, pulse, blood Head, brain, temples, forehead Breath, throat, windpipe, cheeks, tongue, bile Stomach, gut, cramps Skin, hair, shivers, tingle, prickle
Adjectives	Numb, sick, nervous, uneasy Dry, tight, thick, heavy Long, deep, short, shallow Unsteady, shuddering, rasping Quick, fast, painful Cold, tingling Hot, sweaty
Verbs	Felt, thought, urged, warned, paralysed Rose, grew, swept, surged, seized Bubbled, gripped, clutched, choked, strangled Breathed, blew, hissed, sucked, gulped, gasped, tasted Beat, leapt, raced, banged, throbbed, pounded, hammered, quickened Crept, crawled, prickled, scuttled Ran, tore, pumped, drenched Dropped, fluttered, squeezed, tightened, gripped, stabbed

PHRASES – NOUNS AND ADJECTIVES

- Sick with fear
- Throat was dry and tight
- Tongue felt thick and heavy in his mouth
- Fear was like a bitter bile at the back of his throat
- Cold sweat
- Prickle of fear in the bottom of his spine
- Like an electric shock
- Like a lead ball in his stomach

PHRASES – VERBS

- Numb and paralysed by fear
- Dread swept through him like a tidal wave
- Fear settled on him like a dark fog
- Struck dead with terror
- Terror surged through her
- Fear seized him in its jaws
- Thought of the consequences urged him on
- Instincts screamed at him to . . .
- Every nerve in his body warned him not to . . .
- Could taste the fear in the back of his throat
- Gulped air
- Let out a gasp
- Blew out her cheeks to stop herself howling
- Took long, shuddering breaths
- Panic rose in his chest
- Panic bubbled in her throat
- Fear choked him with its murderous hands
- Snaked round his windpipe
- Heart pounded
- Pulse raced
- Missed a beat
- Banged against his ribs
- Heart abandoned his chest to pound in his throat
- Squeezed her heart like a vice
- Blood pounded in her temples
- Drenched in sweat
- Cold sweat poured down his forehead
- Skin crawled
- Hairs prickled on the back of his neck
- Shivers tore down her spine and racked her body
- Like a hundred spiders were scuttling down her back

- Stomach dropped
- Like a moth fluttering inside her stomach
- Doubled over with cramps
- Gripped with anxiety
- Like a volcano erupting inside her

SENTENCES

Every nerve in his body warned him not to go any further.

All his instincts screamed at him to slip away before he was spotted.

He was sick with fear, but the thought of the consequences urged him on.

Her throat was dry, her tongue thick and heavy in her mouth.

Fear choked him with its murderous hands. It gripped at his throat and strangled his breath into short, shallow gasps.

She was struck dead with terror. Her heart was beating painfully fast and banging against her ribs.

Her heart missed a beat, squeezed like a vice by the shock.

As the blood pounded in her temples, her brain quickened and all her senses were alert.

Blowing out her cheeks, she drew a long, shuddering breath and tried to dampen the sense of impending doom.

He felt uneasy. The hairs on the back of his neck prickled with dread and he was drenched in sweat.

Fear settled on her like a dark fog, bringing a chill that crept over her and that no amount of heat could drive away.

The fear was like an electric shock, pumping shivering waves tearing through his body and making his hair stand on end.

He doubled over with cramps. It was as if a lead ball had been dropped in his stomach and was blocking his gut.

Her stomach was gripped with anxiety, like a volcano erupting inside her.

Something was making her feel very uneasy. It was gnawing at her stomach and fluttering as if she had swallowed a butterfly.

SECTION 2 – EXPRESSIONS

WORDS

Nouns	Worry, anxiety, terror, horror
	Look, expression, glance, gaze, stare
	Mouth, teeth, jaw
Adjectives	Alert, sharp, urgent
	Edgy, nervous, troubled, pinched
	Startled, horrified, haggard, contorted
	Pale, bloodless, ashen, expressionless

Verbs

Wore, showed, drained
Froze, dropped, trembled
Bared, clenched, chattered, gnashed

PHRASES – NOUNS AND ADJECTIVES

- ★ Troubled look
- ★ Look of sheer terror
- ★ Startled look
- ★ Face was drawn with worry
- ★ Pinched with terror
- ★ Sharp with anxiety
- ★ Urgent and anxious
- ★ Face was expressionless
- ★ Expression was haggard and drawn

PHRASES – VERBS

- ★ Froze in horror
- ★ Drained of all colour
- ★ Wore a startled expression
- ★ Smile dropped from her face like a theatrical mask
- ★ Cold sweat poured down his face
- ★ Bit her lip
- ★ Lips moved silently in prayer
- ★ Mouth twisted in a scream
- ★ Clenched his jaw
- ★ Jaw dropped open with horror
- ★ Teeth gnashed against each other
- ★ Bared teeth in an edgy grin
- ★ Teeth were chattering like castanets

SENTENCES

Her eyes swept over the scene in front of her and her face froze in horror.

She was rooted to the spot, hands trembling and her face ashen and drenched in sweat.

Her face was expressionless, but inwardly she was fighting to remain calm.

The smile dropped from her face like a theatrical mask, to be replaced by a look of sheer terror.

As she listened to the news, a troubled expression settled on her face.

Her face was drawn and anxious, as she paced backwards and forwards across the room.

Her mouth was twisted in a scream that never came.

The smile suddenly fell from her face and her jaw dropped open.

34 *Emotions: scared, frightened, timid*

She bit her lip to stop her teeth chattering like castanets.

Clasping her hands in her lap, she moved her lips silently in prayer.

He turned his head sharply, raised an eyebrow and bared his teeth in an edgy grin.

SECTION 3 – EYES

WORDS

Nouns	Gaze, stare, glance, trance, twitch, tic
Adjectives	Round, wide, staring, gaping, unblinking Wary, wild, horror-struck
Verbs	Blinked, stared, strained Swept, darted, snapped, flicked, flickered

PHRASES – NOUNS AND ADJECTIVES

- Wide eyes
- Round with terror
- Alert and strained
- As if in a trance
- Staring and horror-struck
- Nervous tic

PHRASES – VERBS

- Widened in horror
- Snapped open in panic
- Narrowed eyes
- Nervous tic flickered beneath her eyes
- Blinked rapidly
- Stared unblinking, horror-struck
- Stared off into the shadows
- Kept eyes fixed to the floor
- Strained to pierce the darkness
- Threw out darting little glances
- Flicked from one to the other
- Darted backwards and forwards
- Swept over the scene in front of him

SENTENCES

His eyes snapped open in panic and he froze to the spot.

He shifted uncomfortably and flicked his eyes from one to the other.

She was horror-struck. She stared unblinking, as if in a trance, and frozen to the spot.

His wide eyes strained to pierce the darkness, darting wildly from side to side.

Drenched in sweat and heart pounding, Kitty kept her narrowed eyes fixed to the floor, unable to meet his cold, unblinking stare.

Eyes round with terror, Robert let out a moan of despair and drew in a deep, shuddering breath.

SECTION 4 – VOICE

WORDS

Nouns	Tone, whisper, gasp, moan Wail, yell, howl, scream, shriek
Adjectives	Silent, numb Wild, urgent, savage, deathly Shrill, high-pitched, harsh, strangled, piercing, quivering
Verbs	Spoke, whispered, mumbled, murmured, muttered Gasped, panted, croaked, spluttered Bleated, whined, pleaded, simpered, whimpered Lowered, rushed, faltered, strained
Adverbs	Tensely, anxiously, hurriedly, desperately, despairingly Weakly, meekly

PHRASES – NOUNS AND ADJECTIVES

- Strangled whisper
- Deathly moan
- Moan of despair
- Thin, high-pitched howl
- High, piercing scream
- Piercing yell
- Wild, ragged wail
- Howl like a wounded dog
- Voice was urgent and shrill
- Shrill and harsh like the shriek of a seagull
- Tone was numb with horror
- Faltering tone
- Full of violence and despair
- Words were a jumbled stream, one rushing into the next

PHRASES – VERBS

- Lowered his voice
- Shrank into silence
- Voice froze in her throat

- Opened her mouth wide in a silent scream
- Spoke in a rush
- Pleaded desperately
- Words came in gasps

SENTENCES

His voice dropped to an urgent whisper.

Her high-pitched scream echoed through the house.

Her voice shook and her words came in gasps.

He let out a long, quivering sigh and shrank into silence.

She spoke in a rush, the words tumbling over each other in a jumbled stream, one rushing into the next.

She flung her head back and screamed – a savage, desperate yell like a wounded dog.

He started to shout. His voice, shrill and harsh like the shriek of a seagull, was full of violence and despair.

SECTION 5 – HANDS

WORDS

Nouns	Pain, agony, surrender Knees, hand, fist, palms, fingers, thumb, knuckles, nails Chest, head, face, eyes, cheeks, mouth, lips Skin, hair
Adjectives	White, pale, tense
Verbs	Bent, leant, curled, drew, hugged Covered, buried Squeezed, pinched, rubbed, pressed, gripped, clutched, crushed

PHRASES – VERBS

- Curled hand into a fist
- Gripped knuckles until they turned white
- Drew knees up and hugged them to his chest
- Buried his head in his hands
- Pressed fingers into his eyes
- Rubbed eyes trying to get rid of the image
- Put his finger to his lips for her to be quiet
- Covered his mouth and whispered through his fingers
- Rammed fingers into her ears to block out the screams
- Ran hand through his hair, tugging it into wild tufts

- Clutched hand to her mouth
- Beckoned him forward with a tense jerk of her fingers
- Raised her shaking hands in the air in an act of surrender

SENTENCES

He clutched his hand to his mouth to stop himself from screaming out.

He shuddered and rubbed his eyes, trying to clear the image of what he had just seen.

He lowered his voice, leant forward in his chair and looked around cautiously before he spoke.

He raised his shaking hands in the air, palms upwards, in an act of surrender.

She screwed her eyes shut tight and rammed her fingers into her ears to block out the screams.

SECTION 6 – BODY

WORDS

Nouns	Statue, corpse
	Legs, feet, knees, hands
Adjectives	Still, frozen, rigid, corpse-like, motionless
	Low, flat, snake-like
	Slow, cautious, tentative
	Fast, frantic, feverish, jerky
	Upright, backwards, forwards
Verbs	Froze, paralysed, stiffened
	Stopped, halted, faltered
	Skidded, slithered
	Sat, crouched, squatted, huddled, flattened
	Moved, walked, tiptoed, treaded, sneaked
	Crept, crawled, groped, edged, clawed, squirmed, crabbed
	Approached, advanced
	Ran, sprinted, darted, bolted, hurtled
	Crashed, dodged, leaped, jerked
	Scrambled, scurried, scuttled
	Struggled, fought, wrenched, staggered, stumbled, clambered, floundered, flailed
Adverbs	Slowly, lightly, quickly, swiftly
	Shakily, cautiously
	Wildly, blindly, helplessly, desperately, relentlessly

34 *Emotions: scared, frightened, timid*

PHRASES – VERBS

- Fear turned her to stone
- Stood rooted to the spot
- Stood utterly still like a living statue
- Sat corpse-like
- Body stiffened and she froze to the spot
- Hung back, paralysed with terror
- Shuddered and went rigid
- Huddled in the darkness
- Squatted like a frozen toad
- Crouched down, afraid to move
- Flattened himself against the wall
- Slithered to a halt
- Skidded to a halt
- Rose on his toes
- Rose shakily to his feet
- Edged forward
- Groped his way forward
- Kept low to the ground
- Crawled over the ground flat on her belly
- Moved forward cautiously
- Took one small, tentative step
- Treaded lightly
- Sneaked along the passage
- Walked slowly back and forth
- Clawed his way up
- Crabbed slowly along the edge
- Squirmed his way between . . .
- Approached cautiously . . .
- Advanced slowly . . .
- Tiptoed along . . .
- Ran wildly
- Bolted out of the room
- Sprinted down the corridor
- Moved at a feverish pace
- Moved with frantic, jerky movements
- Hurtled full pelt
- Scurried like a spider
- Scuttled in a low crouch
- Scrambled away on hands and knees
- Jerked upright
- Leaped to his feet

- Crashed to the floor
- Struggled like a fish in a net
- Wrenched himself free
- Floundered around in the dark
- Clambered up the bank
- Darted and dodged
- Fought his way through . . .

SENTENCES

She sat corpse-like – frozen and motionless.

She moved as delicately as a wild creature stalking its prey.

He padded noiselessly up the stairs in his bare feet.

He crabbed slowly along the ledge and felt the way with his feet.

It was as if time had stopped. He stood perfectly still, frozen to the floor, paralysed by fear.

He lingered in the shadows, motionless – alert and ready to move quickly.

He slithered to a halt and stood with his hands on his hips, head bowed, gasping for breath.

He huddled in the darkness, listening for any sound that might guide him.

She curled herself into a ball, shivering violently, and covered her head with her hands.

He crawled over the ground, keeping low, hardly daring to raise his head.

He moved slowly. Treading lightly, he checked the area around him, searching for any movement.

Flat on her belly, she slithered snake-like out of the room.

Her steps quickened until her feet appeared to be flying.

She scrambled up the bank, chest heaving and gasping for breath.

He ran like a scuttling lizard, with his legs flailing sideways and forwards.

Robert bent over and ran with his bottom in the air, scuttling like a rabbit in a warren.

She stumbled and flung her hand out in front of her – groping for something to stop her falling.

They maintained a feverish pace and surged forward relentlessly.

He started to run, faster and faster, his head down, his arms pumping and his legs a blur of movement.

He darted and dodged through the trees. Blundering and slipping, he fought his way through the undergrowth.

35

Nervous, shy, embarrassed

SECTION 1 – EMOTIONS

WORDS

Nouns	Mind, senses, nerves, confusion, embarrassment Body, heart, breath, throat, tongue, mouth Hands, palms, stomach
Adjectives	Thick, dry, fuzzy Tense, sharp, alert Sweaty, breathless
Verbs	Shook, trembled Pounded, fluttered Gulped, swallowed Shrunk, shrivelled

PHRASES – NOUNS AND ADJECTIVES

- Tongue was thick and fuzzy
- Throat was dry
- Like a nervous rabbit caught in the headlights
- Blizzard of nerves and confusion

PHRASES – VERBS

- Heart pounded
- Heart fluttered
- Held their breath
- Watched with bated breath
- Trembled like a nervous rabbit
- Butterflies fluttered in her stomach

- Body was tense and her senses alert
- Felt as if the whole world was watching
- Insides shrivelled with embarrassment
- Mist descended on his mind

SENTENCES

Her hands were shaking. Butterflies fluttered in her heart and stomach.

A mist descended on her mind. She felt as if she was walking in a blizzard of nerves and confusion.

She felt her body tense and her senses sharpen, as she watched with bated breath.

He tried to speak, but his tongue was thick and fuzzy and pasted to the roof of his mouth.

He felt as if the whole world was watching him, and his insides shrivelled with embarrassment.

SECTION 2 – EXPRESSIONS

WORDS

Nouns	Look, expression, tic, twitch Neck, cheeks, lips, tongue, teeth, forehead, pulse Smile, grin Blush, sweat
Adjectives	Blank, nervous, twitchy, jerky, edgy
Verbs	Crept, ran, rushed Chewed, gnashed

PHRASES – NOUNS AND ADJECTIVES

- Blank expression
- Small nervous tic
- Nervous twitch
- Twitchy smile
- Edgy grin

PHRASES – VERBS

- Blood rushed to her cheeks
- Blush spread from her neck to her face
- Drenched in sweat
- Bared teeth in an edgy grin
- Chewed nervously on her tongue
- Ran a tongue nervously over his lips
- Teeth gnashed against each other
- Cheeks bulged, as she held her breath to slow her pulse

35 *Emotions: nervous, shy, embarrassed*

SENTENCES

Her teeth were gnashing against each other inside her cheeks.

He ran his tongue nervously over his lips and kept baring his teeth in an edgy grin.

She could feel the blood rush to her cheeks and she kept her gaze fixed to the floor.

She blushed, feeling the warmth spread up from her neck, her cheeks, her ears and drenching her in sweat.

Her cheeks bulged, as she held her breath to slow her pulse and calm her nerves.

With beads of sweat running down her forehead, she folded her arms across her chest and chewed nervously on her tongue.

His jaw was trembling, his teeth chattering like castanets, and no matter how hard he bit his lips, he couldn't control either.

SECTION 3 – EYES

WORDS

Nouns	Look, glance, tic, twitch
Adjectives	Nervous, anxious
Verbs	Lowered, blinked, flickered Glanced, exchanged
Adverbs	Rapidly, furtively

PHRASES – NOUNS AND ADJECTIVES

- Small nervous tic
- Nervous glance
- Eyes were downcast

PHRASES – VERBS

- Fixed to the floor
- Blinked rapidly
- Exchanged nervous looks
- Flickered beneath her eye
- Glanced rapidly around him
- Eyes flicked from one to the other
- Looked round furtively

SENTENCES

Her eyes flickered briefly to his face and they exchanged a nervous look.

He found it difficult to meet her gaze and kept his head down and his eyes fixed to the floor.

Glancing rapidly around him, his eyes flicked from one to the other.

SECTION 4 – VOICE

WORDS

Nouns	Giggle, gasp, whisper, murmur, gabble, laugh
Adjectives	Low, deep Quick, urgent, nervous, hissing
Verbs	Spoke, giggled, laughed, stammered, stuttered

PHRASES – NOUNS AND ADJECTIVES

- ★ Urgent whisper
- ★ Low, gasping gabble
- ★ Hissing giggle
- ★ Laugh was a quick, nervous stutter

PHRASES – VERBS

- ★ Words came in gasps
- ★ Sank to a murmur
- ★ Giggled nervously
- ★ Dropped to an urgent whisper
- ★ Stammered nervously
- ★ Took a deep breath
- ★ Words tumbled out in a rush
- ★ Spoke through clenched teeth
- ★ Struggled to keep his voice steady
- ★ Opened his mouth as if to speak, but closed it again

SENTENCES

She faltered, took a deep breath and rushed on.

Her voice sank to a murmur and she tried to hide her embarrassment behind a cloak of dark hair.

Her words came in gasps and tumbled over each other in a low gabble.

He spoke through clenched teeth, struggling to keep his voice steady.

The words tumbled out in a rush, as if he was making himself speak before he lost his nerve.

His eyes darted from one to the other uncertainly and he opened his mouth as if he was about to speak – but closed it again.

SECTION 5 – MOVEMENT

WORDS

Nouns	Neck, shoulders, arms, hands, fingers, nails Head, forehead, brow, mouth, lips Legs, feet
Adjectives	Nervous, sweaty, trembling, jerky
Verbs	Gnawed, twisted, stroked Folded, lowered, hunched Danced, twitched, trembled
Adverbs	Tightly, shakily, nervously, feverishly

PHRASES – NOUNS AND ADJECTIVES

- Sweaty brow
- Trembling lips
- Hunched shoulders

PHRASES – VERBS

- Arms folded tightly across her chest
- Made jerky movements with his hands
- Clicked nails on table
- Gnawed at her fingernails
- Twisted a strand of hair round and round her finger
- Stroked her forehead feverishly
- Wiped a handkerchief across his sweaty brow
- Put a finger on her trembling lips
- Covered her mouth and whispered through her fingers
- Lowered his head and looked intently at his feet
- Neck disappeared into his hunched shoulders
- Twitched nervously
- Feet danced with nervous strain
- Trembled like a nervous rabbit
- Rose shakily to her feet

SENTENCES

She moved with the frantic, jerky movements of a nervous hamster.

He stiffened slightly and twitched from one foot to the other.

She looked round furtively, covered her mouth and whispered through her fingers.

Trembling nervously, she gnawed at her fingernails and looked up without meeting his gaze.

Feeling a blush creeping up his neck and burning his cheeks, he lowered his head and looked intently at his feet.

36

Sad, miserable

SECTION 1 – EMOTIONS

WORDS

Nouns	Sadness, misery, grief, despair, loneliness, regret Heart, throat, lump, sobs
Adjectives	Cold, hollow Painful, horrible
Verbs	Filled, welled, choked, broke

PHRASES – NOUNS AND ADJECTIVES

- ★ Silent, shuddering sobs
- ★ Heart was swollen and bruised
- ★ Felt hollow and cold
- ★ Huge lump in the back of his throat
- ★ Horrible sense of loneliness like a dark fog

PHRASES – VERBS

- ★ Sadness erupted inside him
- ★ Enveloped her like a dark cloud
- ★ Spread through his chest like a dull ache
- ★ Wild grief was building inside her
- ★ Despair washed over him
- ★ Insides curled up and shrivelled
- ★ Hopelessness washed over him
- ★ Coldness settled inside him
- ★ Gripping pain in his heart

- Sob welled up in her throat
- Weight of his grief was crushing his windpipe
- His despair tightened around his chest in a vice-like grip
- All thought and reason had shut down

SENTENCES

The pain of his loss spread through his chest like a dull ache.

A horrible sense of loneliness bled through her.

The gripping pain in her heart was reflected in her haunted expression.

Sadness filled his chest and erupted in a wail of misery.

He buried his head in his hands and tried to block out the sadness erupting inside him.

She felt a rush of anguish surge into her chest and throat, and flood her eyes with tears.

She felt a wild grief building inside her – taking her over – until she could only break down in an agony of weeping.

SECTION 2 – EXPRESSIONS

WORDS

Nouns	Sadness, misery, grief, pain, despair Face, mouth, jaw, chin, lips, teeth Tears, sobs
Adjectives	Sad, unhappy, haunted Wet, red, swollen, blotchy
Verbs	Trembled, wobbled Twisted, tightened, faltered, crumpled Bit, pressed, jammed Welled, poured, spilled

PHRASES – NOUNS AND ADJECTIVES

- Wet and red from weeping
- Swollen and blotchy
- Quivering lips
- Haunted expression

PHRASES – VERBS

- Lips trembled
- Jaw wobbled
- Jaw trembled as she spoke
- Twisted in an unhappy smile

- ★ Pressed lips together
- ★ Bit her lip until she drew blood
- ★ Jammed her knuckles against her teeth
- ★ Expression faltered as her chin started to tremble
- ★ Contorted with pain and misery

SENTENCES

She jammed her knuckles against her teeth.

She pressed her quivering lips together to smother the sob that welled in her throat.

His jaw tightened and his mouth twisted in an unhappy smile.

She tried to hold the smile, but her expression faltered as her chin started to tremble.

She bit her lip to stem the tears that welled up in her eyes and threatened to spill onto her face.

Her face became shadowed with grief and misery as she remembered the last time they had met.

SECTION 3 – EYES

WORDS

Nouns	Grief, tears
Adjectives	Wet, teary, watery, cloudy, glassy, bloodshot, swollen Dull, gloomy, blank, vacant, shadowed, downcast, forlorn
Verbs	Wept, poured, streamed, spilled Filled, blurred

PHRASES – NOUNS AND ADJECTIVES

- ★ Cloudy and sad
- ★ Glassy eyes
- ★ Gloomy and downcast
- ★ Vacant expression
- ★ As if in a trance
- ★ Shiny slug trails down her face
- ★ Wet and bloodshot from weeping

PHRASES – VERBS

- ★ Tears streamed from her eyes
- ★ Spilled out of her eyes
- ★ Blurred his vision
- ★ Scalded her cheeks as they flowed

- Filled with grief
- Stared with glassy eyes
- Screwed eyes shut to hold back the tears
- Stared as if in a trance
- Stared unblinking at the ground in front of him

SENTENCES

Her dark brown eyes filled with grief.

Her lips started to tremble and her eyes filled with tears.

Robert stared at her with glassy eyes and then screwed them shut to hold back the flood of tears.

The pain of her loss filled her chest like a dull ache and her eyes grew clouded and sad.

She was crying again, the tears spilling out of her eyes and leaving shiny slug trails down her face.

His face was shadowed with grief and misery, as he stared unblinking at the ground in front of him.

Without any warning, tears welled up in her eyes and poured down her face, scalding her cheeks as they flowed.

SECTION 4 – VOICE

WORDS

Nouns	Emotion, tone
	Sadness, misery, grief, despair, anguish
	Sob, sigh, whisper, murmur, moan, groan, wail, howl
Adjectives	Quiet, low, grave, solemn, husky, gruff, hoarse
	Shaky, choking, quivering, gurgling, shuddering
	Heartfelt, forlorn
Verbs	Cried, wept, sobbed
	Shook, trembled
	Cracked, crumpled, swallowed, stifled, strangled

PHRASES – NOUNS AND ADJECTIVES

- Wild, ragged wail
- Quiet groan
- Low, gurgling moan
- Moan of despair
- Stifled sob
- Shuddering sobs
- Quivering whisper

- Husky with emotion
- Full of sadness
- Heartfelt sigh
- Unshed tears in her voice
- Tone was forlorn

PHRASES – VERBS

- Let out a quiet groan
- Sobbed softly
- Choked with misery
- Shook and cracked with grief
- Swallowed hard before speaking
- Howled like a wounded dog
- Sob welled up in her throat
- Broke out as a strangled moan
- Uncontrollable sobbing racked her body

SENTENCES

His voice trailed off into a heartfelt sigh.

She broke into a sudden and uncontrollable sobbing.

Her words came in gasps and tears poured down her cheeks.

She rose shakily to her feet and her voice trembled as she greeted him.

When he spoke, his voice was a gruff whisper.

Shaking her head, she slumped to the ground and wept.

With a moan of despair, he buried his head in his hands.

Kitty's voice sank to a murmur, as a single tear trickled down her cheek.

Her eyes were filled with grief and, as she spoke, her voice crumpled with misery.

She swallowed hard before speaking – trying to dislodge the hard lump stuck in her throat.

Despite his efforts to conceal his disappointment, Robert's voice was strained and husky with emotion.

SECTION 5 – MOVEMENT

WORDS

Nouns	Body, head, eyes, lips, teeth Arms, shoulders, elbows, hand, fist, palms, knuckles, fingernails Legs, knees, feet
Verbs	Bit, chewed, rubbed, pressed Sniffed, wiped, brushed

	Bent, stooped, hunched, slumped, slouched
	Rocked, swayed
Adverbs	Quietly, slowly, clumsily, unhappily, frantically

PHRASES – VERBS

- Pressed palms into his eyes
- Bit lip unhappily
- Chewed fingernails
- Bit her knuckles
- Jammed her knuckles against her teeth
- Brushed tears away with a clumsy fist
- Wiped his eyes with the back of his hand
- Shook his head frantically
- Head dropped onto his chest
- Bent over with elbows on her knees
- Hugged her body in both arms
- Entire body was hunched over
- Slouched with hands in pockets
- Slumped like a puppet with its strings cut
- Rocked back and forth quietly
- Swayed on his feet
- Whole body was racked with sobs
- Moved with agonizing slowness
- Moved as if her legs were blocks of wood

SENTENCES

He sank down on the chair and hung his head in despair.

She rocked back and forth, with tears streaming quietly down her cheeks.

He crouched in the corner, tears spilling out of his eyes and snot bubbling in one nostril.

He held his body rigid – jaws tight, back hunched – elbows pressed into his knees.

He sniffed, wiped his eyes with the back of his hand and rose shakily to his feet.

Hugging his body in both arms, he swayed backwards and forwards.

Rubbing her eyes, she brushed away the tears that blurred her vision.

With a moan of despair, she slumped on the floor like a puppet with its strings cut.

He was a picture of despair with his bowed head and stooped shoulders. Shuffling along, he moved slowly, awkwardly, as if his legs were blocks of wood and every movement was an effort.

37

Tired

SECTION 1 – EMOTIONS

WORDS

Nouns	Sleep, tiredness, exhaustion Legs, head, eyes
Adjectives	Tired, sleepy, weary, exhausted Heavy, stiff, corpse-like Dizzy, faint, light-headed
Verbs	Sat, lay, dropped, slumped Dragged, staggered

PHRASES – NOUNS AND ADJECTIVES

- Light-headed with exhaustion
- Legs were heavy like pieces of wood

PHRASES – VERBS

- Sat corpse-like
- Head was swimming with tiredness
- Dragged down by an irresistible urge to sleep

SENTENCES

He didn't think he could go any further. His legs felt like pieces of wood – heavy and stiff.

Exhaustion had made him light-headed. He lay on the floor – dragged down by an irresistible urge to sleep.

37 *Emotions: tired*

SECTION 2 – EXPRESSIONS

WORDS

Nouns	Face, head, chin, eyes, nose, mouth, chest, arms Yawn, saliva
Adjectives	White, pale, grey, deathly, lifeless Wide, gaping
Verbs	Slept, yawned, dribbled Dropped, slumped, stretched

PHRASES – NOUNS AND ADJECTIVES

- Gaping yawn
- Face deathly white and eyes lifeless

PHRASES – VERBS

- Mouth dropped open
- Stretched arms behind his head
- Opened mouth wide in a gaping yawn
- Chin fell onto her chest
- Saliva dribbled out of the corner of his mouth

SENTENCES

She slept with her chin slumped onto her chest, her mouth dropping open and saliva dribbling out of the corner of her mouth.

His mouth open in a wide, gaping yawn, he leant back and stretched his arms behind his head.

SECTION 3 – EYES

WORDS

Nouns	Tiredness, exhaustion, fatigue Eyes, eyelids
Adjectives	Dull, lifeless, tired-looking Heavy, drooping, sagging, heavy-lidded Pink, red, bloodshot
Verbs	Closed, drooped, fluttered

PHRASES – NOUNS AND ADJECTIVES

- Drooping eyes
- Tired-looking eyes
- Sagging eyes
- Dull and heavy-lidded
- Heavy eyelids and bloodshot eyes

PHRASES – VERBS

- Rimmed with red
- Drooped downwards
- Kept closing
- Had difficulty keeping eyes open
- As if heavy weights were forcing them down

SENTENCES

His drooping lids seemed to have heavy weights forcing them down.

His eyes were bloodshot and rimmed with red.

Her face was deathly white and her sagging eyes were lifeless.

SECTION 4 – VOICE

WORDS

Nouns	Sigh, gasps, wheeze
Adjectives	Low, quiet
Verbs	Whispered, sighed, whined, groaned, muttered, mumbled, murmured Gasped, panted, croaked, faltered
Adverbs	Weakly, feebly, painfully

PHRASES – NOUNS AND ADJECTIVES

- Low, painful wheeze

PHRASES – VERBS

- Groaned with every step
- Whined that he couldn't go any further
- Mumbled weakly
- Voice came in painful gasps as he tried to get his breath

37 *Emotions: tired*

SENTENCES

He could barely put one foot in front of the other and groaned with every step.

Her eyes fluttered open and she mumbled weakly.

His vision was blurred. He couldn't do any more. With a sigh, he took off his glasses and closed his eyes.

He kept stopping every few metres – whining that he couldn't go any further.

He slumped with his hands on his knees, gasping for breath; when he eventually spoke, his voice was a low, painful wheeze.

Drenched in sweat, he fell back against the wall. His voice came in painful gasps as he tried to get his breath.

SECTION 5 – MOVEMENT

WORDS

Nouns	Legs, feet, hips
	Chest, arms, hands, shoulders
	Head, chin, mouth, nose
Adjectives	Heavy, stiff, corpse-like
	Tired, weary, exhausted, dizzy
Verbs	Fell, sank, slumped
	Bowed, sagged, stooped

PHRASES – VERBS

- Shoulders stooped
- Head bowed
- Chin fell on his chest
- Dragged his feet across the ground
- Stood with hands on hips
- Chin slumped onto his chest
- Fell back against the wall panting
- Sank to the floor gasping for breath
- Could barely put one foot in front of the other
- Kept stopping every few metres
- Unable to walk another step
- Slumped with his hands on his knees
- Slithered to a halt
- Flicked his tongue round his lips
- Tried to get some moisture to his mouth and lips
- Stretched his arms behind his head
- Pinched the bridge of his nose and closed his eyes

SENTENCES

He slithered to a halt. His throat was parched and his breath was coming in painful gasps.

Unable to walk another step, she slumped forward and lay corpse-like on the floor.

Exhausted and drenched in sweat, he fell back against the wall, hands on hips, head bowed, gasping for breath.

He was so tired he could barely walk, but he kept on moving, dragging his feet across the ground, shoulders stooped and his head slumped on his chest.

Unable to read any more, he took off his glasses, pinched the bridge of his nose and closed his eyes.

Swallowing hard, he flicked his tongue round his lips – trying to draw some moisture to his mouth and lips.

38

Pain

SECTION 1 – EMOTIONS

WORDS

Nouns	Head, breath, throat, chest Stomach, leg Grip, grasp, vice Poison, acid, bile
Adjectives	Sick, dizzy, breathless Claw-like, hammering, overwhelming
Verbs	Gripped, grasped, tightened, contracted, throbbed Churned, gnawed, jerked, writhed

PHRASES – NOUNS AND ADJECTIVES

- Felt dizzy
- Pain was overwhelming
- Like a clenched fist
- Like a vice around his chest
- Like a razor-edged breath
- Like an acid burning his stomach
- As if a poison had taken root in his gut
- Bile at the back of her throat
- Hammering pain in his head

PHRASES – VERBS

- Took his breath away
- Felt a blaze of pain
- Pain twisted in his stomach
- Tore through his stomach
- Stomach was churning
- Stomach contracted like a clenched fist
- Gnawed in his empty stomach
- Tightened like a vice around his chest
- Pain in his leg jerked with a claw-like grasp
- Every nerve in his body screamed at him as . . .

SENTENCES

The gnawing in her empty stomach was making her feel sick and dizzy.

The pain in his leg jerked with a claw-like grip and left him feeling breathless and sick.

It felt like a poison had taken root in his stomach, seeping through his veins and spreading bile to the back of his throat.

Every nerve in his body screamed at him, as the pain gripped his head like a clenched fist.

All thought drained out of him, as the pain tore through his head and left him bent double and writhing in agony.

SECTION 2 – EXPRESSIONS

WORDS

Nouns	Face, eyes, nose, nostrils, mouth, tongue, teeth, lip Muscles, arms, fist, legs Cramps, ache, sore, sting, wound, bruise Pain, spasm, agony, anguish
Adjectives	Wounded, bruised, aching, sore Red, deep Wild, fierce, searing, hammering, stinging
Verbs	Throbbed, ached, stung, pounded, hammered Reddened, twisted, scrunched, tightened Dropped, lolled Bit, gritted Bent, staggered, rocked, buckled, crashed

38 *Emotions: pain*

PHRASES – NOUNS AND ADJECTIVES

- Pained look on his face
- Red in the face
- Fierce grimace

PHRASES – VERBS

- Reddened and twisted in agony
- Nostrils flared
- Deep lines creased the bridge of his nose
- Gritted her teeth
- Mouth was set in a fierce grimace
- Scrunched eyes tight
- Bit his lip until it bled
- Spasm crossed his face
- Mouth dropped open and tongue lolled out

SENTENCES

There was a pained look on his face.

He rubbed his forehead, trying to ease the hammering ache in his head.

As she cleaned the wound, his face reddened and twisted in agony.

He was bent in half by the cramps in his stomach. Holding his breath and gritting his teeth – he staggered to his feet.

As the next of wave of pain surged through his shoulder, he scrunched his eyes shut and bit his lip.

He gasped, as the wave of pain flooded through him. Scrunching his eyes tight and clenching his fists, he rocked backwards and forwards.

The wound had been torn open and was throbbing savagely. Nostrils flared and deep lines creasing the bridge of his nose, he gritted his teeth and got to his feet.

Her mouth dropped open and her tongue lolled out. With one final gasp, her legs buckled under her and she crashed to the floor.

SECTION 3 – EYES

WORDS

Nouns	Whites, sockets, tears
Adjectives	Wide, bulging
Verbs	Shut, squeezed, scrunched
	Rolled, popped, bulged

PHRASES – VERBS

- ★ Squeezed eyes shut
- ★ Bulged in his head
- ★ Rolled in their sockets
- ★ Only the whites were showing
- ★ Looked as if they were going to pop out of his head
- ★ Tears streamed down her face

SENTENCES

Her mouth gaped like a fish out of water and tears streamed down her face.

As she hit the wall, her head was thrown backwards and her eyes rolled in their sockets, until only the whites were showing.

SECTION 4 – VOICE

WORDS

Nouns	Cry, whimper, whine, groan, moan, gasp Scream, yell, shriek, howl, wail
Adjectives	Small, low, ragged Wild, deathly, piercing, high-pitched, ear-splitting
Verbs	Cried, whined, groaned, moaned, whimpered Yelled, howled, wailed Gasped, gulped Let out, uttered, released

PHRASES – NOUNS AND ADJECTIVES

- ★ Low, gurgling groan
- ★ Deathly moan
- ★ Piercing scream
- ★ High-pitched howl
- ★ Wild, ragged wail

PHRASES – VERBS

- ★ Let out a small whimper
- ★ Uttered a low, gurgling groan
- ★ Moaned and writhed in agony
- ★ Released an ear-splitting yell
- ★ Gulped for air
- ★ Words came in painful gasps

38 *Emotions: pain*

SENTENCES

She curled into a ball and howled like a wounded animal.

He winced and put his hands to his head.

He let out a loud, ragged wail and tugged wildly at his hair.

She crouched in the corner, with her arms wrapped around her, and let out a small whimper.

Writhing in agony, he clutched his stomach and groaned.

She bent forward with her hands on her knees. Gulping for air, her words came in painful gasps.

Half-mad with the pain in her back, she released an ear-splitting yell.

SECTION 5 – MOVEMENT

WORDS

Nouns	Head, brow, eyes, sockets
	Stomach, arms, hands, fists, knees, feet, hair
	Ball, heap, ragdoll, puppet
Adjectives	Painful, wild, savage, searing, cramping
	Half-mad, spread-eagled
Verbs	Buried, wrapped
	Tugged, grabbed, twisted, clenched, clutched
	Shivered, shuddered
	Struggled, writhed, thrashed
	Lay, sprawled, slouched, slumped
	Bent, curled, hunched, huddled
	Limped, hobbled, buckled, dragged
Adverbs	Shakily, unsteadily
	Tightly, fiercely, violently

PHRASES – NOUNS AND ADJECTIVES

- ★ Cramping pain
- ★ As limp as a ragdoll
- ★ Like a puppet with its strings cut

PHRASES – VERBS

- Doubled up
- Curled into a ball
- Clutched at her stomach
- Huddled in a heap
- Hunched her shoulders
- Bent over to ease the cramping pain
- Lay spread-eagled
- Sprawled on the floor groaning
- Fell in a struggling heap
- Slouched against the wall
- Slumped to the ground
- Legs buckled under her
- Thrashed around on the floor
- Struggled into a sitting position
- Got unsteadily to his feet
- Limped slowly, dragging foot behind him
- Hobbled to the door
- Buried head in his hands
- Head lolled from side to side
- Clenched his fist
- Shivered violently

SENTENCES

The blistering pain made him crumple into a heap.

He pressed his hands tightly over his eyes to block out the pain.

She crouched in a corner, with her arms wrapped tightly around her.

He thrashed wildly – fighting the pain that came again and again.

He twisted his head and tugged his hair, trying to escape the searing pain.

She writhed on the floor, clutching her stomach. Her eyes rolled in their sockets and sweat streamed from her brow.

She hunched her shoulders and bent forward, hands on knees, gasping for air.

He limped slowly away, with his foot dragging behind him and scraping on the pavement.

His legs buckled under him and he slumped on the pavement, legs splayed and eyes rolling back in their sockets.

Staggering to a halt, she slumped to the ground.

Curled in a ball, he shuddered and shivered violently.

Clutching at his stomach, he doubled over, gasping as the pain shuddered through his body.

Part 3
Creatures

39

Parts, size, shape, colour and covering

SECTION 1 – TYPE AND BODY PARTS

WORDS

Nouns	Head, body, torso, wings, tail
	Arms, hands, fingers, talons
	Legs, feet, toes, hooves, claws
Mammals	Human, monkey, ape, gorilla
	Cat, tiger, lion, leopard
	Dog, wolf, hyena, jackal, coyote
	Tapir, pig, hog, boar, ram, goat, bull
	Horse, donkey, deer, camel
	Racoon, weasel, badger, beaver, hedgehog, rabbit
	Rat, mouse, gerbil
Reptiles	Crocodile, alligator, lizard, iguana, gecko, snake
	Tortoise, turtle
Birds	Vulture, buzzard, eagle, hawk, gull, raven
	Albatross, swan, emu, ostrich, peacock, pelican
	Turkey, rooster, chicken
Insects	Fly, wasp, bee, cockroach, beetle
Arachnids	Spider, scorpion
Fish	Shark, eel, barracuda, piranha
Molluscs	Snail, slug, octopus
Mythical	Dragon, griffin, phoenix, unicorn, werewolf, centaur, Cyclops, boggart, banshee
	Dwarf, elf, goblin, leprechaun, genie, giant, ogre, troll, gorgon, harpy
	Ghost, tree spirit, death spirit, water spirit, household spirit

39 *Creatures: parts, size, shape, colour and covering*

Adjectives

Colour	Black, inky, blue, purple
	Grey, silver, pale, white
	Golden, yellow, bronze, red, crimson, scarlet, brown, copper
	Green, bright green, slime green, poisonous green
Size	Small, little, tiny, minute, elfin, short
	Large, enormous, gigantic, immense, colossal, massive, mammoth
Shape	Narrow, thin, slim, slender
	Wide, broad, stubby, stocky, squat
	Round, oblong, square, serpentine, stretched, flattened
Character	Ugly, vile, hideous, monstrous, repulsive, ghastly, grotesque
	Fierce, brutal, savage, violent, vicious, menacing, merciless, venomous, malicious, ferocious, fiendish, malevolent, frightening, terrifying, petrifying
	Sly, crafty, cunning

PHRASES – NOUNS AND ADJECTIVES

- ★ Half-human, half-hyena
- ★ Part ape, part scorpion
- ★ Slime green body of a lizard and the head of a badger
- ★ Hideous, red creature with eight legs, the head of a fly and a snake for a tail
- ★ Ferocious, rooster-like animal
- ★ Tiny, vicious goblin with a scarlet rat's tail
- ★ Savage spirit that looked like a rooster from behind, but had the front of a hyena
- ★ Terrifying, eight-legged monster with chicken feet and the tusk of a rhino
- ★ Vicious spirit in the shape of a gerbil
- ★ Grotesque yellow badger, with a hawk's head at either end
- ★ Human above the waist, a leopard below and an enormous shell on its back
- ★ Large, winged creature
- ★ Enormous silver hog's body
- ★ Colossal, eight-foot camel
- ★ Massive purple iguana
- ★ Short, trunked creature
- ★ Squat creature with six legs
- ★ Ugly little creature
- ★ Tiny, elfin body
- ★ Minute goblin
- ★ Narrow body of a wolf
- ★ Wide, six-legged creature
- ★ Painfully thin deer, with spider's legs and a bulging stomach
- ★ Hedgehog-like creature, stretched and flattened into the shape of a crocodile

- ★ Huge, round-bodied raven
- ★ Venomous, serpentine creature

SENTENCES

The wasp's head was attached to a black, porcupine-like body.

Scuttling towards him was a huge bronze scorpion.

A hideous creature crawled out from behind the tree. It was part ape and part scorpion.

It had the body of a lizard and the head of a badger.

A winged creature, with a terrifying, demonic face, swooped down from the tree.

The island was guarded by a fierce sea monster with an enormous, humped, serpentine body and a hideous cockroach head.

The three-legged bird had the huge wings of an albatross, the claws of an eagle and hog's tusks.

The vile creature was so terrifying that anyone who looked at it died instantly.

It looked as if there were two creatures twisted together, but as it moved its huge slime green body, Robert could see that it was actually a two-headed monster, with a racoon head at the front and a beetle head at the back.

SECTION 2 – COVERING

WORDS

Nouns	Skin, hide, feathers
	Spikes, spines, quills, arrows
	Studs, horns, plates, lumps, armour
	Scales, tentacles, spots, warts
	Fur, hair, whiskers, mane, beard, tussocks, locks
	Plants, leaves, grass, vines, seaweed
Adjectives	Hairy, woolly, furry, white-furred
	Bare, hairless
	Fleshless, loose-fitting
	Metallic, leathery, scaly
	Slippery, wet, moist, clammy
	Dry, soft, silky
	Long, thick, huge, enormous, trailing
	Sharp, stiff, bony, pointed, stinger-tipped
	Straight, triangular
	Untidy, wild, matted, tangled, torn
	Living, bristling, hissing, flicking
	Venomous, poisonous
Verbs	Covered, grew, clung
	Hung, drooped, trailed, flowed

Stuck up, jutted, sprouted
Wrinkled, polished, glistened, glinted
Oozed, bulged

PHRASES – NOUNS AND ADJECTIVES

- Bronze-skinned
- Skin was black and hairless
- Pale white skin
- Bright, poisonous green skin
- Ill-fitting skin
- Hard, leathery skin
- Dirty, tangled hide
- Bare skin around its face and neck
- Skin as slippery as polished leather
- As wrinkled as a prune
- Furry body
- White-furred wolf
- Furry, brown creature
- Thick, fleecy coat
- Hairy body
- Long black hair
- Long, thick, flowing hair
- Locks of fiery red hair
- Matted, woolly hair
- Thick tussocks of hair
- Hair of living, venomous snakes
- Lion's mane
- Billy-goat beard
- Beard like a dragon
- Hairy whiskers
- Mane and beard like a bison
- Scaly body
- Snake scales
- Scaly, clammy skin
- Dry, scaly skin
- Scales as soft as silk
- Bird feathers
- Feathers the colour of copper
- Gleaming feathers of scarlet and gold
- Mane of thick, black feathers
- Ring of crimson feathers around its neck
- Spikes along its back
- Stiff quill feathers

- Porcupine quills
- Body armour with spikes on its shoulders
- Tough, armour-plated skin with pointed, bony plates
- Triangular plates round its neck
- Enormous tortoise shell
- Stinger-tipped tentacles

PHRASES – VERBS

- Ran from its head to the tip of its tail
- Ran the length of its body
- Drooped in loose folds
- Hung loosely on its skeletal body
- Clung to its fleshless skeleton
- Flowed to her feet
- Stuck up along its spine
- Sprouted from its body
- Jutted out of its back
- Covered in inky, black fur
- Covered in heavy scales
- Covered in sharp, metallic feathers
- Dressed only in leaves
- Hair and beard made from living grass and vines
- Covered in studs, spikes and horns
- Covered in sharp quills
- Studded with bony lumps
- Bulged with green spots that oozed a yellow liquid
- Glistened like wet leather
- Glinted red and gold

SENTENCES

It had thick red feathers around its neck.

Porcupine quills ran the length of its body.

Its hairy whiskers were long, purple and twitching.

It was half-human, half-hyena, with long, wild green hair.

The sun glinted on the sharp spikes sprouting from its legs.

The five-headed, monstrous beast was covered in bulging, green spots.

No-one dared to go near the caves, which were guarded by vicious female monsters, with boar tusks and hair of writhing, hissing snakes.

Below the waist, it was covered in black fur, and above, stinger-tipped tentacles hung from its body.

Grinning maliciously at him was an ugly little goblin, with a sly face and hard, leathery skin covered in warts.

40

Head

HEAD AND FACE

WORDS

Nouns	Head, skull, face
	Skin, flesh, folds
	Horns, tusks, antlers
	Beak, bill, snout, nose, nostrils
	Mouth, jaws, teeth, fangs, tombstones, needles, spikes, tongue
	Whiskers, feelers, antennae
	Suckers, tentacles, blowhole
	Venom, poison, acid, slime
Adjectives	Small, tiny, large, huge, massive, enormous, gigantic
	Wide, broad, thin, slim, long, short
	Rounded, oval, cone-shaped, wedge-shaped, twisted, curling, spiral, corkscrew, hooked, curved, forked
	Bald, knobbly, scaly, rubbery, steel, metallic
	Sharp-beaked, cruel-beaked, horned
	Ape-like, bird-like, reptilian
	Razor-sharp, scissor-like, needle-sharp
	Bulging, sagging, drooping, sprouting, thrusting
	Writhing, twitching, dripping, snarling, slavering
	Ugly, hideous, grotesque, monstrous
	Nasty, cruel, evil, savage, vicious, demonic, malicious, menacing, merciless
	Venomous, stinger-tipped
Verbs	Covered, stretched, grew, sprouted, thrust, hung, drooped, curled
	Bared, revealed, snarled, dribbled, drooled, dripped, slobbered

PHRASES – NOUNS AND ADJECTIVES

- Small, horned head
- Scaly head of a lizard
- Enormous, wedge-shaped head
- Twisted head like a corkscrew
- Cruel-beaked bird's head
- Large, knobbly, bald head
- Narrow head and bulging skull
- Ape-like face with a beak
- Narrow, pointed face
- Long, thin, snarling face
- Small, grotesque face
- Malicious, demonic face
- Deathly pale, scaly skin
- Huge folds of sagging skin
- Some of its flesh was missing
- Horn in the middle of its forehead
- Golden antlers like a stag
- Great, curled horns
- Sharp tusks like a wild boar
- Two long, corkscrew horns
- Central horn like a thrusting sword
- Sprouting, rubbery feelers
- Stinger-tipped tentacles
- Huge, spiralling antennae
- Gigantic, writhing feelers
- Hood of purple skin around its head
- Head crests like red trumpets
- Venom-storing blowhole on top of its head
- Monstrous, slobbering mouth
- Scissor-like jaws
- Razor-sharp fangs
- Thin, needle-sharp teeth
- Savage, needle teeth like spikes on a trap
- Fangs like hypodermic needles
- Teeth like tombstones
- Venomous fangs
- Eagle's beak
- Parrot-like beak
- Needle-sharp, metallic beak
- Hooked, golden beak
- Huge, rounded beak
- Cruel, steel-coloured beak
- Massive, horned bill

- Curved beak as merciless as a dagger
- As sharp as the edge of a blade

PHRASES – VERBS

- Covered in black hair
- Drooped from its face
- Sprouted from its head
- Hung from its head
- Curved from its head like a dagger
- Spiked upwards like a thrusting sword
- Fangs curled beneath its chin
- Filled with drooping tentacles
- Tipped with suckers
- Dripping slime
- Forked tongue flickered constantly
- Tasted the air in search of its prey
- Dripped with blood from its last kill

SENTENCES

Huge folds of sagging skin drooped from its long, snarling face.

Its small, narrow head had a rounded beak like a turtle.

It was small and wrinkled, with a large, knobbly, bald head like a turnip.

A malicious, demonic face peered through the strands of the web.

It had an ape-like face with a beak. Some of its flesh was missing, as if it had been eaten away by acid.

Two long corkscrew horns grew from its cone-shaped head.

There was a single, spiral horn in the middle of its forehead.

Its bulging skull had two corkscrew horns.

Rubbery feelers sprouted from its mouth.

Huge, spiralling antennae erupted from its head.

It had a blunt-snouted head, with a central horn that spiked upwards like a thrusting sword.

Stinger-tipped tentacles hung from its enormous, wedge-shaped head.

A stream of venom shot into the air from the blowhole on top of its head.

Its scaly head was like that of a lizard and was surrounded by a hood of slime green and red skin.

Venomous slime drooled from its razor-sharp fangs.

Savage needle teeth tore at Kitty's legs, like spikes on a trap.

It opened its mouth to reveal thin, needle-sharp teeth.

Fangs curled beneath its chin and dribbled with blood from its last kill.

Its forked tongue flickered constantly, tasting the air in search of its prey.

It had a cruel, metallic beak that curved from its head like a dagger.

41

Eyes

WORDS

Nouns	Pupils, sockets, whites, slits, stalks
	Back, belly, forehead
	Hatred, anger, greed, malice
Adjectives	Black, grey, green, emerald, yellow, golden, orange, brassy, red, fiery, bloodshot
	Large, huge, little, small, beady, raised, bulging, goggling
	Bright, vivid, angry, fierce, gleaming, burning, blazing, flaming, glowing, ferocious
	Cold, dead, evil, staring, piercing, malicious
Verbs	Lit, cast, shone, burned, blazed, gleamed, glinted, glowed
	Looked, glared, drilled, twitched, flickered, bulged

PHRASES – NOUNS AND ADJECTIVES

- Beady black eyes
- Eyes like bulging emerald balls
- Blazing, bloodshot eyes
- Glowing red eyes
- Goggling yellow eyes
- Piercing grey eyes
- Bulging orange eyes
- Eye sockets but no eyes
- Raised, brassy eyes
- Single round eye like a spotlight
- On its belly
- Middle of its forehead
- On top of long stalks

- On rubbery, twitching eye-stalks
- Two raised little bat eyes
- Long slits
- Size of headlights
- Huge, cold eyes
- Malicious, staring eyes
- Flaming red eyes
- Full of hatred and anger
- Bulging and fierce in its hideous face

PHRASES – VERBS

- Dotted along its back
- Bulged out of its skull
- Looked in different directions
- Cast wide beams of light
- Burned like furnaces
- Burned with a cruel light
- Glowed like flickering sparks in the dark
- Glinted with greed
- Gleamed maliciously
- Drilled into her

SENTENCES

Its beady black eyes glinted with greed.

Its red eyes burned with a cruel light from its long, snarling face.

Goggling yellow eyes glinted from rubbery, twitching eye-stalks.

It had a single round orange eye in the middle of its forehead.

Its glowing red eyes were bulging and fierce in its hideous face.

Its eyes were the size of headlights and cast wide beams of light on the ground in front of it.

She closed her eyes to escape the cold, staring eyes that drilled into her from its sharp-beaked bird's head.

Above a curved beak as sharp as a blade, its bulging orange eyes burned like furnaces.

Its eyes were on top of long stalks, which twisted and writhed as they followed Kitty's every movement.

It had piercing red eyes, which glowed like flickering sparks in the dark.

42

Arms and legs

SECTION 1 – ARMS AND HANDS

WORDS

Nouns	Fingers, knuckles, wrists, fingernails, suckers, claws, talons, tentacles, stumps
Adjectives	Long, short, skinny, fat, huge Bird-like, webbed Woolly, brass, steel Sharp, sharp-clawed, curved, hooked Deadly, menacing
Verbs	Dangled, dragged Spread, folded, extended, displayed, wriggled Sharpened

PHRASES – NOUNS AND ADJECTIVES

- ★ Long arms like rippling octopus tentacles
- ★ Short arms like stumps
- ★ Short, skinny, woolly arms
- ★ Short, bird-like arms
- ★ Webbed hands
- ★ Sharp-clawed hands
- ★ Six fingers on each hand
- ★ Suckers on the ends of its hands
- ★ Lifeless hands
- ★ Dead, white fingers
- ★ Fingernails made of brass

- Steel claws
- Razor talons
- Huge, menacing claws as sharp as a dagger
- Hooked claws like coat hangers
- Eagle talons on its fingers were long and deadly

PHRASES – VERBS

- Dragged along the ground
- Folded, bird-like, under its shoulders
- Dangled from its wrists
- Wriggled like mindless maggots
- Displayed its claws

SENTENCES

Its arms were small, useless stumps with webbed fingers.

There were long, deadly, brass talons on the end of her fingers.

Each of its six fingers had claws as sharp as razor blades.

The ends of its fingers were speared by hooked claws like coat hangers.

Its arms were so long its knuckles grazed along the ground.

It had short arms that folded, bird-like, under its shoulders.

Dead, white fingers wriggled like mindless maggots from the end of its octopus tentacles.

As its long arms dragged along the ground, its huge, menacing claws scraped tracks in the earth.

It opened its hand and displayed its claws, which had points as sharp as a dagger.

SECTION 2 – LEGS AND FEET

WORDS

Nouns	Front, hind, footprints, toes, paws, claws, talons, spurs, suction cups
Adjectives	Short, long, tiny, small, large, giant Thick, tree-trunk, thin Scaly, furry Two-legged, four-toed, clawed Agile, clumsy, powerful
Verbs	Faced, pointed, extended Acted as, ended with, tipped with, linked to Crawled, shuffled, scuttled

PHRASES – NOUNS AND ADJECTIVES

- Tree-trunk legs
- Thin, two-legged beast
- Legs of a goat and eagle talons
- Six short, thick legs like a hippo's
- Front legs shorter than the hind legs
- Tiny front legs
- Powerful hind legs and a kangaroo tail
- Cushioned, furry paws
- Long, agile legs and four-toed feet
- Two scaly legs
- Spurs on its front legs
- Lion paws and vulture claws
- Single large foot
- Two scaled chicken feet
- Large tortoise feet
- Seven clawed toes
- Suction cups on tips of toes

PHRASES – VERBS

- Used to crawl on all fours
- Acted as a tripod
- Ended in sharp claws
- Linked to poison glands in its body
- Tipped with vicious talons
- Extended from a thick leg in the middle of its body
- Feet faced backwards and forwards

SENTENCES

The spurs on its front legs were linked to poison glands in its body.

A brown mist gushed from the spurs on its powerful front legs.

A single large foot extended from one thick leg in the middle of its body.

The giant shuffled clumsily on its tree-trunk legs and large tortoise feet.

It was a thin, two-legged beast, with seven clawed toes on each foot.

It had legs like a horse and its cushioned paws were tipped with vulture claws.

It had two scaly legs and giant chicken feet that ended in sharp claws.

Its hind legs were like huge tree trunks, but its front legs were short and skinny and only used when it crawled on all fours.

It had powerful hind legs and feet, which were tipped with vicious talons.

42 *Creatures: arms and legs*

Its powerful hind legs and kangaroo tail acted as a tripod, as it stood motionless, watching them with its darting, red eyes.

Its feet could face backwards and forwards, so it was impossible to tell from its footprints which direction the creature had taken.

43

Wings and tails

SECTION 1 – WINGS

WORDS

Nouns	Bat, beetle, ostrich, eagle, hawk Shoulder, withers
Adjectives	Short, stubby, long, huge, giant Shiny, black, golden Bat-like, leathery, scaly, spiny
Verbs	Grew, burst, sprouted Stretched, flapped, beat, fluttered

PHRASES – NOUNS AND ADJECTIVES

- Wings like an ostrich
- Golden eagle wings
- Short, stubby wings
- Huge, bat-like wings
- Shiny beetle-wings
- Huge, spiny wings
- Long, scaly wings
- Winged death spirits

PHRASES – VERBS

- Sprouted from its shoulders
- Burst from each wither
- Folded its wings against its shoulders
- Dived towards them
- Sent air rushing through the trees

SENTENCES

Long, scaly wings sprouted from its shoulders.

Winged death spirits haunted the forest.

Huge, black, bat-like wings burst from each wither.

It fluttered its shiny beetle-wings and stuck its snarling face through the strands of its web.

It circled above, folded its long, scaly wings flat against its shoulders and dived towards them.

The winged death spirits sent the air rushing through the trees with every beat of their huge, bat-like wings.

SECTION 2 –TAILS

WORDS

Nouns	Lion, peacock, lemur, scorpion, snake
	Spear, club, oar, whip, rudder, corkscrew, pine cone
	Tuft, stinger, spines, tail feathers
Adjectives	Large, thick, heavy, long, tall, broad, flat
	Scaly, bony, barbed, spiked
	Stiff, rigid, whip-like
	Scarlet, fiery, golden
	Poisonous, venomous
Verbs	Thrashed, tossed, whipped, jerked, beat, lashed

PHRASES – NOUNS AND ADJECTIVES

- ★ Thick, heavy tail
- ★ Scaly corkscrew tail
- ★ Barbed, oar-like tail
- ★ Long, stiff, rudder-like tail
- ★ Snake's head at the end of its tail
- ★ Long lemur tail
- ★ Glittering, golden tail
- ★ As long as a peacock's
- ★ Long tail with a spear at the end
- ★ Club at the end of its tail
- ★ Poisonous tail stinger
- ★ Scarlet and gold tail feathers
- ★ Broad, flat tail like a squashed pine cone

PHRASES – VERBS

- Ended in a scorpion's sting
- Tipped with four tall, poisonous spines
- Dragged along the ground
- Thumped on the ground
- Used its tail to swing through the trees
- Thrashed the air, searching for its target

SENTENCES

Its thick, heavy tail dragged along behind it. The club at the end thumped on the ground with every step.

Its tail was broad and flat like a squashed pine cone. The spikes studded along its length made it a lethal weapon.

It hung from the branch by its long, lemur-like tail and swung towards them, baring its needle-sharp teeth.

Its four poisonous spines were thrust upwards like spears – thrashing the air – searching for their target.

44

Smell and sound

SECTION 1 – SMELL

WORDS

Nouns	Smell, stink, vapour, stench, odour
	Meat, flesh, water, plants, seaweed, smoke, acid, chlorine, sulphur, decay
Adjectives	Foul, strong, bitter, rotting, decaying, poisonous, pungent, putrefying
Verbs	Smelt, stank, reeked
	Rose, seeped, wafted, released
	Clung, surrounded
	Choked, coughed, retched, vomited

PHRASES – NOUNS AND ADJECTIVES

- Rotting flesh
- Stench of decay
- Foul-smelling vapour
- Pungent odour of decay

PHRASES – VERBS

- Stank of rotting meat
- Reeked of foul water
- Smelt of rotting plants and seaweed
- Clung to it like a rotting cloak
- Reeked of chlorine
- Smelt of smoke and sulphur
- Surrounded by the stench of poisonous acid

- Polluted the air with each beat of its wings
- Gave off a pungent odour

SENTENCES

Its breath stank of rotting meat.

The dragon's breath smelt of smoke and sulphur.

It gave off a pungent odour of decay and rotting flesh.

A foul-smelling vapour polluted the air with each beat of its wings.

The stink of rotting meat and decay clung to the beast like a rotting cloak.

Its fur reeked of decaying plants and foul water from years spent in the swamps.

Its breath stank of rotting meat and the blood from its last kill dripped from its fangs.

She retched as the creature drew near and the stench of decay and rotting flesh wafted towards her.

Even though it was invisible, she knew the death spirit was near, from the pungent odour of decay and rotting flesh that surrounded it.

SECTION 2 – SOUND

WORDS

Nouns	Hiss, whistle, moan, cry, howl, yell, scream, cackle, laughter Hoot, squawk, call, roar, bark, trumpet
Adjectives	Loud, high-pitched, shrill, ear-splitting, piercing, thunderous Crazy, deathly, mournful, demonic, venomous, blood-curdling
Verbs	Rung, echoed Tore, ripped, pierced, slashed

PHRASES – NOUNS AND ADJECTIVES

- Loud, hooting call
- Deathly moan
- Venomous, hissing noise
- Shrill, whistling sound
- Demonic cackle
- Piercing squawk
- Blood-curdling growl
- Terrifying yell
- Trumpet roar
- Piercing scream
- Thunderous cry
- High-pitched, human scream
- Ear-splitting shriek

44 *Creatures: smell and sound*

PHRASES – VERBS

- ★ Let out a mournful howl
- ★ Rang in his ears
- ★ Echoed through the night
- ★ Pierced the silence

SENTENCES

The sound of its piercing squawk rang in his ears.

It threw back its head and let out a mournful howl.

A loud, hooting call echoed through the night.

A blood-curdling howl ripped through the air.

The silence was pierced by a high-pitched scream high in the trees.

The hideous beast had imitated her father's voice to lure her into its den.

45

Movement

WORDS

Nouns	Legs, feet, footprints Unicorn, dragon, sheep, whale, lizard, spider, coconut Dust, mist, cloud
Adjectives	Large, enormous, giant, tiny
Verbs	Walked, moved, slithered, dragged Moved, ran, slithered, rolled, skied, rode, flew, floated
Adverbs	Slowly, quickly, clumsily

PHRASES – VERBS

- Rode on a giant whale
- Rode on a sheep
- Flew through the air in a giant coconut
- Passed in a swirl of dust
- Left no footprints
- Ran in pecking strides like a scuttling lizard
- Dragged its clawed foot over the ground
- Slithered very quickly in both directions
- Locked the jaws of its two heads together
- Rolled like a hoop
- Moved around on a pair of dancing spider's legs
- Moved around by skiing on its enormous feet
- Floated across the snow like a mist
- Yellow cloud covered its movements

SENTENCES

It floated across the snow like a mist and left no footprints.

It covered its movements by spurting a yellow cloud out of its snout.

It moved towards them and then passed by in a swirl of dust.

One moment it was standing upright on its hind legs and then – it locked its two ends together and rolled like a hoop towards him.

It walked slowly – clumsily dragging its clawed foot over the ground.

There was a rush of air as the witch flew over his head in a huge coconut. Using a skull to steer the vessel, she circled above and screeched with laughter.

As he drew closer, the spirit vanished in a cloud of mist and reappeared behind him.

46

Habitat

WORDS

Nouns	Castle, church, graveyard, grave, house, fireplace, boot, pipes, sewer, drains Forest, trees, trunks Hills, mountains, rocks, caves, tunnels, underground Swamp, creek, lake, river, pools, sea, ocean, seashell
Adjectives	Dark, damp, swampy Ruined, deserted, haunted
Verbs	Lived, lodged, inhabited, guarded

PHRASES – NOUNS AND ADJECTIVES

- Hill-dwelling creature
- Trunks of large trees
- Dark caves and tunnels
- Rock crevices
- Ruined castles
- Deserted graveyards
- Swampy habitats
- Deep pools
- Rivers with dangerous currents
- Seashell hidden by seaweed caves

PHRASES – VERBS

- Lived in the mountains
- Guarded the treasures of the dead

46 *Creatures: habitat*

- Inhabited ruined castles
- Tunnelled underground and uprooted trees in its path
- Lurked in swamps and creeks
- Came out of the water at night
- Stood in the middle of the ocean
- Lodged itself in a house and lived in the boots

SENTENCES

It stood in the middle of the ocean and, at a distance, appeared to be an enormous rock.

It hid in the rocks and only came out at night to search for prey.

They found the tiny creature living in a seashell hidden by seaweed caves.

It lived underground and tunnelled through the earth, uprooting trees in its path.

The lake was guarded by a huge, humped monster that stretched from shore to shore. Its humps looked like islands dotted across the water.

The hag lived in a house guarded by a fence of human bones, lit by skulls with glowing eyes.

The vicious spirit had sneaked into their house and was living in the boots.

47

Abilities and actions

SECTION 1 – CHANGING APPEARANCE

WORDS

Nouns	Animal, human, man, woman, werewolf Insect, bird, raven Ghost, spirit, shape-shifter, shadow, mist, smoke Body, torso, shoulders, arms, hands, legs, feet Nose, beak, talons, claws Wings, hair
Adjectives	Tall, huge, small, tiny, normal, abnormal Bat-like, reptilian Hairy, scaly, invisible
Verbs	Rose, flew, drifted Grew, stretched, sprouted, shrank Changed, transformed, disguised Cut, severed, detached

PHRASES – VERBS

- Grew or shrank at will
- Transformed from a human to an animal and back again
- Detached its upper body in order to fly at night
- Turned feet to face backwards
- Arms transformed into huge front legs
- Wings sprouted from her shoulders
- Nose stretched into a sharp beak
- Nails stretched into pointed talons

- Sprouted thick, dark hair on its face
- Rose from the grave as a wisp of smoke
- Made herself invisible
- Wore a pointed hat that made her invisible
- Transformed into a mist and drifted away
- Changed its colour to blend with its surroundings

SENTENCES

The spirit rose from the grave as a wisp of smoke and appeared like the corpse lying beneath the ground.

He could grow or shrink at will. One moment he was an enormous man and the next, the size of a blade of grass.

The only sign of her presence was the tinkle of the tiny silver bells, which were attached to the pointed hat she wore to make herself invisible.

As his face sprouted thick, dark hair, his limbs twisted and writhed. He crouched down on his arms, which had transformed into huge front legs.

Her black cloak spread, as wings sprouted from her shoulders. Her nose stretched into a sharp beak and, flapping her wings, she flew into the trees – transformed into a raven.

He appeared as a normal human during the day, but at night, his head and neck detached from his body and flew about with huge, bat-like wings, leaving his severed torso hidden in the house.

It was impossible to track, as it could turn its feet to face backwards and still run at incredible speeds.

SECTION 2 – ACTIONS

WORDS

Nouns	Human, children, owner, death fairy, house spirit
	Death, dreams, nightmares, sign, omen, danger
	Body, blood, mind, voice, soul
Verbs	Fed, ate, drank, drained, devoured
	Stole, buried
	Copied, imitated

PHRASES – VERBS

- Fed on dead bodies in graveyards
- Drank the fresh blood of cattle
- Ate its tail, which grew back
- Travelled vast distances in a flash of smoke
- Could read the future

- Played tricks on its owner
- Imitated the voice of any human it had heard
- Stole the souls of dead bodies before they were buried
- Seeped into the minds of children
- Devoured dreams and twisted them into nightmares
- Appeared as an omen of death

SENTENCES

The evil spirit seeped into the minds of children, to devour their dreams and twist them into nightmares.

The death fairy had sneaked into the house where the funeral was being held and stolen the soul of the dead body before it could be buried.

It was able to imitate any human voice it had heard and had captured many victims by luring them into the forest using the voice of a loved one.

It was impossible to follow, as it could travel vast distances in a flash of smoke.

The huge lizard could hide for months. It stayed alive by eating its tail, which grew back ready for the next meal.

They knew it had returned. Every morning there was another fresh carcass lying in the field, its blood drained by the beast, as it fed on the fresh blood of the cattle to stay alive.

She shivered, as fear like ice spread through her veins. She knew that a sighting of the dog was an omen of death.

48

Weapons and destruction

SECTION 1 – WEAPONS

WORDS

Nouns	Prey, victim Stare, skin, flesh, mouth, teeth, jaws, tongue Tail, legs, spines, warts Breath, saliva, slime, acid, poison, venom Harp, song
Adjectives	Sticky, slimy, rubbery Venomous, poisonous, sizzling, toxic Huge, deadly, powerful, savage, lethal Sharp, pillar-like, barbed
Verbs	Spat, shot, sprayed, spurted, squirted, belched Trapped, lured, lassoed Froze, paralysed, killed Tore, crushed, struck

PHRASES – NOUNS AND ADJECTIVES

- ★ Icy breath was like a mist
- ★ Poisonous saliva
- ★ Powerful stream of acid
- ★ Deadly poison from the warts on its skin
- ★ Venomous spines on its legs
- ★ Trail of sticky slime
- ★ Pillar-like teeth
- ★ Savage teeth like barbed spikes on a trap

- Club on the end of its tail
- Long snout was like a vacuum hose
- Huge, rubbery tongue

PHRASES – VERBS

- Stare turned him to stone
- Froze him to the spot
- Instant death if looked into its eyes
- Paralysed prey with venomous spines
- Crushed the life out of the body with its teeth
- Tore the flesh from prey with its savage teeth
- Spat out a powerful stream of acid
- Squirted a deadly poison
- Blew up like a balloon
- Squirted brown acid from its eyes
- Poisonous saliva dripped from its jaws
- Sucked the blood out of its prey
- Sucked out the heart of its sleeping victim
- Laid a trail of sticky slime to trap its prey
- Lassoed its victims with the silk thread from its mouth
- Played enchanting songs on its harp

SENTENCES

Poisonous saliva dripped from its savage jaws.

It had laid a trail of sticky slime to trap its prey.

It closed its pillar-like teeth around the body and crushed the life out of it.

The warts on its skin split open and it squirted its deadly poison.

It blew up like a balloon and squirted brown acid from its eyes.

Its savage teeth were like barbed spikes on a trap and tore the flesh from its prey.

Its long snout was like a vacuum hose and sucked the blood out of its prey.

Its prey was paralysed by the venomous spines shooting from its legs.

Women and children were lured into the lake by the enchanting songs it played on its harp.

He kept his eyes fixed to the floor, avoiding her stare, which he knew would turn him to stone.

Whipping its head around, it spat out a stream of acid, which sizzled as it hit the ground at his feet.

It flicked its huge, rubbery tongue, prodding and poking, until it found the chest and sucked out the heart of its sleeping victim.

Robert's legs were jerked from under him, as he was lassoed by the silk thread from its mouth. It snaked around his legs and wound round and round, until his feet were locked together by the sticky ball at the end. Waving his arms wildly, he grasped for a hold as he was dragged towards the cave and the spider's web.

Robert's muscles were locked. The icy breath had fallen like a mist and frozen him to the spot. He was unable to move, unable to run. He stood motionless, as the beast towered over him.

SECTION 2 – DESTRUCTION

WORDS

Nouns	Heart, head, reflection
	Light, mirror, moon, fire, salt, garlic, dagger, potion, rooster
Verbs	Died, killed, stabbed, chopped, burned
	Sprayed, smeared, sprinkled
	Heard, looked, drank, touched

PHRASES – VERBS

- Frightened of the light
- Scared of fire
- Stabbed in the heart with a silver dagger
- Heard the crow of a rooster
- Looked at itself in the mirror
- Touched metal
- Sprinkled salt or smeared garlic on it
- Had to drink a special potion every twelve hours or it died
- Chopped off its head, burned it and dumped the ashes into the sea

SENTENCES

It could only be killed by stabbing it in the heart with a silver dagger.

It was immune to normal weapons, but needed to drink a special potion every twelve hours, otherwise it would die.

The only way it could be killed was by chopping off its head, burning it and dumping the ashes into the sea.

It was frightened of the light and would only emerge in the dark.

The crow of the rooster would kill it, so as dawn approached, it returned to its lair deep underground.

It crumpled in a heap, pressing its scaly fingers into its eyes, to avoid looking into the mirror she was thrusting in its face.

Kitty grabbed the piece of metal and thrust it towards him. As he backed away, she lunged and struck him on the arm. Shrieking, he fell to the ground. As she watched, poised to strike again, he crumpled into a ball and shrivelled, until only a pile of clothes remained.

Part 4
Additional vocabulary

49
Adverbs

An *adverb* is a word that *describes* a *verb*, an *adjective* or another *adverb*.

They describe *how, when, where*. This section will focus on adverbs that explain *how*, as these help to describe a character's emotions and resulting actions, movements and speech. They can also be used when using *personification*.

Adverbs that describe *when* and *where* have been included in the section on 'Connectives'.

EXCITED, HAPPY

- Excitedly, eagerly, enthusiastically, vivaciously, effusively
- Quickly, loudly, energetically, jauntily
- Happily, cheerfully, merrily, joyfully, gaily, gleefully, chirpily, jovially, blissfully, joyously, jubilantly, deliriously, elatedly, ecstatically, buoyantly, euphorically, exuberantly
- Brightly, radiantly

DETERMINED

- Determinedly, intently, diligently, earnestly, thoroughly, knavishly, single-mindedly
- Repeatedly, continually, doggedly, relentlessly, persistently, staunchly, tenaciously, unswervingly, unwaveringly, resolutely

SYMPATHETIC, CARING

- Quietly, softly, gently, calmly, patiently, soothingly
- Kindly, warmly, sweetly, dearly, lovingly, fondly, tenderly, adoringly, kind-heartedly, generously, considerately, sensitively, compassionately, solicitously
- Sympathetically, comfortingly, consolingly, supportively, coaxingly, cajolingly, encouragingly, reassuringly
- Politely, thoughtfully, truthfully, honestly, sincerely, earnestly, wisely, meaningfully

- Faithfully, loyally
- Sadly, seriously, worriedly, solemnly

ANGRY, AGGRESSIVE, IRRITATED, IMPATIENT

- Angrily, crossly, madly, wildly, roughly, fiercely, furiously, heatedly, thunderously
- Aggressively, forcefully, violently, savagely, viciously, brutally, ferociously
- Sharply, rudely, insultingly, offensively, obnoxiously, derisively
- Sternly, tensely, irritably, impatiently, tetchily
- Acidly, sourly, tartly
- Defiantly, indignantly, quarrelsomely, antagonistically

COLD, EVIL, SLY, ARROGANT

- Coldly, coolly, icily, frostily, stiffly, cold-heartedly, stonily
- Acidly, jeeringly, caustically, scornfully, mockingly, sneeringly, tauntingly
- Evilly, cruelly, wickedly, spitefully, brutally, brutishly, murderously, ruthlessly, mercilessly, grotesquely, hideously, noxiously, malevolently
- Sinisterly, vilely, bloodthirstily, demonically, sadistically, remorselessly, fiendishly, masochistically, macabrely, cold-bloodedly, cold-heartedly
- Slyly, craftily, cunningly, shiftily, deceitfully, sneakily, deviously, cagily, stealthily, furtively, covertly, clandestinely
- Arrogantly, vainly, boastfully, pompously, triumphantly, victoriously

SCARED, FRIGHTENED, TIMID

- Quickly, briskly, rapidly, speedily, hastily, swiftly
- Wildly, urgently, frenetically, frantically, hysterically
- Uneasily, doubtfully, tensely, hesitantly, worriedly, reluctantly, suspiciously
- Shakily, weakly, limply, timorously

NERVOUS, SHY, EMBARRASSED

- Nervously, anxiously, cautiously, warily, carefully, uncertainly, tentatively
- Doubtfully, reluctantly, apprehensively
- Shakily, weakly, limply, helplessly, queasily

SAD, MISERABLE

- Sadly, miserably, bleakly, gloomily, glumly, woefully
- Seriously, solemnly, sombrely, soberly, gravely
- Quietly, silently, mutely, hollowly, croakily, tearfully
- Hopelessly, bleakly, mournfully, forlornly, despondently, dejectedly, resignedly, dispiritedly, mirthlessly, morosely, morbidly
- Tragically, desperately, despairingly

TIRED

- Sleepily, tiredly, wearily, drowsily
- Slowly, weakly, feebly, limply, sluggishly, exhaustedly, jadedly, lethargically, listlessly

PAINFUL

- Weakly, wearily, limply, shakily, unsteadily
- Painfully, queasily, helplessly, mortally, fatally
- Sharply, tightly, frantically

50
Connectives

SETTING THE SCENE

- A year ago
- A month ago
- Last week
- One evening towards the end of summer . . .
- The first promise of spring began to stir, when . . .
- Bitterly cold winds scattered the leaves and announced the arrival of winter.

MOVING THE ACTION ON A FEW DAYS, WEEKS, MONTHS

- The next few days . . .
- The next couple of days passed . . .
- For the first few days,
- Over the next few days,
- For two days and nights,
- After days of (travelling, waiting) . . .
- In just a few days,
- More than a day went by before . . .
- The days that followed were . . . (a nightmare)
- On the fourth morning,
- The following day,
- The next day . . .
- A day later . . .
- After a day's rest,
- The rest of the day was . . .

(Day can be substituted with week or month)

MOVING THE ACTION ON A FEW HOURS

- As the hours passed, he began to grow more and more (nervous)
- Hours later
- Hour after hour they trudged on through . . .
- It was almost three hours since . . .
- Through the hours that followed . . .
- After several hours,
- The time limped by while he waited for . . .
- In just a few hours
- Within an hour

CHANGING THE TIME OF DAY AND MOVING ON TO THE NEXT DAY

NIGHT TIME

- That evening (night),
- Later that night,
- It was beginning to get dark . . .
- As darkness fell,
- As the sun began to fall,
- At the end of the day,
- As the light started to fade,
- It was almost dusk when . . .
- It was getting darker by the moment.
- She spent the night . . .
- Before they were swallowed in the darkness, they . . .
- They travelled through the night, not daring to stop despite their exhaustion.

MOVING ON TO THE NEXT DAY

- He slumped down and fell into a deep sleep.
- He sank into an exhausted sleep.
- That night he dreamed of . . .
- Huddled under the bedclothes, he eventually fell asleep.
- He stared into the darkness, reliving the day's events until he was finally overcome by tiredness.
- . . . was the last thing he saw before he finally fell asleep.

MORNING

- The following morning,
- When morning came . . .
- When he opened his eyes the next morning,
- The sun was rising in the sky.

- After hours of darkness, the sun finally rose.
- The dawn of the new day was grey and overcast.
- It was daylight when he woke.
- It was so early that no-one was stirring.
- A faint glimmer of light began to creep out of the gloom.
- It was still dark when he was jolted awake by . . .
- The sound of . . . made him open his eyes.
- Just before dawn he was awakened by . . .
- He woke with a start to . . . (loud voices and tramping feet).
- He opened his eyes slowly, the memories of the previous day's events throbbing in his head.

LATER IN THE DAY

- After breakfast,
- In the middle of the afternoon,
- It was late in the morning when . . .
- The sun was still high in the sky when they reached . . .

CONNECTING ACTION SCENES

FIRST ACTION

- First of all,
- At first,
- The first thing he did was . . .

ALTERNATIVES FOR NEXT, THEN

- Later,
- A second later,
- Within seconds,
- For a fraction of a second,
- A minute passed . . .
- For one short moment,
- Within a few minutes,
- Shortly after that . . .
- Before long,
- Not long afterwards,
- Just then,
- Next moment,
- The next thing he knew . . .
- He hesitated a moment and then . . .

INSTANT REACTION

- At once,
- Almost at once,
- At the same time,
- At that very moment,
- As if on cue,
- Immediately,
- Instantly,
- Wasting no time, he . . .
- Without a second's hesitation,
- Not a moment too soon,
- Already he was . . .
- Almost from the moment when they . . .
- Even as he spoke (watched, listened) . . .
- As he watched (listened, waited, walked, ran, left, approached),
- Suddenly,
- Without warning,
- All of a sudden,
- Quickly,
- Abruptly,
- Without delay,

CONCLUDING THE ACTION

- At last,
- In the end,
- After it was over,
- After all of that,
- Eventually,
- When he got back,
- When he looked back,
- When he had finished,
- For a long time, he . . .
- When he finally,
- In the final moments before . . .
- Looking neither left nor right, he (walked) . . .
- Without even a glance,
- He waited a while and then . . .
- From then on,
- From that day on,
- From that day forward,
- Ever since,
- The months that followed were . . .
- Six months later,

50 *Additional vocabulary: connectives*

CHANGING SETTING

LEAVING

- Leaving the (wood) behind, he . . .
- He left the last of the houses behind and . . .
- With each step, his home fell further and further behind him.
- He turned and walked out of the room (house, building).
- The sea gradually slipped away.

THE JOURNEY

- As they travelled north,
- They set off travelling south towards . . .
- They headed for . . .
- The first leg of the journey took them . . .
- After an hour or so on the road,
- He walked for hours before he came to . . .
- Hour after hour they trudged on . . .

NEW SETTING

- Far off in the distance,
- About half a mile away,
- Within a few miles,
- A little further on,
- In the distance,
- Some distance away,
- Every so often he saw . . .
- Sweeping views of . . .
- Looming in the distance . . .
- Towering above her,
- Just beyond the . . .
- All around them were . . .
- As far as the eye could see were . . .
- Stretching endlessly before her were . . .
- The gloom lifted to reveal . . .
- Blocking the path were . . .
- When they finally reached the other side,
- By the time they reached,
- As they approached,
- They came to a place where . . .
- A little further on,
- Within a few miles,
- They had reached . . .

- Ahead of him,
- In front of him,
- Above him,
- Overhead,
- Below him,
- Beneath,
- Underneath,
- Behind him,
- At the other side,
- Across the . . .
- Opposite him,
- Beyond the
- Next to him . . .
- Near the . . .
- On the edge of the . . .
- Outside,
- Inside,
- Once inside,
- On one side,
- Away to the right (left),
- Between

Part 5
Grammar in a creative context
'The forest'

Overview

The chapters in Part 5 provide models (poems, sentences, passages) that teach pupils how to embed description and imagery in their writing by using phrases and sentence structures in accordance with the requirements of the National Curriculum, but in a creative context. The whole unit has been based on a forest setting.

CHAPTER 51 – POETRY

This starts with modelling the structures in a variety of poems, which provides an ideal opportunity for developing a vocabulary bank for that particular setting. It also enables the focus to be broken down into small 'chunks,' to be imitated, practised and, therefore, absorbed.

CHAPTER 52 – MODELLED SENTENCES

The vocabulary accumulated through writing the poems is then used in a series of modelled sentences. Punctuation and sentence structure are important to convey meaning, paint a clear picture and create an atmosphere. The curriculum requirements have, therefore, been split into three categories:

1. Detail (D)
2. Flow (F)
3. Impact (I)

The DFI sentences can be used to:

★ examine incorporating the structure into a sentence, and experiment with its placement
★ discuss the requisite punctuation
★ describe another setting
★ collect a number of sentence structures and descriptions in an action frame to form the basis for a piece of writing.

Each sentence is on a display card for class demonstration and discussion.
All of the words in each sentence have been printed onto a flash card for experimenting with:

- ★ constructing the sentence
- ★ innovating the sentence.

They can also be used to focus on the choice of verb, adverb, fronted adverbial, prepositional phrase, etc. For example:

- ★ Circle the focus.
- ★ On blank flash cards, write alternatives and experiment by substituting them with the original.
- ★ Discuss the merits of each.

A limited vocabulary has been used in order to demonstrate the effectiveness of different sentence structures, orders, length, detail, etc. When writing, pupils must remember *APE – audience, purpose and effect*. Experimenting with a number of the models provides an invaluable opportunity to discuss how different structures and degree of detail are appropriate in different contexts and at different points within a text.

CHAPTER 53 – ACTION FRAMES

Why does a final piece of creative writing not always match up to the fantastic, imaginative ideas for a story at the brainstorming stage? Why is it so difficult to maintain the threads of a story and the creativity? Inadequate planning is more often than not the explanation. Using *action frames* provides a system that limits the breadth of the planning required, but gives it far more focus. The story can be broken down into individual sections, then those sections broken down even further into 'scenes'. The action frame also helps to develop the plot and descriptions in far more detail by providing a prompt to consider the following:

- ★ Are there any questions that need to be answered?
- ★ Is there any additional description that can be included?

The forest setting has been used to develop a story involving a wolf chase. A model of an action frame has been included to demonstrate the types of questions to consider when planning, along with a collection of descriptive phrases and ideas for each scene. A blank action frame is included on the companion website (www.routledge.com/cw/wilcox).

CHAPTER 54 – SETTING/CHARACTER, INTERACTION AND REACTION (S/C-I-R)

Effective writing:

- ★ describes the setting
- ★ moves the characters through the setting
- ★ describes the characters' reactions to what they see or the events in which they are involved.

The work on poems, modelled sentences and the action frame have then been used to write an example piece of text.

Other example passages for S/C-I-R have been included on the companion website. Their purpose is to demonstrate how to balance a description in respect of setting, character, action and emotions. Some of the plots and locations have been specifically chosen to provide opportunities for cross-curricular writing.

Each example has been split into basic, individual sentences to be used for:

- ★ experimenting with combining and varying order, structure and length
- ★ trying different ways of starting sentences.

The S/C-I-R passages can also be used to stimulate discussion:

- ★ How do they end?
- ★ Who is the main character? Why are they at the location?
- ★ How are they structured? Consider choice of words, phrases, conjunctions, length of sentences.
- ★ Highlight descriptions of setting, character, interaction and reaction to examine how they are interwoven.

They may also be used to prompt further writing:

- ★ Write the ending.
- ★ Create character descriptions and profiles.
- ★ Use the example and the action frame to scaffold a similar piece of writing.
- ★ Rewrite the passage in the present tense or first person.

Writing Tips and Hooks provide additional assistance for linking writing, signalling an event, and building suspense and atmosphere. They can be found on the companion website (www.routledge.com/cw/wilcox).

51

Poetry

Poems for:

- ★ **Vocabulary development**
- ★ **Target phrases and clauses**
- ★ **Sentence structure**
- ★ **Experimenting with:**
  - ☆ **Word, phrase and clause order**
  - ☆ **Repetition for impact.**

FORBIDDEN FOREST I

(NOUN PHRASES, ADJECTIVES AND VERBS)

A gloomy, twisted labyrinth
Dense, towering, endless
Circled, spread, engulfed
Tangled thicket, twisting trails

A sharp, barbed barricade
Spiky, spiny, needle-sharp
Grabbed, clutched, tripped
Bleached branches, rotting roots

Flitting, leafy shadows
Shivering, shuddering, shaking
Flickered, flashed, faded
Ghostly eyes, quivering shapes

Haunting, prickly murmur
Soft, faint, muffled
Sighed, hummed, whistled
Whispered secrets, hissed threats

Stiff, icy fingers
Sharp, gnarled, dagger-like
Pulled, tugged, grasped
Wooden tentacles, bony fingers

Damp, stinking reek
Bitter, foul, rank
Seeped, surged, lingered
Rancid fumes, retching cough

FORBIDDEN FOREST II

(EXPANDED NOUN PHRASES, ADJECTIVES AND VERBS)

A dark, tangled maze,
With hidden tunnels and secret paths
Spread, stretched, arched
Gloomy, eerie, menacing

A tangled, thorny web,
With barbed barriers and spiked traps
Grasped, clutched, scratched
Pointed, prickly, razor-sharp

A misty, brooding cloak,
With flickering figures and shuddering shadows
Floated, swayed, danced
Crooked, ghostly, sinister

A frosty wintry breeze,
With rustling leaves and snapping twigs
Whispered, whined, groaned
Chilly, gusting, stammering

A mucky, swampy bog
Of sticky mud and squelching sludge
Slid, slithered, squirmed
Wet, slimy, syrupy

A smoky, peaty stench
Of rotten eggs and decaying mushrooms
Rose, wafted, choked
Damp, festering, rancid

51 *Grammar in a creative context: poetry*

THE ENCHANTED FOREST

(NOUN PHRASES, ADJECTIVES AND VERBS)

A breathtaking, vibrant forest
Bright, vivid, spectacular
Emerald cloaks, colourful creepers
Lit, painted, covered

A rich velvety layer
Gold, blue, purple
Blazing carpet, dazzling blossoms
Sparkled, glistened, shimmered

Warm, gentle breeze
Calm, peaceful, soothing
Fluttering leaves, dancing blossoms
Sighed, rustled, murmured

Smooth, soft stroke
Sleek, shiny, glossy
Swaying feathers, silky carpet
Tapped, brushed, tickled

Fresh, sweet scent
Aromatic, fragrant, divine
Delicate fragrance, rich perfume
Rose, wafted, drifted

HAIKU

Dark, dense labyrinth
Tangled thicket, twisting trails
Sharp, spiky, spiny

Tiny bells of blue
A swaying sapphire tide
Tinkling in the sun

A sea of colour
Vivid velvety layers
Gold, orange and red

CINQUAIN

Shadows
Gloomy, eerie
Hidden tunnels, lost paths
Sinister shapes, crooked figures
Ghostly

Welcome
Glory of spring
Pale ivory clusters
Dazzling, delicate, scented bells
Snowdrops

Waves
Spring daffodils
Dancing in the warm breeze
Long, yellow, tubular trumpets
Stunning

A TOUCH

(SYNONYMS AND APPOSITIVE PHRASES)

A touch, a warm breath, brushes my face
A touch, a bitter, icy gust, stings the back of my neck
A touch, a needle-sharp point, scratches my hand
A touch, a sleek slap, slithers across my shoe
A touch, a swish of hairy wings, grabs at my hair.

THE ANCIENT YEW TREE

(PREPOSITIONAL PHRASES AND EXPANDED NOUN PHRASES)

Over the medieval churchyard, it guards,
with its brown, scaly trunk.
Across the ground, it crawls,
with its knuckled, gnarled roots.
Into a vaulted ceiling, it spreads,
with its thick, splintered stem.
Over the wall, it reaches,
With its bony, arm-like tentacles.
Inside the enormous trunk, it hides
With its secret, ancient hollow.

51 *Grammar in a creative context: poetry*

SENSES POEM

(TENSES: PRESENT PERFECT AND PRESENT CONTINUOUS)

I have heard the leaves rustling in the wind.
I have heard their whispered threats.
I have heard the snapping of a twig.
I have seen the darkened spaces.
I have seen the ghostly shadows cloaked in mist.
I have touched the dagger-like thorns.
I have smelled the decaying carpet of rotting leaves.
I have felt the squelching mud around my ankles.
And a strange sensation is gripping the back of my neck.

She has heard the alarm call for the forest.
She has heard the birds singing at dawn.
She has heard their joyful chorus.
She has seen the sun rise in an explosion of orange.
She has touched the liquid diamonds of the morning dew.
She has felt the crunch of frosty leaves beneath her feet.
She has smelled the sweet scent of pine needles.
And a wonderful glow of happiness is pulsing in her veins.

THE CHASE I

(ADVERBS, PREPOSITIONAL PHRASES AND COMPOUND VERBS)

Slowly,
towards the ruined archway,
he slunk and slithered.

Suddenly,
in the trees, a flickering movement,
he glimpsed and noted.

Urgently,
under the cover of a bush,
he sank and dropped.

Anxiously,
between the prickly thorns,
he crouched and hid.

Instantly,
to the other side of the bush,
he spun and whirled.

Frantically,
out of the reach of the claws,
he jerked and ducked.

Quickly,
away from its slavering jaws,
he scuttled and scurried.

Desperately,
through the tangled undergrowth,
he darted and dashed.

Constantly,
in the slimy swamp,
he slipped and stumbled.

THE CHASE II

(SUBORDINATE CLAUSES, COMPOUND VERBS AND PREPOSITIONAL PHRASES)

In case someone was watching,
he crawled, and slithered
closer to the ruined archway.

While he was looking for the entrance,
he glimpsed and noted
a flickering movement in the trees.

When he spotted the movement,
he froze, and waited
in the shadows.

Before he could be spotted,
he ducked, and crawled
under the cover of the bush.

Because he was terrified of the thundering steps,
he crouched, and huddled
between the prickly thorns.

When it got close to where he was hiding,
he spun, and rolled
to the other side of the bush.

Because it had spotted his movement,
it clawed and thrashed
at the undergrowth.

As it attacked,
he ducked and dodged
away from the dagger-like claws.

While it was thrashing at the undergrowth,
he scuttled and scrabbled
out of his hiding place.

Before it could spot him,
he darted and hurtled
down the twisting trail.

Because the path was uneven,
he slipped and stumbled
towards the entrance.

THE CHASE III

(FRONTED ADVERBIALS, COMPOUND VERBS AND PREPOSITIONAL PHRASES)

As quietly as he could,
he slunk and slithered, crept and crawled,
closer to the ruined archway.

Out of the corner of his eye,
he peered and peeked, glanced and glimpsed,
a flickering movement in the trees.

Without waiting a moment longer,
he stopped and froze, watched and waited,
in the shadows.

As quick as lightning,
he ducked and sank, dived and crawled,
under the cover of the bush.

With every thudding step towards him,
he crouched and sprawled, hid and huddled,
deeper and deeper between the prickly thorns.

Moments later,
he spun and whirled, rolled and slid,
to the other side of the bush.

A hair's breadth from his face,
it clawed and thrashed, sliced and carved,
through the undergrowth.

Not a moment too soon,
he jerked and ducked, swayed and dodged,
away from the dagger-like claws.

As quickly as he could,
he scuttled and scurried, scrambled and scrabbled,
out of his hiding place.

Without looking back,
he darted and dashed, bolted and hurtled,
down the twisting trail.

Again and again,
he slipped and stumbled, tripped and tumbled,
on the uneven path.

ACTIVE AND PASSIVE

Towering trees formed dark tunnels.
Dark tunnels were formed (by. . .)

The huge canopy blocked out the light.
The light was blocked out (by. . .)

The tangled thicket created secret paths.
Secret paths were created (by. . .)

The gnarled trunks concealed an ancient secret.
An ancient secret was concealed (by. . .)

Bleached, wooden tentacles blocked the path.
The path was blocked (by. . .)

A blanket of mist shrouded the trees.
The trees were shrouded (by. . .)

51 *Grammar in a creative context: poetry*

CONJUNCTIONS

When the spidery tangle of trees and bushes smothers the path;
When rotting leaves hide the roots that wriggle across the ground;
When the thick tangled branches spread and twist to form dark
overhead tunnels and secret paths;
When the ceiling of thick branches shuts out the sky;
When the path is covered in darkness;
When the branches twist and grate against each other like rusty hinges;
When the creepers strangle the trees,
then the forest has become a forbidden, impenetrable maze.

Until you have seen the magnificent forest of majestic trees like vivid
green umbrellas;
Until you have observed their beautiful green cloaks;
Until you have glimpsed the brightly coloured creepers like party streamers;
Until you have spotted the swaying tide of blazing bluebells;
Until you have stared in amazement at the pale ivory snowdrops with
their dainty drooping bells;
Until you have marvelled at the glistening icicles like liquid diamonds
hanging from the branches,
then you haven't fully wondered at the magic of nature.

FORBIDDEN FOREST

(PRESENT PARTICIPLE PHRASES AND PREPOSITIONAL PHRASES)

Arching tunnels stretching endlessly towards the shadows,
scratching barriers spread across the trails,
tangling trap clutching at limbs.
The menacing forbidden forest, a dark secretive maze, looms ahead.
At dusk,
in the ghostly grey,
in the shivering shadows,
with a sinister dance,
from the whistling breeze.

THE STORM

(APPOSITIVE PHRASE AND PARTICIPLE PHRASES)

The wind, a frosty wintry breeze, whined and howled,
rushing through the undergrowth,
rustling the leaves,
bending the branches,
stealing the leaves,
chasing the fallen leaves in circles.

USING THE INFINITIVE

Wherever he looked, wherever he moved,
the tangled, thorny barriers were a spiked trap:
to grasp at his arms,
to clutch at his ankles,
to scratch at his face,
to capture him in their barbed spider's web –
a prickly barricade guarding the trail.

52

Modelled sentences

Detail, flow, impact (DFI)

SECTION A – DETAIL

- ★ Expanded noun phrases (ENP) and similes
- ★ Relative clauses
- ★ Appositive phrases
- ★ Fronted adverbials
- ★ Prepositional phrases

EXPANDED NOUN PHRASES (ENP) AND SIMILES

The secret, ancient forest loomed ahead of them.

They were faced with **a dark, dense, impenetrable forest**.

The leafy shadows flickered eerily in the moonlight.

The colourful blossoms danced gleefully in the wind.

Clusters of dazzling yellow daffodils nodded their heads in greeting.

Thickets of gnarled, vicious vines blocked the **narrow** path.

The oak tree had a trunk *like melting candle wax.*

The yew tree had a trunk *like an enormous cavern.*

Cloaked in mist, the trees looked *like ghostly, stooped figures.*

Carpeted in bluebells, the forest floor looked *like a swaying sapphire tide.*

He was greeted by **wave after wave of dazzling yellow daffodils.**

He was greeted by **wave after wave of the nodding yellow heads of dazzling daffodils.**

The entrance was blocked by **wave after wave of vicious thorns.**

The entrance was blocked by **wave after wave of the piercing barbed needles of vicious thorns.**

It was **a secret, ancient forest** with **huge towering trees.**

The forest floor, with its thick layer of pine needles, muffled her footsteps.

The forest floor, with its layer of crispy golden leaves, crunched under her feet.

The ceiling of thick tangled branches, *like a crooked arch*, covered the path in **flickering shadows**.

The carpet of pale ivory snowdrops, *like dainty drooping bells*, covered the clearing in **a rippling white cloak**.

She had entered **a mystical, magical forest of ancient yew trees with enormous crooked trunks**.

She waded through **a swaying tide of blazing** bluebells: their delicate, fragrant scent wafted through the air.

RELATIVE CLAUSES

The wind, **which hissed through the trees**, sounded like whispered threats.

The wind, **which sighed through the trees**, sounded like soothing whispers.

The forest floor was a writhing, buzzing cloud of bugs **that flitted and scuttled through the undergrowth.**

She skipped through the crispy golden leaves, **which crunched under her feet.**

She edged deeper into the tangled thicket, **whose branches twisted together to form a gloomy tunnel.**

She crept into the shadows, **where her footsteps were muffled by a thick layer of pine needles.**

The forest, **which had magnificent ancient yew trees and narrow, twisting trails,** was mystical and magical.

The hunting howl, **whose loud hoot pierced the silence,** suddenly flew above them like a white shadow.

The track, **which seemed to get narrower with every step,** was littered with fallen trees, patches of bramble and strips of swampy ground.

They headed deeper into the forest, **where the path narrowed and where the tangled spider's web of thorns had blocked the path.**

APPOSITIVE PHRASES

The forest floor, **a layer of crispy golden leaves**, crunched under her feet.

It was an ancient forest, **a magical forest**, with magnificent towering trees.

Ivory snowdrops, **dainty drooping bells**, carpeted the forest floor.

They waded through a blazing carpet of bluebells, **a swaying, knee-deep tide,** whose delicate, fragrant scent lingered in the air.

The forest floor, **a writhing, buzzing carpet**, was covered in flitting, scuttling bugs and beetles, midges and termites.

The forest floor, **a thick layer of pine needles**, muffled her footsteps as she moved through the shadows.

52 *Grammar in a creative context: modelled sentences*

FRONTED ADVERBIALS

Ahead of them, a narrow, uneven path twisted through the trees.

In the moonlight, the trees were like crooked, ghostly figures.

In the shadows around the trees, the squelching mud clutched at their feet.

Beneath his feet, the tangled undergrowth grasped at his ankles.

Beneath his feet, the tangled undergrowth grasped at his ankles, making him slip, stumble and fall constantly.

Above the trees, clouds like fluffy cotton balls drifted across the sky, while below, autumn's crackling leaves rushed across the ground.

All of a sudden, an icy wintry breeze whined and creaked through the bare branches.

During the storm, the petals had been shaken off the bush, and lay like a carpet of pink confetti on the floor.

In the blink of an eye, the storm arrived to bow the trees, shake their branches and steal their leaves.

Within minutes, the branches were bare: stripped of their autumn cloaks.

Every morning in November, dewdrops like liquid diamonds dangled from the branches.

PREPOSITIONAL PHRASES

The sound of the wind **among the trees** ceased abruptly.

Their path **through the dense undergrowth** wound in and out.

Their path through the dense undergrowth wound in and out: **around the tangled, thorny barriers; over the trunks of fallen trees; under low branches; through the gloomy vault** formed by the huge oak trees.

The forest **to her left** was an endless dark labyrinth of trees.

The forest **to her left** was an endless dark labyrinth of trees, but **to her right,** the moonlit clouds glowed through the branches.

SECTION B – FLOW

- ★ Coordinating conjunctions
- ★ Subordinating conjunctions
- ★ Word, phrase, clause order
- ★ Participle phrases
- ★ Parentheses
- ★ Semi-colon
- ★ Colon

COORDINATING CONJUNCTIONS: FANBOYS (FOR, AND, NOR, BUT, OR, YET, SO)

BEGINNER

The forest was a dark tangled maze, **and** it was impossible to find a way through.

He was now in the middle of the forest, **and** surrounded by blackness on all sides.

The branches swayed in the wind, **and** their leaves fluttered like graceful butterflies.

They had found a path, **but** their progress through the tangled thicket was slow.

The forest was usually full of sound, **but** it had fallen strangely silent.

There was nothing she could do, **so** she stayed absolutely still.

INTERMEDIATE

He quickened his pace, **but** the ground was uneven.

He quickened his pace, but the ground was uneven **and** he stumbled.

He quickened his pace, **but** the ground was uneven **and** he stumbled, crashing to the ground.

It was easy to imagine something hiding in the shadows **or** someone watching her from behind the trees.

She was intrigued by the rich perfume that wafted towards her, **so** she followed the scent until she came across a blazing carpet of bluebells.

ADVANCED

He kept looking over his shoulder, **for** in his mind every shadow in the wood had grown eyes.

There was a growing unease among them as they wound their way through the wood, **for** its dark recesses could conceal any number of dangers.

He did not see the vine stretching across the path, **nor** the fallen tree covered in rotting leaves.

Neither the thick layer of pine needles **nor** the carpet of leaves could totally muffle their footsteps.

He was crouched in the shadows, **yet** ready to move quickly.

His knees were rubbery, **yet** he kept moving as quickly as he could.

His knees were rubbery, his arms and legs splattered with sticky, squelching mud that clung to his feet, **yet** he kept moving as quickly as he could.

There was nothing she could do, **so** she stayed absolutely still **and** hoped she wouldn't be seen, **for** she knew the slightest movement would give her away.

SUBORDINATE CLAUSES

If he stopped and listened, he could hear the branches creaking in the wind.

If he waited any longer, it would be getting dark.

If he waited any longer, it would be getting dark, and hide what lay behind the trees.

If he waited any longer, it would be getting dark, hiding what lay behind the trees – watching and waiting.

He did not see the roots that wriggled across the ground **because they were hidden by layers of rotting leaves.**

When winter came, icy frosts coated the trees, the bushes, the undergrowth.

An eerie gloom filled the clearing **when patches of misty light shone through the gaps in the trees.**

When he took a step forward, he could feel the oozing mud of the swamp suddenly squelching beneath his feet.

Before winter had spread its chill over the forest, clusters of purple and pink blossoms had covered the bushes.

After the sun had spread its glittering rays, the forest was bathed in a hazy golden light.

While she had stumbled through the tangled thicket, the sun had fallen like a sinking stone, and a black cloud had been drawn across the sky.

The wind pounded at the trees **until it had bent their branches and stolen their leaves**.

Although it was the middle of the day, the ceiling of thick branches shut out the light.

Where the branches had spread to form an arched ceiling, the ground was a muddy swamp.

As winter spread its icy breath over the forest, dewdrops like liquid diamonds clung to the branches.

The branches began to form a gloomy tunnel **as she edged deeper into the thicket.**

PARTICIPLE PHRASES

The forest, **spreading in all directions,** was a gloomy, twisting labyrinth.

Tearing at her arms and legs, the sharp, barbed barricade was a spider's web of needle-sharp thorns.

Hissing through the trees, the wind sounded like whispered threats.

Flickering in the moonlight, the leafy shadows looked like ghostly eyes.

Grasping at her clothes, tearing at her arms and legs, the stiff, dagger-like thorns were sharp fingernails.

The dense undergrowth tugged at her feet, trying to trip her.

The dense undergrowth tugged at her feet, **trying to trip her, throwing up gnarled, ankle-twisting roots and impenetrable walls of thorns and brambles.**

Swinging her legs, wrapping them around the branch, she pulled herself on to it.

Swinging her legs, wrapping them around the branch, she pulled herself on to it, then reached from branch to branch until she found a fork in the branches where she could sit and keep watch.

Leaping up, Scarlett threw herself at a lower branch of the tree.

Leaping up, Scarlett threw herself at a lower branch of the tree, **grasped the branch and scrambled upwards.**

Resting on his hands and knees, he sucked in air.

Resting on his hands and knees, his shoulders heaving, he sucked in air.

Resting on his hands and knees, his shoulders heaving as he sucked in air, Tom slowly raised his head.

PARENTHESIS

(There are also examples within the other sections)

The branches, **gnarled bony fingers**, reached an arm-like tentacle over the wall.

Ahead, they spotted a narrow path **– an uneven, treacherous, ankle-twisting path –** disappearing into the thicket.

Clusters of vivid, colourful blossoms**, purples, reds, blues and yellows,** cloaked the forest.

Like a carpet of jewels **(amethysts, rubies, sapphires),** clusters of dazzling blossoms painted the forest floor in a rainbow of vivid colour.

The yew tree – **huge, ancient, scaly** – climbed almost horizontally out of the ground.

SEMI-COLON

He was crouched in the shadows; he was ready to move quickly.

They moved deeper into the forest to where the path ended, and Scarlett halted; she wondered whether she should double back or follow the mat of creeping, dark green weed.

Usually, the forest was full of sound; it had suddenly fallen strangely silent.

He slid and scrambled up the bank; his feet were struggling to get a grip in the mud.

There was nothing she could do; she stayed absolutely still.

It was easy to imagine something hiding in the shadows; to imagine someone watching her from behind the trees.

COLON

There was a growing unease among them as they wound their way through the wood: its dark recesses could conceal any number of dangers.

He kept looking over his shoulder: in his mind every shadow in the wood had grown eyes.

His foot caught on a vine across the path: a vine dotted with vicious thorns, concealed by the dense undergrowth like cunning tripwire.

He was searching for a single yew tree in the centre of the forest: an ancient yew, with a gnarled, splintered trunk that had created a hollow cavern in its centre.

It was a dense, dark forest with eerie mazes and dangerous traps: secret paths and hidden swamps, impenetrable walls of thorns and brambles.

Vicious vines, like barbed wire, blocked the clearing: their needle-sharp thorns clutched at the arms and legs of anyone who dared to enter.

As branches swayed in the wind, he quickened his pace: his mind imagined that every shadow in the wood had grown eyes.

52 *Grammar in a creative context: modelled sentences*

SECTION C – IMPACT

- ★ Changing the order
- ★ Opening adjectives
- ★ Delayed adjectives
- ★ Opening adverbs
- ★ Delayed adverbs
- ★ Compound verbs
- ★ Repetition and emphasis

CHANGING THE ORDER

They had entered a secret, ancient forest.

A secret, ancient forest loomed before them.

Frozen liquid diamonds hung from every branch.

Hanging from every branch were frozen liquid diamonds.

Magnificent towering trees guarded the entrance to the ancient wood.

Guarding the entrance to the ancient wood were magnificent towering trees.

The entrance to the ancient wood was guarded by magnificent towering trees.

The forest had a carpet of pale ivory snowdrops with dainty drooping bells.

Pale ivory snowdrops, with dainty drooping bells, carpeted the forest.

The forest was carpeted by pale ivory snowdrops with dainty drooping bells.

The trees were cloaked in mist that made the trees look like ghostly, stooped figures leaning towards each other.

Cloaked in mist, the trees looked like ghostly, stooped figures leaning towards each other.

Vicious vines, like barbed wire, blocked the clearing.

Like barbed wire, vicious vines blocked the clearing,

The clearing was blocked by vicious vines like barbed wire.

OPENING ADJECTIVES

Prickly and **needle-sharp**, the undergrowth was a thorny spider's web.

Towering and **majestic**, the trees stood tall and proud.

Rich, vivid and **velvety**, the blossoms painted the bushes with splashes of dazzling colour.

As dry as bone, the blanket of dead leaves crunched under his feet.

Clad in their beautiful, fiery autumn cloaks, the trees swayed in the wind: their leaves fluttered like graceful butterflies.

Deeper and deeper, darker and darker, the trail twisted and turned through the forest: under the gloomy vault formed by the huge oak trees; across the dense undergrowth and around the tangled, thorny barriers.

Desperate, he searched for the trail between the spidery knot of trees and bushes.

DELAYED ADJECTIVES

The trees, **towering** and **majestic**, stood **tall** and **proud**.

A thicket, **tangled, gnarled** and **thorny**, guarded the entrance.

Blossoms, **rich**, **vivid** and **velvety**, painted the bushes with splashes of **dazzling** colour.

The undergrowth, **prickly** and **needle-sharp**, was a **thorny** spider's web.

Trunks, **thick, twisted** and **splintered**, spread into an arched ceiling.

OPENING ADVERBS

Up and up, the trees stretched towards the sky.

Overhead, the huge canopy of treetops joined together like a crowd of vivid green umbrellas.

Instantly, the ground was painted with flickering shadows.

Around and around, the leaves swirled as the frosty gusts chased them along the ground.

Soon, the gusts of frosty air will arrive to steal the leaves from the branches.

DELAYED ADVERBS

The trees stretched **up and up** towards the sky.

The huge canopy of treetops **overhead** joined together like a crowd of vivid green umbrellas.

The leaves swirled **around and around** as the frosty gusts chased them along the ground.

The gusts of frosty air will **soon** arrive to steal the leaves from the branches.

Clusters of purple blossoms drooped **sleepily** from the branches: **drowsy and dozy** in the warm summer sun.

The trees tossed their branches **upwards** and flung their leaves to the sky.

The ground was **instantly** painted with flickering shadows.

COMPOUND VERBS

The trees **floated, swayed and danced** in the moonlight.

The haunting, prickly murmur of the wind **sighed through trees**, **whistled through the branches** and **crackled through the canopy.**

The stiff, icy fingers of the thorns **pulled, tugged and grasped at his clothes, hair and arms.**

The stiff, icy fingers of the thorns **pulled at his clothes**, **tugged at his hair**, **grasped at his arms.**

The damp, stinking reek from the swamp **seeped from the ground**, **surged through the trees** and **lingered in the air.**

The fiery scarlet leaves **fluttered in the breeze**, **quivered on their branches and floated to the ground** to dance on gusts of frosty air.

The ceiling of thick branches were locked together, **shutting out the light, covering the path in shadows**, **painting flickering shadows on the trees.**

REPETITION AND EMPHASIS

Rain-drenched, fresh, vibrant, blooming with new growth, spring had enveloped the forest.

Dazzling, breathtaking, spectacular golden blossoms hung in masses from vivid green stems.

Prickly and needle-sharp, tangled and thorny, the undergrowth was a spiked spider's web.

On and on, wave after wave of blazing bluebells greeted them as they entered the clearing.

On and on, mile after mile, they trudged through the gloomy vault: across the dense undergrowth, around the tangled, thorny barriers, over the trunks of fallen trees, under low branches.

Viciously, venomously, the vines, like barbed wire, grasped at the arms and legs of anyone daring to enter.

Gently, soothingly, the wind sighed through the trees, stirred her hair and tickled her face.

The matted creepers **slithered along the floor and around the trunks,** strangling them in their slimy grasp.

The morning dew **crept up the trunk and around the leaves** to hang like liquid diamonds.

Every morning in November, when winter had spread its frosty chill over the forest, the dewdrops like crystal earrings dangled from the branches.

When the thick tangled branches spread and twist to form dark, overhead tunnels and secret paths; **when** the creepers strangle the trees; **when** darkness covers the paths, the forest has truly become a forbidden, impenetrable maze.

Until you have seen the magnificent forest of majestic trees with their beautiful green cloaks; **until you have glimpsed** the brightly coloured creepers like party streamers; **until you have stared** in amazement at the pale ivory snowdrops with their dainty drooping bells, you haven't fully wondered at the magic of nature.

Wherever he looked, **wherever he stepped,** the tangled, thorny barriers threatened to clutch at his ankles, to grasp at his arms, to scratch at his face.

Wherever he looked, spring was ready, **to wake** the forest from its wintry slumber, **to thrust** emerald shoots out of the ground, **to paint** the hills in reds, yellows and greens, **to sprinkle** tiny diamonds on the streams.

The deeper he went into the forest, the more he realised that it would be impossible **to find a way through** the gloomy, twisted labyrinth, **to negotiate** the tangled thicket, **to find** a way out.

53

Action frames

The wolf chase

BLANK:			
Action Frame	**EVENTS/IDEAS:**	**THINK ABOUT:** **Describe when, how, why, what, where** **Use powerful verbs**	**Vocabulary/phrases**
1.		Describe location. What does the character hear? What does the character see? How does the character feel? What does the character do?	

BLANK:			
Action Frame	**EVENTS/IDEAS:**	**THINK ABOUT:** **Describe when, how, why, what, where** **Use powerful verbs**	**Vocabulary/phrases**
2.		What does the character do? Describe what the character: • Sees • Hears • Smells • Touches How does the character feel?	

BLANK:			
Action Frame	**EVENTS/IDEAS:**	**THINK ABOUT:** **Describe when, how, why, what, where** **Use powerful verbs**	**Vocabulary/phrases**
3.		How does the character feel? What can the character hear, see, smell, touch? What does the character do?	

BLANK:			
Action Frame	**EVENTS/IDEAS:**	**THINK ABOUT:**	**Vocabulary/phrases**
4.		What does the villain look like? Describe the location. How does it attack? How does the character escape? How does she move? How does she feel? Does the character have any help?	

BLANK:			
Action Frame	**EVENTS/IDEAS:**	**THINK ABOUT:**	**Vocabulary/phrases**
5.		How does the character move? What obstacles does she face? How does she feel?	

BLANK:
BUILDING A SCENE:

OUTLINE:			
Action Frame	**EVENTS/IDEAS:**	**THINK ABOUT:** **Describe when, how, why, what, where** **Use powerful verbs**	**Vocabulary/phrases**
1.	Lost in the middle of a forest and it is getting dark The forest has gone quiet – hears a noise Spots a movement through the trees	Describe the location. What does the character hear? What does the character see? How does the character feel? What does the character do?	Dark, tangled maze of narrow paths and jagged, thorny barriers Deeper she went, the darker it became Forest had been full of noise – birds fluttered in the trees; squirrels scampered from branch to branch, but eerie, throbbing silence as dusk fell Heart jumps at every creak and rustle Kept glancing over shoulder Sudden tingling sixth sense Glanced to left – glimpses a flickering movement Stops dead in her tracks

OUTLINE:			
Action Frame	**EVENTS/IDEAS:**	**THINK ABOUT:** **Describe when, how, why, what, where** **Use powerful verbs**	**Vocabulary/phrases**
2.	Hears a creature howling Spots a wolf Hides	What does the wolf do? What does the character do? Describe where the character hides. How does the character feel?	The next thing she knew . . . Forest exploded - howling came from all directions at once Branches snapped like gunshots Crashing through the undergrowth Heading straight towards her For one brief moment . . . Frozen to the spot Heart thudded in her chest Watched in horror as . . . A huge white wolf hurtled towards her through the trees Blind instinct took over from sheer panic Flung herself under the nearest bush Clawed at the ground with her fingers Impossible to bend her legs Pushed with her toes Spikes scratched her arms and legs and face Ignored pain and burrowed deeper into the middle of the bush

OUTLINE:			
Action Frame	**EVENTS/IDEAS:**	**THINK ABOUT:** **Describe when, how, why, what, where** **Use powerful verbs**	**Vocabulary/phrases**
3.	Hidden in the bush Waits, listens and watches Hears the wolf coming closer	How does the character feel? What can the character hear, see, smell, touch? What does the character do?	Tried to steady her breathing. Wanted to get up and run but knew she couldn't Sweat collected on forehead, trickled down the side of her nose into his eyes Squeezed eyes shut, blinked rapidly Didn't dare to raise her hand Hardly dared to breathe Pins and needles stabbed her legs Could hear the wolf's paws thudding closer to where she was crouched in the bushes Could see its ears twitching Could feel its warm, rancid breath wafting against her face Could smell its stale, decaying breath Waited and watched – didn't move a muscle Craned her neck so she could see through the branches For what seemed like an eternity . . .

OUTLINE:			
Action Frame	**EVENTS/IDEAS:**	**THINK ABOUT:**	**Vocabulary/phrases**
4.	Starts to edge her way out of the other side of the bush Comes face to face with the wolf Wolf attacks Evades wolf and is rescued by an owl	How does the character get out of the bush? What does the wolf look like? How does it attack? How does the character escape? How does the character move? How does the character feel?	Inch by inch . . . She edged her way backwards out of the bush Stopped every few seconds to listen for any sounds Just as the undergrowth became less dense . . . A sudden noise behind Scarlett made her whirl round Found herself face to face with the wolf Slavering jaws, pair of long, dripping fangs Claws sliced the air in front of her face Jaws plunged towards her outstretched arm Ducked, scuttled frantically backwards on her elbows Blur of white plummeted out of the night sky Plunged its talons into the wolf's face Launched herself off the ground Broke into a wild, stumbling run Tried to put as much distance between herself and the wolf as possible Horror-struck Hesitated for a brief second Wave of adrenalin surged through her body

OUTLINE:			
Action Frame	**EVENTS/IDEAS:**	**THINK ABOUT:**	**Vocabulary/phrases**
5.	Runs for her life Slips and stumbles	How does the character run? What obstacles does the character face? How does the character feel?	Darted and dodged through the trees Blundered and slipped Fought her way through the undergrowth Grasped at her ankles Lungs were burning Legs were aching Didn't dare stop Even when she fell over a tree root Stumbled onto her face Staggered back to her feet Never once did she turn and look back Just kept on running Chest heaving and gasping for breath

OUTLINE:
BUILDING A SCENE:

<table>
<tr><th colspan="4">MODEL:</th></tr>
<tr><th>Action Frame</th><th>EVENTS/IDEAS:</th><th>THINK ABOUT:
Describe when, how, why, what, where
Use powerful verbs</th><th>Vocabulary/phrases</th></tr>
<tr><td>1.</td><td>Scarlett is lost in the middle of a forest and it is getting dark

The forest has gone quiet and she hears a noise

She spots a movement through the trees</td><td>Describe Scarlett's location.

What does she hear?

What does she see?

How does she feel?

What does she do?</td><td>Dark, tangled maze of narrow paths and jagged, thorny barriers
Deeper she went, the darker it became
Forest had been full of noise – birds fluttered in the trees; squirrels scampered from branch to branch, but eerie, throbbing silence as dusk fell
Heart jumps at every creak and rustle
Kept glancing over her shoulder
Sees a flickering movement to her left
Sudden tingling sixth sense
Glanced to left _ glimpses a flickering movement
Stops dead in her tracks</td></tr>
<tr><td colspan="4">As the night drew a grey cloak across the sky, Scarlett found herself in the middle of the forest, a dark, tangled maze of narrow paths and jagged, thorny barriers that spread, stretched and arched above her. The deeper she went the darker it became. Up until then, the forest had been full of noise: birds fluttering in the trees, squirrels scampering from branch to branch. But as dusk fell, an eerie silence descended on the forest. Scarlett couldn't shake off the sensation that she was being followed. She kept glancing nervously over her shoulder. Every shadow had grown eyes; every branch looked like bony fingers. At every creak and rustle her heart jumped. A sudden, tingling, sixth sense made her glance to her left, and out of the corner of her eye, Scarlett glimpsed a flickering movement. She stopped dead in her tracks.</td></tr>
</table>

MODEL:			
Action Frame	**EVENTS/IDEAS:**	**THINK ABOUT:** **Describe when, how, why, what, where**	**Vocabulary/phrases**
2.	Scarlett hears a creature howling Spots a wolf Hides	What does the wolf do? What does Scarlett do? Describe where she hides. How does she feel?	The next thing she knew . . . Forest exploded – howling came from all directions at once Branches snapped like gunshots Crashing through the undergrowth Heading straight towards her For one brief moment Frozen to the spot Heart thudded in her chest Watch in horror as A huge white wolf hurtled towards her through the trees Blind instinct took over from sheer panic Flung herself under the nearest bush Clawed at the ground with her fingers Impossible to bend her legs Pushed with her toes Spikes scratched her arms and legs and face Ignored pain and burrowed deeper into the middle of the bush

The next thing she knew, the forest exploded. It was as if the howling was coming from all directions at once. Branches snapped like gunshots. Something was crashing through the undergrowth and heading straight towards her. For one brief moment, Scarlett was frozen to the spot; her heart thudded in her chest. She watched in horror as a huge white wolf hurtled towards her through the trees. Then, blind instinct took over from sheer panic and she flung herself down under the nearest bush. She clawed at the ground with her fingers and hauled herself through the spider's web of jagged thorns. It was impossible to bend her legs, so she pushed with her toes. Gradually, she burrowed deeper and deeper into the bush, ignoring the pain as the needle-sharp spikes grabbed at her clothes and tore at her arms, her legs, her face.

MODEL:			
Action Frame	**EVENTS/ IDEAS:**	**THINK ABOUT:** **Describe when, how, why, what, where**	**Vocabulary/phrases**
3.	Scarlett is hidden in the bush Waits, listens and watches Hears the wolf coming closer	How does she feel? What can she hear, see, smell, touch? What does she do?	Tried to steady her breathing. Wanted to get up and run but knew she couldn't Sweat collected on forehead, trickled down the side of her nose into his eyes Squeezed eyes shut, blinked rapidly Didn't dare to raise her hand Hardly dared to breathe Pins and needles stabbed her legs Could hear the wolf's paws thudding closer to where she was crouched in the bushes Could see its ears twitching Could feel its warm, rancid breath wafting against her face Could smell its stale, decaying breath Waited and watched – didn't move a muscle Craned her neck so she could see through the branches For what seemed like an eternity

Scarlett tried to steady her breathing. And waited. And watched. She wanted to get up and run, but she knew she couldn't, even though she could hear the thudding of the wolf's paws on the hard ground as it moved closer and closer to where she was crouched in the bushes. Then nothing. Not a sound. As quietly as she could, Scarlett craned her neck so she could see through the undergrowth. She gasped as she saw that the wolf was standing just the other side of the bush: so close she could see its ears twitching, could feel its warm, rancid breath – a stale, decaying stench – wafting against her face. Slowly, it raised its head and sniffed the air. Its yellow eyes glowed like flickering sparks from the shadows. Sweat had collected on Scarlett's forehead and was trickling down the side of her nose into her eyes. Squeezing her eyes shut, she blinked rapidly, not daring to raise her hand, hardly daring to breathe. For what seemed like an eternity, she stayed frozen to the spot. Pins and needles were stabbing her legs, and she knew she would have to move soon. But, all of a sudden, the wolf turned its back, and stalked off into the trees. Scarlett felt sure that it had picked up her scent; knew that she was hiding in the bushes. She could hardly believe her luck.

MODEL:			
Action Frame	**EVENTS/IDEAS:**	**THINK ABOUT:**	**Vocabulary/phrases**
4.	Scarlett starts to edge her way out of the other side of the bush Comes face to face with the wolf Wolf attacks Scarlett evades wolf and is rescued by an owl	How does Scarlett get out of the bush? What does the wolf look like? How does it attack? How does Scarlett escape? How does she move? How does she feel?	Inch by inch She edged her way backwards out of the bush Stopped every few seconds to listen for any sounds Just as the undergrowth became less dense . . . A sudden noise behind Scarlett made her whirl round Found herself face to face with the wolf Slavering jaws, pair of long, dripping fangs Claws sliced the air in front of her face Jaws plunged towards her outstretched arm Ducked, scuttled frantically backwards on her elbows Blur of white plummeted out of the night sky Plunged its talons into the wolf's face Launched herself off the ground Broke into a wild, stumbling run Tried to put as much distance between herself and the wolf as possible Horror-struck – hesitated for a brief second Wave of adrenalin surged through her body

Inch by inch, Scarlett edged her way backwards out of the bush, stopping every few seconds to listen for any sound of the wolf; ready to dive back into the bush should it return. It seemed to take for ever, but eventually the thorny barrier became less dense, and Scarlett was able to bend her legs and crawl rather than slither. With a sigh of relief, she knew she was near the exit. Above her, a hunting owl burst from the tree with a loud hoot. Raising her head, Scarlett caught sight of the owl flying above her like a white shadow, and then her heart sank. A stench of rancid breath had wafted towards her. Whirling round, Scarlett found herself face to face with the wolf. She had little time to react before it struck and its claws sliced the air in front of her face. Horror-struck, she watched as its slavering jaws plunged towards her outstretched arm. It was like watching a film in slow motion. Before the wolf's fangs had reached her arm, a blur of white plummeted out of the night sky, and plunged its talons into the wolf's face. For a brief second, she hesitated. Then, a wave of adrenalin surged through her body, and she scuttled frantically backwards on her elbows, launched herself off the ground and broke into a wild, stumbling run, trying to put as much distance between herself and the wolf as possible.

MODEL:			
Action Frame	**EVENTS/IDEAS:**	**THINK ABOUT:**	**Vocabulary/phrases**
5.	Scarlett runs for her life Slips and stumbles	How does she run? What obstacles does she face? How does she feel?	Darted and dodged through the trees Blundered and slipped Fought her way through the undergrowth Grasped at her ankles Lungs were burning Legs were aching Didn't dare stop Even when she fell over a tree root Stumbled onto her face Staggered back to her feet Never once did she turn and look back Just kept on running Chest heaving and gasping for breath
Scarlett darted and dodged through the trees. Blundering and slipping, she fought her way through the undergrowth that grasped at her ankles. Her lungs were burning, her legs aching, but she didn't dare stop. Even when she fell over a tree root and stumbled onto her face, she soon staggered back to her feet. Never once did she turn and look back: just kept on running; eyes wide and wild; chest heaving and gasping for breath.			

54

Setting/character, interaction and reaction (S/C-I-R)

The wolf

SECTION A

As the night drew a grey cloak across the sky, Scarlett found herself in the middle of the forest. Dark and tangled, a maze of narrow paths and jagged, thorny barriers spread, stretched and arched above her. The deeper she went, the darker it became. It was an endless labyrinth of towering trees – an unending green blanket steeped in shadow. As the forest closed in around her, Scarlett's unease grew. She knew that its recesses could conceal any number of dangers. Up until then, the forest had been full of noise: birds fluttering in the trees, squirrels scampering from branch to branch. But, as dusk fell, an eerie silence descended on the forest. Scarlett couldn't shake off the sensation that she was being followed. Every few steps, she kept glancing nervously over her shoulder, probing the forest for any flicker of movement, expecting to see something hideous behind every tree. Every shadow had grown eyes; every branch looked like bony fingers. At every creak and rustle, her heart jumped. A sudden, tingling sixth sense made her glance to her left, and out of the corner of her eye, Scarlett glimpsed a flickering movement. She stopped dead in her tracks, and scanned the gap between the trees.

The next thing she knew, the forest exploded. It was as if the howling was coming from all directions at once. Branches snapped like gunshots. Something was crashing through the undergrowth, and heading straight for her. For one brief moment, Scarlett was frozen to the spot, her heart thudding in her chest. She watched in horror as a huge, white wolf hurtled towards her through the trees. Then, blind instinct took over from sheer panic, and she flung herself down under the nearest bush. Clawing at the ground with her fingers, she hauled herself through the spider's web of jagged thorns. It was impossible to bend her legs, so she pushed with her toes. Frantically, she burrowed deeper and deeper into the bush, ignoring the pain as the needle-sharp spikes grabbed at her clothes, tore at her arms, her legs, her face.

Scarlett tried to steady her breathing. And waited. And watched. She wanted to get up and run, but she knew she couldn't, even though she could hear the thudding of the wolf's paws on the hard ground as it moved closer and closer to where she was crouched in the bushes. Then nothing. Not a sound. As quietly as she could, Scarlett craned her neck so she could see through the undergrowth. She gasped as she saw the wolf was standing just the other side of the bush: so close she could see its ears twitching, could feel its warm, rancid breath – a rotting, decaying stench – wafting against her face. Slowly, it raised its head and sniffed the air. Its yellow eyes glowed like flickering sparks from the shadows. Sweat had collected on Scarlett's forehead, and was trickling down the side of her nose into her eyes. Squeezing her eyes shut, she blinked rapidly, not daring to raise her hand, hardly daring to breathe. For what seemed an eternity, she remained motionless. Pins and needles were stabbing her legs, and she knew she would have to move soon. But, all of a sudden, the wolf turned its back, and stalked off into the trees. Scarlett felt sure it had picked up her scent: knew she that she was hiding in the bushes. She could hardly believe her luck.

Inch by inch, Scarlett edged her way backwards out of the bush, stopping every few seconds to listen for any sound of the wolf: ready to dive back into the bush should it return. It seemed to take for ever, but, eventually, the thorny barriers became less dense, and Scarlett was able to bend her legs, and crawl rather than slither. She knew she was near the exit, but her feeling of unease suddenly returned. Haunting and prickly, a breath of wind sighed through the undergrowth, whistled through the trees, and grated against the branches. With a loud hoot, a hunting owl burst from the trees. Raising her head, Scarlett caught sight of the owl, a white shadow, above her, and then, her heart sank. A stench of rancid breath had drifted towards her. Whirling round, Scarlett found herself face to face with the wolf. She had little time to react before it struck, and its claws sliced the air in front of her face. Horror-struck, she watched as its slavering jaws plunged towards her outstretched arm. It was like watching a film in slow motion. The wolf's teeth were millimetres from her arm when a blur of white plummeted out of the night sky, and thrust its talons into the wolf's face. For a brief second, Scarlett hesitated. Then, with a wave of adrenalin surging through her body, she scuttled frantically backwards on her elbows, launched herself off the ground, and broke into a wild, stumbling run, trying to put as much distance between herself and the wolf as possible.

Scarlett darted and dodged through the trees. Blundering and slipping, she fought her way through the undergrowth that grasped at her ankles. Her lungs burning, her legs aching, she gasped for air. But she didn't dare stop. Even when she fell over tree roots and stumbled with a thud onto her face, she soon staggered back to her feet. Never once did she turn and look back: just kept on running, gasping for breath.

SECTION B – INDIVIDUAL PASSAGES AND SENTENCES

PASSAGE 1

As the night drew a grey cloak across the sky, Scarlett found herself in the middle of the forest. Dark and tangled, a maze of narrow paths and jagged, thorny barriers spread, stretched and arched above her. The deeper she went, the darker it became. It was an endless labyrinth of towering trees – an unending green blanket steeped in shadow. As the forest closed in around her, Scarlett's unease grew. She knew that its recesses could conceal any number of dangers. Up until then, the forest had been full of noise: birds fluttering in the trees, squirrels scampering from branch to branch. But, as dusk fell, an eerie silence descended on the forest. Scarlett couldn't shake off the sensation that she was being followed. Every few steps she glanced nervously over her shoulder, probing the forest for any flicker of movement, expecting to see something hideous behind every tree. Every shadow had grown eyes; every branch looked like bony fingers. At every creak and rustle, her heart jumped. A sudden, tingling sixth sense made her glance to her left, and out of the corner of her eye, Scarlett glimpsed a flickering movement. She stopped dead in her tracks, and scanned the gap between the trees.

1

SENTENCES 1

The night drew a grey cloak across the sky.

1

Scarlett found herself in the middle of the forest.

1

The forest was a dark, tangled maze of narrow paths.

1

Jagged, thorny barriers spread, stretched and arched above her. 1

The deeper she went, the darker it became. 1

It was an endless labyrinth of towering trees. 1

It was an unending green blanket steeped in shadow. 1

The forest closed in on her. 1

Scarlett's unease grew. 1

She knew that its recesses could conceal any number of dangers. 1

The forest had been full of noise.

1

Birds had fluttered in the trees.

1

But as dusk fell, an eerie silence descended on the forest.

1

Squirrels had scampered from branch to branch.

1

Scarlett couldn't shake off the sensation that she was being followed.

1

Every few steps, she kept glancing nervously over her shoulder.

1

She probed the forest for any flicker of movement.

1

She expected to see something hideous behind every tree.

1

Every shadow had grown eyes.

1

Every branch looked like bony fingers.

1

Her heart jumped at every creak and rustle.

1

A sudden, tingling sixth sense made her glance to her left.

1

Out of the corner of her eye, Scarlett glimpsed a movement.

1

She stopped dead in her tracks.

1

She scanned the gap between the trees.

1

PASSAGE 2

The next thing she knew, the forest exploded. It was as if the howling was coming from all directions at once. Branches snapped like gunshots. Something was crashing through the undergrowth, and heading straight for her. For one brief moment, Scarlett was frozen to the spot, her heart thudding in her chest. She watched in horror as a huge, white wolf hurtled towards her through the trees. Then, blind instinct took over from sheer panic, and she flung herself down under the nearest bush. Clawing at the ground with her fingers, she hauled herself through the spider's web of jagged thorns. It was impossible to bend her legs, so she pushed with her toes. Frantically, she burrowed deeper and deeper into the bush, ignoring the pain as the needle-sharp spikes grabbed at her clothes, tore at her arms, her legs, her face.

2

SENTENCES 2

The next thing she knew, the forest exploded.

2

Branches snapped like gunshots.

2

Something was heading through the undergrowth.

2

It was heading straight towards her.

2

For one brief moment, Scarlett was frozen to the spot.

2

It was as if the howling was coming from all directions at once.

2

Her heart was thudding in her chest.

2

She watched in horror.

2

A huge, white wolf hurtled towards her.

2

It came through the trees.

2

Then, blind instinct took over from sheer panic.

2

She flung herself down under the nearest bush.

2

She clawed at the ground with her fingers.

2

She hauled herself through the spider's web of jagged thorns.

2

It was impossible to bend her legs.

2

She pushed with her toes.

2

Frantically, she burrowed deeper and deeper into the bush.

2

She ignored the pain from the needle-sharp thorns.

2

They grabbed at her clothes.

2

They tore at her arms.

2

They tore at her legs.

2

They tore at her face.

2

PASSAGE 3

Scarlett tried to steady her breathing. And waited. And watched. She wanted to get up and run, but she knew she couldn't, even though she could hear the thudding of the wolf's paws on the hard ground as it moved closer and closer to where she was crouched in the bushes. Then nothing. Not a sound. As quietly as she could, Scarlett craned her neck so she could see through the undergrowth. She gasped as she saw the wolf was standing just the other side of the bush: so close she could see its ears twitching, could feel its warm, rancid breath – a rotting, decaying stench – wafting against her face. Slowly, it raised its head and sniffed the air. Its yellow eyes glowed like flickering sparks from the shadows. Sweat had collected on Scarlett's forehead and was trickling down the side of her nose into her eyes. Squeezing her eyes shut, she blinked rapidly, not daring to raise her hand, hardly daring to breathe. For what seemed an eternity, she remained motionless. Pins and needles were stabbing her legs, and she knew she would have to move soon. But, all of a sudden, the wolf turned its back, and stalked off into the trees. Scarlett felt sure it had picked up her scent: knew she was hiding in the bushes. She could hardly believe her luck.

3

SENTENCES 3

Scarlett tried to steady her breathing. 3

She waited and watched. 3

She wanted to get up and run. 3

She knew she couldn't. 3

She could hear the thudding of the wolf's paws on the hard ground. 3

It moved closer and closer to where she was crouched in the bush. 3

Then nothing. 3

Not a sound.

3

Scarlett craned her neck.

3

She could see through the undergrowth.

3

She gasped.

3

She saw the wolf was standing just the other side of the bush.

3

It was so close she could see its ears twitching.

3

She could feel its warm, rancid breath.

3

It was a rotting, decaying stench.

3

It wafted against her face.

3

Slowly, it raised its head.

3

It sniffed the air.

3

Its yellow eyes glowed like flickering sparks from the shadows.

3

Sweat collected on Scarlett's forehead.

3

It was trickling down the side of her nose into her eyes.

3

She squeezed her eyes shut.

3

She blinked rapidly.

3

She didn't dare to raise her hand.

3

She hardly dared to breathe.

3

She remained motionless for what seemed an eternity.

3

Pins and needles were stabbing her legs.

3

She knew she would have to move soon.

3

All of a sudden, the wolf turned its back.

3

It stalked off into the trees.

3

Scarlett felt sure it had picked up her scent.

3

She was certain it knew she was hiding in the bushes.

3

She could hardly believe her luck.

3

PASSAGE 4

Inch by inch, Scarlett edged her way backwards out of the bush, stopping every few seconds to listen for any sound of the wolf: ready to dive back into the bush should it return. It seemed to take forever, but, eventually, the thorny barriers became less dense, and Scarlett was able to bend her legs, and crawl rather than slither. She knew she was near the exit, but her feeling of unease suddenly returned. Haunting and prickly, a breath of wind sighed through the undergrowth, whistled through the trees, and grated against the branches. With a loud hoot, a hunting owl burst from the trees. Raising her head, Scarlett caught sight of the owl, a white shadow, above her, and then, her heart sank. A stench of rancid breath had drifted towards her. Whirling round, Scarlett found herself face to face with the wolf. She had little time to react before it struck, and its claws sliced the air in front of her face. Horror-struck, she watched as its slavering jaws plunged towards her outstretched arm. It was like watching a film in slow motion. The wolf's teeth were millimetres from her arm when a blur of white plummeted out of the night sky, and thrust its talons into the wolf's face. For a brief second, Scarlett hesitated. Then, with a wave of adrenalin surging through her body, she scuttled frantically backwards on her elbows, launched herself off the ground, and broke into a wild, stumbling run, trying to put as much distance between herself and the wolf as possible.

4

SENTENCES 4

Inch by inch, Scarlett edged her way backwards out of the bush.

4

She stopped every few seconds. 4

She listened for any sound of the wolf. 4

She was ready to dive back into the bush should it return. 4

Eventually, the thorny barriers became less dense. 4

It seemed to take forever. 4

Scarlett was able to bend her legs. 4

She could crawl rather than slither. 4

She realised she was near the exit.

4

Her feeling of unease suddenly returned.

4

Haunting and prickly, a breath of wind sighed through the undergrowth.

4

It whistled through the trees.

4

It grated against the branches.

4

There was a loud hoot.

4

A hunting owl burst from the trees.

4

It was a white shadow above her.

4

Her heart sank.

4

A stench of rancid breath had drifted towards her.

4

She whirled around.

4

Scarlett found herself face to face with the wolf.

4

She had little time to react before it struck.

4

Its claws sliced the air in front of her face.

4

She was horror-struck.

4

She watched as its slavering jaws plunged towards her outstretched arm.

4

It was like watching a film in slow motion.

4

The wolf's teeth were millimetres from her arm.

4

A blur of white plummeted out of the night sky.

4

It thrust its talons into the wolf's face.

4

For a brief second, Scarlett hesitated.

4

Then, a wave of adrenalin surged through her body.

4

She launched herself off the ground.

4

She broke into a wild, stumbling run.

4

She tried to put as much distance between herself and the wolf as possible.

4

She scuttled frantically backwards on her elbows.

4

PASSAGE 5

Scarlett darted and dodged through the trees. Blundering and slipping, she fought her way through the undergrowth that grasped at her ankles. Her lungs burning, her legs aching, she gasped for air. But she didn't dare stop. Even when she fell over tree roots and stumbled with a thud onto her face, she soon staggered back to her feet. Never once did she turn and look back: just kept on running, gasping for breath.

5

SENTENCES 5

Scarlett darted and dodged through the trees.

5

She blundered, slipped and fought her way through the undergrowth.

5

It grasped at her ankles.

5

Her lungs were burning.

5

Her legs were aching.

5

She gasped for air.

5

She didn't dare stop.

5

She fell over a tree root.

5

She stumbled with a thud onto her face.

5

Never once did she turn and look back.

5

She just kept on running.

5

She was gasping for breath.

5